K9 Stole My Trousers

To Mike
Very best wish

[signature: Bob Baker]

K9 Stole My Trousers

an autobiography
Bob Baker

fantom
publishing

First published in 2013 by Fantom Films
fantomfilms.co.uk

A catalogue record for this book is available from the British Library.

Hardback edition ISBN: 978-1-781961-01-8

Typeset by Phil Reynolds Media Services, Leamington Spa
Printed and bound by CPI Group (UK) Ltd, Croydon, CR0 4YY

Jacket design by Paul Tams. K9 used with the consent of BBC Worldwide, with thanks to
Matt Nicholls and Edward Russell. Wallace and Gromit © Aardman Animations Ltd and
used with permissions, with thanks to Gabrielle Ruffle.

Photographs appear on plates between pages 102 and 103.

To my darling Marie, who suggested writing this book and made damn sure I finished it!

Contents

Foreword

'THAT BOB BAKER,' SAID Michael O'Hagan judiciously, as we tucked into brunch recently at Berries in Miami's 27th Avenue (steak and eggs, home fries, toast and muffins, Bloody Marys and Buck's Fizzes with coffee on the table), 'was underestimated as a writer.'

Pamela Salem agreed. 'He was talented in all sorts of ways,' she said thoughtfully. 'Should have been better known.' I had often felt this, and wondered if it was partly my fault.

In 1969 as a new Programme Controller at Harlech Television, I had been given the task of running a local service and also of showing my area, the West of England, on the ITV network. This latter task had never been attempted by the company from whom Harlech TV had wrested the licence; and, without whingeing on about the politics of the situation, there was little encouragement from the big five major networking companies, who shared the network slots amongst themselves. One under-supplied area of programming for ITV, however, was the children's programming, particularly children's drama: and this became my first target. Working in Bristol, we needed local writers, and Bob Baker and Dave Martin were a godsend to me. Their early work for us was almost exclusively in children's television, and I still wonder if that label stuck long after Bob's successes in so many other areas.

Talented, inventive, fairly malleable (well, Bob was) and hugely energetic fast workers, they were ready to turn their hands and typewriters to anything. They loved to stick around at rehearsals and filming, take part if possible, help in any conceivable way they could. It started with a short play that was witty and tender, then a massive rewrite on a children's series, then various series of their own and many other scripts. Eventually, by which time Harlech had established itself as a leading supplier, two of their major television films won us awards and rave notices from the national critics.

Personally they were wildly different. Dave was laconic, adding the darker elements to all their writing, often uncompromising, sometimes confrontational. Bob was warm and unfailingly humorous, energetically charging through creative impasses, always in quest of a solution to fit everybody. He knew all too well, probably without much liking it, that while a poet and to some extent a theatre writer can write for himself, in television you write for an audience. Not what you want to write, but what they want to see. Or, more irritatingly, what your colleagues think the audience want to see.

After a long and productive partnership, they went their separate ways. Bob became our main script editor and supervisor, and started inevitably producing as well, with great success. After helping Harlech Televion to get off the ground, he has worked for many other employers; I am flattered that he remembers his early days fondly enough to ask me to write this note.

Patrick Dromgoole
April 2013

CHAPTER ONE
Crisis

IT'S 1968 AND I am a member of a film company. We called ourselves Hexagon Films; we even had printed letterheads, and a logo! Now that's smart.

We were all in our early twenties: a group of like-minded friends, who simply wanted to make and/or be in films, to hopefully somehow gain employment in the industry as directors, cameramen… or even perhaps writers? To be honest, I had no real idea at all of what I wanted to be; I'd entertained the idea of being a director, but felt the dark shadow of my glaringly inappropriate background, sans formal education, sans drama, sans English literature all pulling against me. I'd have embarrassing visions of trying to be clever, but being totally out of my depth and making a bloody fool of myself. Best keep my specific ambition vague, I felt, just see how things go; but I knew I desperately wanted to be in and part of film making…

I'd finished art college some three years before and, not wishing to be a schoolteacher, had gone into several schemes to make a living – whilst still keeping my artistic avenues open, as it were. By this time I had a family (myself, my wife Vicki and three children) so I needed some way of making money. Until then, we had been relying on an inheritance to keep us afloat. We knew it wouldn't last forever.

One way of earning a living which I felt pretty confident about was buying, then doing up, totally derelict Georgian houses in the Clifton area of Bristol; having acquired the first one for forty pounds, it seemed like a good idea. I did a deal with a builder. He does the reconstruction, takes

1

out his costs from the sale and we split what's left. Simple as that… Unless of course, you can't sell the bloody house. Unfortunately I'd started this business during the 1966 Harold Wilson Labour government. They were definitely going to sort out the British economy, however painful it might be. Ouch! The pound is, yet again, in deep trouble. Another recession! Then the pound is devalued! This caused the banks to be very tight-fisted and there was a complete ban on mortgage lending for houses over fifty years old. What was I to do with my refurbished two-hundred-year-old property? No choice but to wait… and wait… for either a buyer with cash or until the ailing pound sterling revived… which might take a long time.

My other life was the pretend one of being a professional film-maker. It was the thing I was passionate about, and took over my entire mind day and night. I'd chosen to do animated films because it was a way of creating an expansion of vision without expansion of cost. Hexagon Films included, besides myself, Malcolm Windsor, Tony Vann and Bill Stair; John Fortune had been part of the original company but he'd left to go to Cambridge and future fame in satire shows. We decided – before we'd seen Terry Gilliam's *Python* work – to do a film in pictures cut from magazines and specially taken photographs. The original story idea came from the highly volatile but highly talented member of our group, Bill Stair. It was fashionably titled *Case History of a Real Life Commercial* (shortened to *Case History*), an allegory of how men can easily be seduced into violence, not thinking of the consequences. Here our character pays the ultimate price.

We made the film on the animation rostrum I'd had built in my basement. It was designed and constructed by a good friend of mine, Ron Fuller, a brilliant toy-maker. He made it from marine plywood timber, cycle parts, chains and pulleys driven by an electric motor. Sadly, innovative as Ron's structure was, it was totally the wrong technology and unfortunately, when the camera was attached, it caused the whole structure to wobble – not something you particularly want in animation work.

We had no alternative but to wait for the wobble to subside before continuing a shot, thus considerably lengthening what was a very slow process anyway! However, you get used to it and somehow cope in your own way. So, our first effort, *Case History*, was counted a success. It was hailed by audiences at the Bristol University Film School and at other showings. It was then selected to be shown at an experimental cinema event at the Edinburgh Festival.

We were extremely proud of this and duly travelled up to Edinburgh in a hired minibus to bask in our glory. We'd imagined it would be seen by thousands of people at a venue somewhere near Princes Street, but we searched practically every inch of Edinburgh trying to find out where the hell it was showing! Eventually to our chagrin we found it was a very 'fringe' event taking place in a junior school way out in the suburbs. Furthermore, we were the only ones in the audience... However, one thing did come from it.

Unbeknownst to us, *Case History* was seen by Sir Arthur Elton, who for many years ran the acclaimed Shell Films documentary unit. He expressed an interest in the film and in us, as film-makers. He apparently suggested he might be able to help us 'get on'. Sir Arthur lived in the family seat at Clevedon, very close to Bristol, so we met up with him to find out what he might be able to do for us. Sir Arthur was a kindly man and did his utmost to get our film on TV. His erstwhile Shell Films partner John Grierson was going to show *Case History* on his TV programme *This Wonderful World*. Sadly he didn't manage to do this, but it all seemed to be part of a surge toward... something.

We finally got a short clip of *Case History* on our local West Country News, but they failed to pay us the going rate which got us pretty pissed off. Again unknown to us, John Boorman had seen the clip and asked to see the whole thing. At that time Boorman worked at the BBC in Bristol doing documentaries, including *The Newcomers*, a very well received film about a young couple (journalist A.C.H. Smith and his wife) fetching up in Clifton – what might be called the artistic quarter of Bristol, which could boast having in residence writers such as Peter Nichols, Charles Wood and Tom Stoppard.

We met with John Boorman at the BBC West Studios. He was highly impressed by our work and asked us if we could do more films in a similar style to *Case History*, to be put into a late-night satirical show he was preparing. We were cock-a-hoop! This was it! We were on our way to fame, fortune and our rightful place in history! I was on cloud nine! There I was, the movie mogul, riding my bike to the BBC with my briefcase on the handlebars and, when there, pausing only to remove my cycle clips before going in for my meeting with John to discuss some point in the scripts.

I was still racked with doubt about my own abilities. I thought, why don't I just ask him for a job on his programme? It would have hardly been fair on the others in Hexagon Films, but needs must when the devil drives as they say. However, I did manage to avoid asking to be taken on by Boorman; and then came news that the programme he'd envisioned had been abandoned when he was asked to direct the feature film *Catch Us If You Can* featuring the Dave Clark Five: not a particularly outstanding film, but enough for John Boorman to start his career in earnest – in Hollywood. He left for LA… and so did Bill Stair…

We realised that Bill had been quiet for too long and that something must be afoot. And lo! that was it. Bill had been having separate meetings with John Boorman and got himself taken on board. I could see that Bill had the quirky kind of mind that John Boorman appreciated and when in Hollywood, he, with contributions from Bill, wrote the outstanding *Point Blank*. For that I could forgive anything. How could we blame Bill for going off on his own? We'd all reached a kind of chicane in our careers and somebody had to go. Besides, after all, hadn't I entertained the very same thoughts?

After Bill left, Hexagon melted away. Malcolm too went to LA, to do a research degree at UCLA. John Fortune was at Cambridge in 'Footlights' and very soon about to open at the Establishment Club in Soho. Tony Vann continued his work at British Aircraft Corporation. I began to feel a little lost, but I continued to use the animation rostrum to make short films. I was contacted by a guy called Bill Mather who asked me if I would help him make some thirty-second cartoon shorts called *The Digger* that he was doing for the BBC children's programme *Vision On*, fronted by the venerable Tony Hart. Also at this time I was joined by Laurie Booth, who was a trusted cameraman on several short films I'd made. Soon, other animators were asking to use – and pay to use – my rostrum. It wasn't a living, and it wasn't really what I wanted to do.

Came the day when an illustrator who did work on the *Radio Times* – black and white drawings for the inside pages – asked me if I would help him make a film. He was willing to pay for my time and I agreed. The subject was the poem by George Crabbe, *Peter Grimes*. I'd heard of the opera but was unfamiliar with the poem. On reading it I was tremendously excited. What a fantastic story! How, I wondered, was he going to capture the sheer energy and violence of the piece? To my utter dismay, he showed me a sheaf of rather stolid black and white drawings of scenes from the story. I was even more amazed to find that his intention was simply to pan over and zoom into various parts of these drawings. No animation whatsoever! Thus, surely, making the dullest of dull films – not even in colour! Then I thought, hang on, if he wants to pay me, so what? However, I was still pretty despondent about being involved in making a film with so little energy, especially given the source material… It was too good to waste on what I felt was a crap way of doing it.

It was at this time that I'd finished the first of my house rebuilding projects. It was the 'nib' point of a long triangle of Georgian houses set on a steep hill running down from Clifton to Hotwells. This tiny house, rather like a slice from a cake, had previously been a shop, so the ground floor was refurbished as one and stocked with all the things we hoped people had forgotten to buy at the supermarket. In addition the shop stayed open till nine in the evening. I usually did the 'dog watch' from seven until closing at nine.

During these stints, I'd got to know a fellow who always came in around nine o'clock to get a packet of Gaulois, which he practically chain-smoked. He was a pleasant, easy-going, confident man and we often talked of ideas and things we wanted to do – ambitions etc. I told him I wanted to make movies – not animated, not TV, but real ones, like you see in the cinema. I gathered that he himself was an advertising copywriter with one of the best advertising agencies in Bristol, Harrison Cowley, and was earning what I regarded then as a fortune. I also understood from him how he hated advertising, the whole grubby world of 'making lies sound plausible'. I must say I was pleasantly surprised, and agreed entirely with the way he felt. He told me he wanted out of it as soon as possible to write something 'good', something 'positive'. In short, he thought he was in a dirty world and needed to cleanse himself.

He told me he was born in Birmingham and had been, like me, on the poor side of the tracks when he was young; however, unlike me, he, like his father before him, had passed his eleven-plus, and to the delight of his parents went to grammar school too. It was, as he told me, a time of deep contemplation about life and death. This did him no harm, and indeed only fired him up to be successful in whatever he decided to do. On leaving grammar school with good A level results he went on to Bristol University to study English and Philosophy. Unfortunately around that time he was diagnosed with TB and spent a long time in hospital until he was finally cured by the magic of antibiotics, missing nearly three years out of his course because of it. After university he decided he wanted to be a writer, and took work as a flyman in the Bristol Old Vic, where he learned a lot about the art of the playwright, of writing structure, as well as going on drinking binges with the likes of Peter O'Toole and Richard Harris during their stint there as actors before going on to become famous in the movies…

One evening I got to telling him about the short films I'd made and my wish to 'get into films', and told him about the ideas I had for future projects. I remember mentioning this crazy guy who wanted to do *Peter Grimes* and about the way he was emasculating the entire story. My newfound friend knew the poem and agreed with me that it was a pretty pathetic way to treat it. He then said, 'Why don't we write it?' I wasn't quite sure if he meant it, or if it was one of those throwaway lines that will be forgotten by the next day.

I was to find that he did mean it. To prove it, he gave up his well paid job, went on the dole and started writing *Peter Grimes*. I sidelined the animated version, letting the fellow down very lightly… At last I was doing the real thing. I was heading in the right direction. I suddenly felt good. Oh, and my friend's name? David Martin…

We needed a place to write. David's wife Celia was very accommodating, and was happy for us to use their dining room. Celia was used to writers – her father was one, Denis Constanduros. (He and his aunt Mabel wrote *The Huggetts*, a successful series of movies in the forties and fifties.) However, we found it difficult working on their dining table. So we decided to find somewhere else.

At that time I was playing in a rock group and our agent John Miles ran an office in Clifton. He was always happy to ease his rent by letting the unused rooms in his office suite, so Dave and I rented the back rooms of 81 Whiteladies Road. We each worked in a separate room and met up for script reviews and ideas conferences. At that point, we didn't actually work together. We went over the script that Dave had written and I made points and suggested amendments.

Grimes was finished, and I decided to use a connection I'd made in my student days: namely director Clive Donner, who I met when he came to Bristol to shoot *Some People* in 1962. I was asked by my film lecturer at college if, as a Bristolian and member of a rock band, I could show his friend Clive Donner some locations and dance venues he might use in the film. I was delighted, and as I got to know Clive my brief expanded. He asked me to read the script. I read it and thought, what a load of rubbish.

To my amazement, it was a pretty thin story to promote the Duke of Edinburgh's Award Scheme: all very well, but the writer had created cardboard cliché so-say working-class kids who were all totally unbelievable characters. The girls involved suddenly and incredibly give up going to dances and generally having a good time… to do knitting classes! Ton-up leather-clad motorbike boys give up driving their bikes having seen the error of their ways and take up some mindless award-scheme event like canoeing…

Clive asked me what I thought of the script. I reasoned, I either tell him the truth and get told to bugger off, or I lie… I told him exactly what I thought, and added a few suggestions; suddenly I got quite animated, slating them for totally missing what youth was about: it was about taking risks – doing a ton-up and why not? They'd be seen as heroes in other circumstances. When I'd finished, there was a long silence. Clive smiled and said, 'Thank you, Bob.' He then got the writer to do a complete rewrite of the script incorporating some of the things I'd suggested. I was then invited to be a regular visitor on set, watching and learning how the real pros do it. I was amazed and learned a lot from it. It starred Kenneth More and his wife to be Angela Douglas, David Hemmings, Ray Brooks and soon-to-be-*Doctor-Who*-companion Anneka Wills, who was the then girlfriend of satirical comedian, John Fortune. Small world!

I approached Clive with *Grimes* and he suggested I take it to the producer of *Some People*, James Archibald, which we duly did. We had a favourable reply from him, but nothing concrete. We drove to Aldeburgh, the setting of the piece, to get the feel of the place and do a bit of research; and, as we lunched in a pub, we got talking to a couple of people and told them what we were up to. One guy turned to us and said: 'Is it anything to do with Mr Archibald?' It seems James Archibald actually lived in

Aldeburgh, only a few doors away from where we were standing. A good sign we felt.

Never ones to stand still, we sent it to other possible producers, including a company called Eyeline Films, suggested to us by a bit of a rogue, Acker Bilk's recalcitrant brother and agent, Dave Bilk, whose claim to filming fame was that in a short film with Acker, shot in Czechoslovakia, he'd ripped off the Czech government for about fifty thousand pounds.

The news from Eyeline began to get better: the finance was beginning to fall into place, and a director had expressed an interest and wish to make *Grimes* – one Michael Reeves, who'd just finished filming the cult horror movie *Witchfinder General* which had been very well received. He would be the perfect man for the job.

Things couldn't get better. Could they? Sad to relate, Michael Reeves died suddenly and unexpectedly at the age of only twenty-five! With this kingpin removed the project began to unravel and sadly went the way of so many film projects.

Dave and I cursed our bad luck. But hang on, it was our first attempt at writing a feature film and the thing damn nearly came off! It was not a time to sit and mope – we must get on and do more films. Our rooms at Whiteladies Road began to buzz, we wrote severally and together and began to accumulate so many scripts and storylines that we were at a loss to know where or who to send them to. I remember in frustration we sent one script outline to simply 'BBC London' in the vague hope that somebody would get it to the right department. We then decided it might be a good idea to get an agent.

Also sharing the offices was a man of sartorial elegance – always dressed in a suit pressed razor sharp, crisp white shirt and tie – whose engaging habit was rolling pennies over and over each other in the fingers of one hand. His name was Jim Buckingham, a genial gent, who, to add to his attributes, was a pilot at the local aero club. Jim was a man of the pop world, hoping to be the next Brian Epstein; his aspiration was to discover a hit group, or chart-topping song. Jim often travelled to London with us and shared the petrol money. He'd then go to a recording studio in Savile Row, where he shared a cupboard with a mildly successful songwriter, Clive Westlake, Jim's partner in a music publishing company. During conversations on our trips to London, Jim offered himself as our agent.

Since we didn't know any other agents, we accepted. Jim, of course, had no more idea about the world of film, drama producers and commissioning processes than we did.

It was at this time that I was at my most political, and I felt outraged by the Vietnam war. Perhaps influenced by Dave, I became more and more anti-American. We decided to make an anti-war film, to be shot more or less like a newsreel. It was a sort of 'what if it happened here?' scenario, with American troops fighting in a jungle-type location before in the final scene they emerge into a typically British village and start rounding women and children up. It was titled *Search and Destroy* and was obviously an extremely low-budget enterprise – we could only just afford the hire of costumes. A BBC designer with sympathetic views, Chris Robilliard, joined us and made replica M16 rifles. We then rounded up all our friends, dressed them in US military uniforms hired from a local 'militaria' store and got them to take direction from us. They included a good friend of ours, one Keith Floyd, a flamboyant would-be chef, who played the officer – the 'Lootenant'.

As I've already mentioned, at this time I'd met a young cameraman and keen film-maker, Laurie Booth, who ran a camera shop in Bath. Laurie offered himself as cameraman, which we accepted with pleasure; and since Jim Buckingham had offered himself for aerial shots (!) we put a rather apprehensive Laurie in the plane with him. We had real trouble with co-ordination, having no radio link, so we tried hard to signal Jim as he flew by as to what to do. The location for this sequence was the Severn riverbank. To our surprise and amazement Jim landed his plane alongside us! My heart was in my mouth as the plane disappeared from view in a dip... but thankfully it reappeared on the other side. We gave Jim and Laurie updated instructions (we were running very late!); Jim then took off and duly made two or three passes at around twenty-five feet...

We spent three days shooting *Search and Destroy*. Then, when we came to see the 'rushes', we had a nasty shock. Our second cameraman (who shall be nameless!) shooting the ground sequences put the zoom lens on the camera but for some reason didn't tighten it up; consequently to see the picture upright through his eyepiece, he had to hold the camera skewed to the left. The result was that all the shots were done sideways! A totally hopeless mess and one which brought our heartfelt film to a grinding halt. There was no way we could reshoot the original sequences.

During this interim period, Dave and I did loads of extra work on BBC films; and Celia managed to persuade one film unit to take on Keith Floyd as location caterer, coming up with *coq au vin* and *boeuf bourguinon* on the menu – something which pleased the production people, but your 'sparks', your 'grips' and your 'chippies' failed to appreciate, and insisted on having their 'sausage an' mash'.

Dave also got us some occasional work from his previous employers, the advertising agency he'd worked for. One was for a new football boot from the Tuf boots people, called 'Tufspin', which had a swivelling ring of studs on the ball of the foot to cut down on knee injuries. Laurie Booth joined us as cameraman when we went to Highbury, the Arsenal ground, to film a match (it being the year 'The Gunners' had won the double, FA and League Cup). We interviewed the manager, Bertie Mee, then shot film of the Arsenal captain rushing about in the new boots. The film was a success, but sadly the boot was a failure: they couldn't build the spinning stud-wheel strong enough.

Jim Buckingham heard about a new company taking over the local TV franchise from TWW (Television Wales and the West). This was to be Harlech Television. The new Programme Controller, Patrick Dromgoole, a man steeped in drama, was hoping to stage a series of half-hour plays by new authors in the region. Jim had managed to fix it for us to take Mr Dromgoole to lunch... instead of the other way around! It was a case of struggling writers taking rich TV mogul out to lunch. Dave and I had an immediate affinity with Patrick and during the lunch he outlined the fantastic plans he had in mind for the fledgling HTV. He ended by asking us to submit a play for consideration in his half-hour play slot.

We set to work and I realised that Dave already had a play in mind and he started writing it. He encouraged me to write one too, but again that dark cloud of insecurity hung over me. I genuinely felt that anyone reading my stuff would think it ridiculously naïve and quietly pass it by. Anyway, I wrote a play called *Whistle For It*. I'd culled it from the reminiscences of wartime Bristol as told by my work colleague Alec, when I was at the Co-op. Dave had written a sharp, clever satire about big business with a powerful central character. It was called *Everybody Does it for the Company*. We sent both plays to Patrick Dromgoole, and after a week or so we were summoned to talk to him about our submissions. He had chosen the play he'd like to do and to my utter shock and surprise, it was mine... with a few minor changes of course: we were to set it in the present day and build up one of the characters.

In order to make these amendments, a sea change had taken place in my relationship with Dave. As we toiled on the rewrites we got to know how each other's mind worked, and found we could anticipate plots and story arcs, almost as if one of us had run ahead in the script being written and mark out points for the story to run smoothly on to.

From that day on, we wrote and constructed stories together. Dave did the typing because he was two-handed and knew about things like punctuation and had a good idea of how to vary story pace. But it was more than that. We got on well together and shared a similar sense of humour, but somehow from different directions: Dave's was intelligent, flinty and sharp; mine, perhaps more what we now call 'street' – and when the two met head on, magic would sometimes happen.

Working with Patrick was exciting and informative. He invited us to rehearsals of *Whistle For It* and I watched in awe as he drew performances out of the actors (one of whom went on to be quite successful: Brian Cox, no less!). The play was to be transmitted live, so it was put together rather like a theatre performance, the only pause in action being the commercial break. Since we were around so much, Patrick made us extras in the pub scene. So, that meant we'd taken our first televised play from writing and then rewriting through rehearsal and on to performing in it as it went out on air. We went on to work with Patrick in one way or another until he retired in the nineties.

Meanwhile, back at the ranch in Whiteladies Road, we were scheming an epic: the story of King Arthur – the real Arthur. It was a personal version of that mist-shrouded era between the fifth and sixth centuries AD. It was going to be an epic on the scale of those being made at that time, like *The Vikings*, or *King Alfred* which Clive Donner was filming in Ireland. Surely, we felt, the world could use another wild extravaganza? Between gathering research for the Arthur project we turned our eyes to another epic, this time about the Siege of Mafeking. A book out at the time traced the history of how Baden-Powell literally besieged himself at Mafeking. By chance we'd come across a handwritten diary of a woman who'd been in the besieged town. This served as a good starting point for our screenplay.

11

We had a call from Patrick Dromgoole who asked us to help him out of a delicate situation. In his bid to open up the station to regional talent, he'd embarked on a children's series proposed by Charles Wood. A superb period piece set in the time of the Monmouth Rebellion (1685), it concerned a troupe of travelling players, one of whom is dying; she tells her son that he is the illegitimate son of the Duke of Monmouth, who himself is the illegitimate son of Charles I and has now raised a rebellion against James II to make himself King. Called *Pretenders*, it was the boy's search with his sister Perfect to find his father in the middle of a bloody rebellion. Stirring stuff indeed.

Patrick's problem was that the HTV publicity trumpeted the fact that on *Pretenders* they were to use 'thirteen West Country authors', and indeed he had done so; but hardly one of them had written for TV before, so they came up with what they knew about – stage plays: plays with heaps of static scenes full of very fine dialogue. But this was an action adventure serial to be completely filmed on location! Our job was to edit the series, and edit it severely, in terms of excess dialogue, dead scenes and costly set-ups.

I guess we upset quite a few writers in that exercise. I must say, when we had to rewrite Charles Wood's episode I felt nervous about, shall I say, restructuring, the work of such a distinguished writer? However, I could see Dave smiling to himself, enjoying every minute as we hammered it into shape.

In the end the serial looked good and went down well. All were pleased with the result. Again Patrick made us part of the Film Unit, and here too we became extras in lots of scenes. Perhaps too often? In some cases, to save money, we'd use extras as, say, soldiers in the morning, then redress them as peasants in the afternoon. This led to an amusing situation where I appeared as a rebel, taking a shot at someone, then on the reverse the victim is me again as a soldier… I shot myself!

With *Pretenders* under our belts we went back to our film epics and TV plays at the office. We were still not earning much and gladly took on film extra work to help out on the finance side. We got lots of jobs since Dave's wife Celia worked as a costume designer with the BBC and so Dave and I would be in various filmed shows that she worked on. She eventually formed an extras agency for a while.

One day, as we sat there surrounded by scripts, half-finished scripts, ideas written in ink, piles of notes and pictures to stimulate the imagination, we had a phone call from the BBC from a man called Trevor Ray, who told us that a play called *A Man's Life* had ended up on his desk. This was the play we'd sent off to 'BBC London' a whole year before… He said he'd read it and enjoyed it and so had some of his colleagues in the office. After warning us that since it was about military hardware – tanks – it might be a little too high on budget, he then asked: would we like to meet them at the BBC?

So, one day in the spring of 1970, Dave and I travelled to London, very excited and full of hope that the BBC would be producing our film. The title *A Man's Life* was taken from the then current Army recruitment advertisement, 'It's a Man's Life in the British Army'. Our story was written from anecdotes told to us by Keith Floyd about the time he spent as an officer in the Royal Tank Corps.

We were cordially greeted in the BBC bar by producer Derrick Sherwin, script editor Terrance Dicks and assistant Trevor Ray. We were on about our fourth gin and tonic when, among stories of their National Service, Terrance Dicks again reminded us that using tanks could prove too expensive. Armoured cars were suggested. 'No, that's fine,' said I, 'armoured cars are fine.' I began to think we'd cracked it.

Derrick Sherwin then looked me in the eye and said: 'Do you know what we do?'

'No,' I replied. 'But about these tanks, armoured cars will be fine.'

He carried on looking at me and then said: 'We do *Doctor Who*.'

'Great!' said Dave. 'Now about these tanks…'

Derrick then said, 'Would you like to write a *Doctor Who*?'

We were utterly bemused and said, 'Yes, of course; now about these tanks…'

Apart from our half-hour regional play for HTV and script editing on *Pretenders*, our writing partnership had not gone much further. However, we were still buoyed up by the fact that the first thing we'd ever written together, *Peter Grimes*, came so close to production.

So here we were, about to embark on a fantastic career in television: ironically, something we'd tried to avoid at the start. Dave was reasonably pleased we were doing *Doctor Who*, but I was cock-a-hoop. I would be writing something I'd loved from my early teens – science fiction – and for a programme I'd watched since its inception in 1963. I'd been captivated by it from the beginning. All its special effects drawbacks were forgiven, because there were brilliant scripts, powerful stories, quirky characters and strange other worlds and the creatures they found there. For me it was like a garden of delights.

Dave and I embarked on *Doctor Who* with tremendous energy, letting our imaginations streak away. Ideas were pouring out, white hot. It was then that we found ourselves no longer free thinkers; we were now bound to a system, and in particular we were harnessed to the one-page outline story idea, possibly the most difficult thing for a writer to accomplish, especially when you're new to it. Our one-pagers often stretched to five, six, even ten pages! Such was the difficulty of condensing the idea, story arc and plot…

The other thing we learned was that *Doctor Who* at that time was an extremely low-budget show. Our first attempt was what we thought a terrific action-packed science fiction idea, but the reaction from Terrance Dicks was: 'No! We can't do that! We're not MGM!' He was referring to a scene we'd put in of a spaceship hitting a fairground, sending the ferris wheel spinning off into Hyde Park, exploding and killing scores of bystanders… Not until we learned to curb our excesses would we be allowed to actually write a script. As newcomers to *Who*, we needed to be beaten into shape; it took the best part of a year to finally get the story commissioned, and during that time we'd gone from a seven-part, to a six-part and then finally a four-parter.

This whole year of us presenting ideas then having them rejected made us feel very discouraged. I could tell that Dave was beginning to tire of it and made the odd remark like: 'This isn't what I started writing for.' I felt a little worried by this as, for me, this was the chance I'd longed for.

The thing which concerned me is that I well understood that Dave didn't care much about the money involved. When we began writing, as mentioned, Dave happily gave up his lucrative job in advertising copywriting without a qualm; and, furthermore, he reasoned that since there were two of us, if you halve the pay we'd be getting, we were earning about as much as a corporation dustman! He said he'd be better off on the dole…

It was true and I knew it was true. I, on the other hand, really wanted this *Doctor Who*. Firstly, I was extremely keen to get a paying job, anxious to provide for the family after faffing around for so long after college. Secondly, it would mean I was writing science fiction – and for a hit network series. Jesus! Could anyone wish for more? Yes. Dave could. Who could blame him? He wanted to write serious hard-hitting drama, like Pinter, Charles Wood and Peter Nichols, not what he perceived as kiddies' melodrama! I too desperately wanted to write something 'important', though I knew not what at that point. I suppose I wanted to write *Casablanca* amongst other things. But I also craved the sheer thrill of writing sci-fi, something I was sure I'd be good at; and of course the kudos, for me, of just writing *Who*.

I feel that Dave realised this and maybe tempered his independent spirit (for which I had huge respect and admiration) to accommodate my feelings. It wasn't as if we really disagreed that much and in fact I don't suppose we ever openly discussed it.

This was the most nerve-racking part of our partnership, one that was beginning to look like a non-starter... because there was a moment, a point, when there might never have been a Bob Baker and Dave Martin writing partnership, and that was the threat facing us at our very first major commission.

So there I was at a crossroads. Was I to continue a most unexpected career in writing with Dave? Or go back to pretending to make a living, by making animated films in my basement?

I think I may have managed to placate Dave by suggesting, but not necessarily meaning, that this would be our only foray into the *Who* world. I suggested we get it out of the way so that we could get on with all the other projects we'd dreamt up. Dave accepted this, and we managed to keep submitting new single-page story ideas and, with difficulty, we curtailed our riotously extravagant and expensive set-pieces. The other element which entered the equation was that whilst all these rejections pissed me off, they made Dave *really* angry; and so a new spirit took hold of our work, along the lines of: 'Of course we can bloody do this!'

And so we did.

BOB BAKER

The 1971 *Doctor Who* season saw episode one of *The Claws of Axos* by Bob Baker and Dave Martin transmitted on March 13th. As I sat with my wife and three children I began to reflect...

How had I, a working-class lad from Bristol with no visible education, i.e. no O or A levels or degrees... whose only writing so far was cut in stone with hammer and chisel... come to be writing for one of the most popular series on television?

CHAPTER TWO
'Cry God for Hanham, Kingswood and St George!'

I WAS BORN IN St George, an eastern suburb of Bristol, adjoining the districts of Hanham and Kingswood. It is a hotchpotch of council housing and private thirties semis plonked into an old coal-mining and quarrying district full of tiny cottages and smallholdings linked by narrow lanes with names like Meg Thatcher's Lane, Quarry Lane and Casey Bottom Lane. St George is bordered on the south by the River Avon at Crew's Hole (don't ask!) and stretches north to Fishponds and eastward into Hanham and open countryside beyond towards Bath.

I was born and brought up at number 152 Hillside Road with my mother Roma, father Stanley, my older brother Roger and 'Our Gran'…

'Coldest road in Bristol, Hillside Road,' my grandmother would moan on arrival every time after she'd walked the half mile from the bus stop. The road was a kind of east-west corridor and when a bitter east wind came it just howled down the road.

The house was a new build (1936) pebble-dashed semi-detached with two bedrooms, bathroom and box room upstairs and two reception rooms downstairs. The 'front room' as we called it was virtually unused and shining with new furniture. It was always a bit of a shock to come downstairs one morning and find the fire burning in the front room. This would usually be because we were having the back room chimney swept.

The back room was the living-cum-dining room where we listened to the radio and later watched television, and where Gran had 'her' chair. It was where our lives were lived, where Dad did his painting and weekend signwriting, where I kept my toys, where we ate and drank, laughed and cried – Mum's domain – under Gran's supervision and criticism of course; and where, in winter, there was endless innuendo about why the fire wasn't drawing, how Mum hadn't laid the fire properly or how the coal was 'slack', a kind of cheap coal dust that hardly burned at all and gave off a damp sort of smell.

My parents bought their house in 1936 for about two hundred and fifty pounds. They had a private mortgage with the builder who'd built about sixteen houses and then built himself a smart bungalow at the bottom of the road with a view over the district. The house was supposed to have been for Mum and Dad to bring up their family, but Gran, Mum's mum, came over for the weekend when World War Two started and stayed thirty-nine years! Amazingly, before I was born in 1939 they'd let two of the rooms to lodgers, the Bigwoods, but they left when I was born, because they too had produced an offspring at the same time. It seems that overcrowding wasn't seen as a problem; and after all, my mother had previously shared a tiny house in Montpelier, central Bristol, with her father, mother and six siblings. So, what was a few lodgers? Also, of course, the rent helped to pay the mortgage. Thankfully they got on well together and we kept in touch with the Bigwoods for several years afterwards.

I remember very little about the early part of the war, just some misty memories of the blackout and being taken into our Anderson shelter, when I recall seeing searchlights sweeping the sky. The wailing air raid siren was the clearest memory and that sound still manages to chill me. I loved aeroplanes from a very early age (and still do!) and had quite a collection of Dinky toy aircraft and several picture books of warplanes. When I was about five, I could recognise most of the regular aircraft that flew over the house, usually training planes, but occasionally something more exciting, a Spitfire or Hurricane perhaps, would fly over. I also recall a Sunday school charity concert in which my mother got on the stage and sang the ballad, *Always*. I was mesmerised. I didn't even know she could sing! I also remember, or think I do, a children's Christmas party at a nearby chapel where I received a present of a pull-along Donald Duck.

Towards the end of the war, Dad was in Holland with the RAF waiting with his trusty sewing machine (Dad's Air Force skill was repairing canvas-covered aircraft) to move into Germany with the advancing Allies. In summer, Mum and I used to take long bus-rides from the Tramway Centre to the end of a line, any one, just to see what was there, go for a walk, then get the bus back again. Most of the time we'd end up sitting in a park, or on the huge expanse of green parkland above Clifton, a bequest to the citizens of Bristol, Durdham Downs – always called, simply, The Downs.

In 1944/5 one side of the Downs was given over to US servicemen, who lived in a Nissan-hut 'city'. I was often embarrassed as I, as an imaginary cowboy, galloped my 'horse' through gullies and up draws and into imaginary forests to come upon a couple, a 'Yank' as we called them and an English girl, in a loving clinch. I would pull up my reins and head off in some other direction. On seeing any American serviceman, out would come the automatic request: 'Got any gum chum?' I was always too embarrassed to ask. Then, the one time I did, I obviously picked an 'ornery Yank' who was clearly not in a good mood. He totally ignored me.

I also recall watching the Home Guard – just after their name was changed to Civil Defence – doing training drill in our street. When the order rang out from the sergeant to 'Take cover!' one man with his rifle took his cover in our side alley. I just watched him mesmerised, wishing I was old enough to tote a gun…

The war in Europe ended in May 1945 and we had a VE (Victory in Europe) Day street party, when all the neighbours brought food out and the children all sat on long benches borrowed from the school. It was more subdued than the VJ (Victory over Japan) Day in August. This time, the war was really over and servicemen were coming back. A huge street party again, but this time everyone donned fancy dress and lots of the neighbours got pretty tipsy. And who could blame them?

With the war over, instead of joy and cheer, there was grinding hardship, if anything worse than in the war. It was as if we felt things should get better after an illness, but it didn't. 1946 crawled through to the coldest winter in living memory – those who had suffered so much during the conflict suffered again.

The late forties were still a time of fragile recovery from the ravages of WWII, but the feeling of hope only began as the decade changed to the fifties, entering the second half of the century. I remember, in my last year at junior school, writing the '50' numbers that looked warm and rounded figures. Things were definitely going to get better! Weren't they?

As a family we were mostly in a state of near poverty, which could be an acute embarrassment – not being able to pay bills, begging for credit, little of which I understood at the time. Dad had come home from the war determined to start his own signwriting business, but building that business up seemed to take ages. Sometimes there would be no work at all, hence the hard financial interludes. We were the last family in the street to get a television set, the last family to get 'the ITV'. I well remember my mother being distraught at being unable to discuss the ITV commercials and soaps with the neighbours, and of course there was no way of making out you had ITV because of the tell-tale aerial.

One of the worst embarrassments of near poverty for me was when we'd run out of coal – this was because Mum had ordered less than we needed to save money. Then came the inevitable: 'Bob, go up to the coal-yard and get us a hundredweight of nutty slack.' This meant bringing the sack of coal back on a push-cart, one with steel rims that made a horrible noise like a tumbrel on the way to the guillotine. I kept my head down as I paraded through the neighbourhood, knowing that everybody knew what I was doing and why… The return journey was worse, the noise of the empty cart was twice as loud, so I used to devise very long alternative routes to take the cart back.

We were also the last family to get a car. Dad didn't really take to car driving. I think he missed the open-vista-vision of the motorbike. He took the driving test eight times before he passed. Dad's car claustrophobia got worse as he got older and he would often sail past our intended turning because he would only look straight ahead out through the windscreen.

At around age twelve or so, I began to realise what a pain in the ass it must have been for Mum to be constantly criticised in her own home by Gran. In the scullery (which is what we called the kitchen), Mum cooked with Gran hovering over everything as a kind of sous chef who was in charge! Then there was the sacred washing. According to Gran, God had pretty much ordained that washing was done on Mondays; Gran insisted on it – the world would end if it wasn't so… On a rainy day, there would be mutterings from Gran: 'Don't you think we'd better get the washing out Rome? I should do it now Rome – the rain's goin' off now.' It sounded benign, but it was in fact a sort of passive-aggressive order. Before that age, Gran was my idol; she was the one who told and sang nursery rhymes to me, most of which I remember to this day. Having a grandparent, or in some cases both grandparents, in the house was pretty much the norm for most houses in the street.

Gran was born in 1886 and delighted in describing herself to strangers as 'an old Bristol d'oman' (a dialect contraction of 'old woman') – or rather, 'I'm only an old Bristol d'oman.' The clue is in the 'only': a lack of self-worth, born of years in service as a housemaid in what she called 'big houses'. She married William Coleman, described on the marriage certificate as 'general labourer'. He had in fact previously been in the Army, the Gloucestershire Regiment, and was stationed at Horfield Barracks in Bristol. Sadly he spent less and less time at home, preferring the pub, and – typical of many men at that time – spending all his wages there, thus forcing Gran to go to work to bring up the six children. Mum was born in 1913, the youngest of six – there were seven but tragically one died in a house fire. By 1914 William was fighting on the Western Front and in 1917 was wounded in a mustard gas attack. Demobbed on convalescent grounds, the poor sod coughed and spluttered his way through to 1919 before he died. The oldest son, my uncle William Jr who was in the Machine Gun Corps, also died in 1919 of the effects of gas in exactly the same way.

To my parents, Gran was both help and hindrance. She helped out with the housework in so many ways, but was strangely lacking when Mum and Dad wanted some much needed respite time on their own. All would be carefully planned down to the last detail on how Gran would feed and look after Roger and me whilst they were away; but regularly, as early as three days into the break Gran would contact them feigning some kind of illness, which would bring them rushing back, only to find – surprise, surprise! – there was nothing wrong with her at all: the sore throat/ stomach pains/dizzy spells had all mysteriously disappeared.

Another annoying trait was Gran's refusal to use the lavatory in our house. She kept a commode in her bedroom, a place that habitually smelled of Eau de Cologne. The commode was of dark polished wood and looked like an ornate chair. After use, Gran would empty it in the toilet and flush it. Equally odd was the fact that she could not spend a second of the day without wearing a hat of some description, often a smart thirties-style felt hat with feathers. To see her in an apron, wringing out the washing wearing a posh hat was absolutely bizarre!

Gran had also put herself in charge of all washing up. My friend Malcolm, who lived just up the road, reminded me recently of how he used to call for me to go to Sunday school, but I was rarely ready and Gran would offer him a cup of tea; when he put the cup to his lips she would whisk the saucer away to wash it up, then hover over him waiting for him to finish his tea so she could wash up the cup!

Stanley, my dad, was born in Tickenham, a small village on the road from Bristol to the sedate Victorian seaside town of Clevedon. He went to school in Bedminster, and when he left at fourteen was put as an apprentice signwriter. He was obviously pretty good at his job and was taken on as a full-time employee by Jones and Bence, a local 'motor factors'. During the thirties he worked for various other companies, painting the lettering on the sides of vans varying in size from small delivery vans to furniture removal lorries. He also did ladder work on shop fronts and was forever being asked to paint boards for church service times and various other sign and poster work. I used to watch him working; it was fascinating to see the easy way he had with a paintbrush, how he rolled his wrist to form the rounded letters – sweeping an 'S' in one deft movement – then watching him do gold-leaf work, which I came to do myself in later years. All this work was usually propped up on a dining chair in the front room or living room and always done at the weekend. Our Sunday smelled of paint and turpentine. He never seemed to stop working.

I didn't really know Dad until he got back from Germany in 1946. He'd been stationed in Rennesberg with an RAF unit charged with the repair of aircraft that were canvas-covered, small communications types – in this case it was Austers of an Air Observation Squadron. He also repaired wooden-built Mosquito bombers or fighters when they got shot up in battle, or just following general wear and tear. During the last year of the war his unit followed the Army across Holland and into Germany. Dad rarely spoke about the war, but his only 'weapon' you might say was not a machine gun, but as already mentioned an industrial-size sewing machine!

Whilst in Germany he became ill with a kidney problem and was sent back to the UK for an operation. This was done at Cossham Hospital in

Bristol, which was within easy walking distance from home. I visited him in hospital, but all I remember is his locker... it had a kind of sweet, damp smell of old biscuit. I was usually given one as I left and it would crumble in my fingers; it's amazing how that sweet, damp odour has stayed with me.

After Cossham, Dad was sent to convalesce at a hotel in Morecambe Bay where he did lovely little watercolour paintings from his window. That was the thing about Dad: he was a very good self-taught artist and was really happy when he had a job requiring a design or picture illustration on the side of a van or shop window. I remember a field of cows for a milkman; a cornucopia for a fruit and veg shop, and roses for a florist. He was very much at home doing florid Gothic-type lettering and gilding, but these jobs were few and far between. His last job after he retired was when that venerable chef Keith Floyd (before his years of fame) started up a business in Bristol called 'Floyd's Feasts', a sort of gourmet home-delivery service; Dad painted his delivery van in Gothic lettering with black shading and gold highlights.

Dad came home from Germany for good one evening in May 1946. I was playing in the lane at the back of Hillside Road when I remember seeing a huge blue greatcoat and backpack going into our garden gate. I just left my friends and ran towards him.

Soon after, with my Mum, Roger and I, he went through the souvenirs he'd brought back from the war, an amazing pile of weird things including a Nazi knife with an inlaid swastika. I remember thinking – without an inkling of what it meant – what a good design it was, a little diamond shape of blood-red Bakelite and a black swastika in a white ground. Dad said we had to dig it out, and so we did; the little diamond-shaped motif stayed around for years at the bottom of one drawer or another. Other things were range-finder sights, a clear plastic sheet covered in lines and numbers with a spinning protractor – something to do with firing torpedoes from a U-boat, I was told. There was a bubble compass like a gargantuan wristwatch. Also I remember he brought a pack of Bakelite strips, like rulers, most of them about a foot long, some smaller; this became my building set with which I built bridges for my toys and defences for my Dinky-toy army. They were old aeroplane parts but they were fantastic things to play with.

I was very close to my mother and I know she probably had perhaps fonder feelings toward me than my older brother; and I was a little put out when this man, who'd come from out of the blue, with bristly chin, started getting close to Mum. I felt positively jilted and my attentions turned to an ever-willing Gran. It was Gran who bounced me on her knee and sang me the nursery rhymes I still remember to this day; Gran who hid little misdemeanours I'd committed, even taking the blame on occasion.

When Dad came home it was time for a realignment of relationships. Mum had allowed Gran to dominate her during the war years and she still threw her weight about from time to time, but my father used sarcasm and humour which took the wind completely out of her sails. I had no idea what was going on and gradually realised that my Gran, my companion and confidante, was becoming the hate figure in the house. My Mum resented the way she regimented all domestic life, like the aforementioned mandatory Monday washing. Dad tried to intervene in the early years, but gradually even he gave up. I suppose basically Mum, as the youngest of seven children, was still scared enough of Gran to – however unwillingly – obey her edicts.

In many ways Stan was frustrated. He had a load of talent but with a very limited artistic outlet for it. Certainly he wouldn't have dreamed of going to art school or anything, probably feeling that he was not worthy of such a status or that he didn't deserve it or something. Judging by his background, a simple working-class upbringing, it is a bit of a mystery where Dad's artistic flair came from. He did portraits too. I remember him doing one of Gran asleep in the chair, and my mother hating the smell of the oil paint in the living room.

I'll never forget the time I was out doing some watercolour painting – emulating the old man – when the local chimney-sweep stopped and looked at what I was doing and asked me my name.

'Not Stan Baker's son?'

'Yes,' I replied.

'Ol' Stan painted my photo!' In fact Dad painted loads of pictures for people and never sold one. He gave them away: pictures of flowers, the odd portrait and clipper ships in full sail. That was his favourite subject matter, since he worshipped the work of Montague Dawson, a fine painter of dramatic seascapes and sailing ships. Dawson was the doyen of *The Homelover's Book*, a collection of popular prints for sale.

Dad used the ancient and tried methods of 'projecting' a small picture up to a large size by squaring it up and matching square for square for accuracy. He collected art books: not that many, but enough for me to know who Rembrandt or Leonardo De Vinci were; and as I grew older I looked at them more and more – including a book called *Beauty in the Human Form*, a book of nude photographic studies – with the naughty parts blurred out…

We never really discussed art much until my brother and I got into modern painting. Then it became an argument with Dad. He believed that anything after the Pre-Raphaelites at the turn of the century was rubbish – 'especially that bloody Picasso! A kid could paint that!' Dad would rave, but to have discussed it at all was probably something unique and special to our family in dear old St George.

Stanley was the illegitimate child of a Tickenham lady, a farmer's daughter, who gave him for official adoption by a childless couple in Bedminster. I know very little of this arrangement and Dad wouldn't talk about it since to him it was a source of deep shame. Being born out of wedlock was seen in the 1930s as a stigma, the kind of thing people whispered about. So he spent a lifetime shielding this secret – even into the seventies when it was no big deal to have illegitimate children and in fact began to become the norm.

I discussed this with Mum after he died; that, and where Dad might have got his artistic bent from. She told me that my father's father had probably been a craftsman who designed ceiling roses, who lived in Tickenham. It sounded made-up rather than fact, but I bought into this. Then, when I researched the family tree on the internet, I found that the Bakers were all farm people and that the parish records in Tickenham, a tiny village which was all very agricultural, showed that illegitimacy was rife and there was probably interbreeding as well.

Dad had a second name which I only discovered when I came across his birth certificate. His full name was Stanley John Horler Baker. On a casual visit to Tickenham, I thought I'd take a look at the churchyard; going through the headstones I found loads of memorials to the family 'Horler' – it appeared to be a common surname in the Tickenham area. So Miss Mary Baker, the grandmother I never met, possibly gave her son the family name of her lover? A local boy, one of the Horlers? They were, apparently, all farming types too – no artists as far as I could tell.

25

Mary Baker continued to live in Tickenham until she passed away in the sixties. Whenever Mum and I used to travel to Clevedon on the bus for a day out, she'd always point out a cottage on Tickenham Hill with a criss-cross pattern in the tiles and tell me that was my dad's 'auntie's house'…

The whole business came to a head when I was about to get married to my first wife Vicki. Dad got into a complete panic because it was a bit of a posh church wedding and for some reason he thought that he would have to reveal his past in the marriage registration document. He took a lot of convincing before he agreed to attend.

Dad was normally a pretty placid type who could take a joke against himself, but underneath he revealed a nasty temper when he felt cornered. He didn't hit me often, but when he did I knew I'd done something really bad. As I got older, though, if I thought I might be in for a whack I'd run away from him and he'd end up laughing.

Dad had a reputation amongst the men around us, uncles, cousins and acquaintances, that he was a 'real gentleman'; but one time to my utter amazement my mother told me that when I was born he was probably having an affair with a lady from the ARP Warden's Post, where he was the head warden. I was truly shocked. He was, it seems, a bit of a ladies' man! This jolted my memory and I remembered a time when my dad took me out for a walk and we ended up in a house in Glebe Road, about a mile away from where we lived; a smiling lady answered the door and I was put in the front room with a tin of biscuits – a tin! After some time I was taken back home. I recall two such visits. On the other hand it could have been quite above board, but my mum went very quiet when I told her about it. This was long after Dad died.

All my early recollections of my mother, Roma – an unusual name usually anglicised to 'Rome' – are very warm ones. She was the one who was always there, always ready with a hug or a surprise when I was feeling down. Like one wet, boring November Saturday: I couldn't go out with my friends and I got so miserable that she opened one of my Christmas presents, a bright red tinplate toy double-decker bus. I was placated; and later on, to my shame, I found ways to manipulate her genuine kindness.

All I can remember is having good times with Mum. We went to the pictures every Monday and Thursday, when the film programmes changed. We had several cinemas within easy walking distance from our home. The Kingsway, a bit of a fleapit, was the nearest, then the very smart

Odeon at Kingswood, all very art deco; and the Park Cinema at St George's Park. Walking back home we'd discuss the film we'd seen and get quite critical at times.

Mum gave me the mostly pleasurable task of going to the corner shop to get the groceries every Friday evening. I got on really well with Mrs Jarrett who ran the local grocery shop and off-licence, a tiny place with beer and cigarette sales on the right, a dark cavern of bottles and barrels and the ever present sweet, damp, dank smell of draught beer delivered through a copper funnel into an empty bottle by the always smoking Mr Jarrett who seemed to keep tatty roll-ups stuck to his lips all the time!

The left side was all sweetness and light; a large window lit a leg of ham on a china pedestal, bacon, bread, various cold meats and on the other end cakes and 'fancies' like cream horns, doughnuts, currant buns and scones. Shelves behind the counter were packed high with tinned food and packets and boxes, a veritable collage of shapes and colour. This side smelled of warmth, flour, bread and sugar and sweets.

When times were hard in the Baker household, particularly in the late forties and early fifties, I could always tell because the money Mum gave me for the groceries was a ten-shilling note; normally, I took a pound. This was accompanied by the shopping list and a request at the bottom for credit... asking if we can pay so much toward the bill and pay the rest off in the following week. I didn't feel any shame at first, but as I got older I realised when there was a sudden silence after Mrs Jarrett read the list. I felt nervous and embarrassed because there might be a chance that she'd refuse to give the credit and send me back without the groceries. I'm pleased to say that it never happened.

Mum was a super cook; her speciality was baking cakes and pastries. The family came round in droves of a Sunday to partake in Auntie Roma's lovely cakes for Sunday tea. Officially the family came to see Gran, as the matriarch of the family – only the Coleman family, since there were no Baker family as such. So I met with all my cousins, second cousins, aunts and uncles on a regular basis. It was always exciting when a crowd of them turned up. We had loads of fun: we'd play cards or sometimes look at old photographs. The cousins and a friend of theirs, all ex-Paratroopers, might do their party piece which was a comedy re-enactment of *Henry V* (after the Olivier film) 'galloping' on chairbacks! Even I was allowed to do my party piece, an impression of marching Chinese soldiers I'd seen on the news at the cinema: they raised both arms on each step! This usually got a laugh. Occasionally there were even jokes against Gran, but she was deaf and couldn't hear them.

A typical fifties Sunday might begin with pottering about in the garden; my father would start work on something as per usual. As a signwriter, in the days before photocopying, he was inundated with requests for shop signs, information boards and posters for various events. Meanwhile Mum, supervised by Gran, would prepare The Sunday Lunch! Always called 'dinner'. We'd have a joint of meat, which, along with lots of other essentials, was still rationed – if you didn't get to the butcher's early, all the best stuff had gone.

As dinner was being prepared, we'd listen to *Two-Way Family Favourites* – Cliff Michelmore and Jean Metcalfe playing requests for British servicemen in Germany and, further afield, Malaya and Korea where the war lasted until 1953. An amazing variety of choices were to be heard, ranging from the Glasgow Orpheus Choir with *All in the April Evening* to Spike Jones' comedy music, a bit of classical and an Irish folk song perhaps and of course the hit Tin Pan Alley popular music (decided on sales of sheet music, not records!) – Frankie Laine, Doris Day or Johnnie (*Cry*) Ray. Thinking back, I realise that as young people we were exposed to a wide range of music, whereas now everything is popular music except from very specialised channels, like Classic, or Jazz FM.

As far as eating was concerned, the fare was pretty much mapped out for the week. At the Sunday dinner table would be a tiny joint. Beef, served in minuscule slices accompanied by fantastic Yorkshire pudding, along with veg from the garden and spuds, boiled and roast. We chewed to the strains of *The Billy Cotton Band Show*, with me hoping to listen to Archie Andrews before I went to Sunday school (a 'must' at a time when evangelist Billy Graham was as popular as, say, Marilyn Monroe). On Monday we always ate what was left of the joint, cold, with bubble and squeak. Tuesday, egg and chips; Wednesday, spam/corned beef and chips; Thursday, liver and mash; Friday, shop-bought fish and chips or cod in parsley sauce. Saturday would be sausage and chips. Breakfast was always cereal or porridge with treacle on it, toast and jam. A cooked breakfast was a rarity in our house, but as mentioned, the Sunday tea was the focal part of the week. Tinned fruit with thin bread and butter, then a slice of Mum's caramel, coffee, Dundee or chocolate cake, washed down with copious cups of tea. As we became a little more affluent in the mid fifties we occasionally used to get a 'box of fancies' from our local baker. What a feast!

From age five until eleven, I attended Air Balloon Hill Junior School – always compressed by locals to Airbloonill. I can only just remember the early years, when the school was run by a tyrant. Yes, a tyrant. A totally humourless cow who insisted she was called 'Madam'… Her actual name was Mrs Robinson, but she would be called nothing else but 'madam' by pupils, teachers or parents. She often wielded a stick and used it whenever she thought appropriate. Madam was a wartime stopgap replacement, obviously over her retirement age, who took charge during the war to release younger teachers for the services or war work. She was an ugly woman with thick glasses and a large wart on her cheek – she could have stepped out of a Roald Dahl horror story! She rode a sturdy bike to school each day before taking the reins of duty for God and Country.

In total contrast to her were the very young teachers, who'd just finished training. My earliest memories are of Miss Horne, a sleepy-eyed lady all of twenty-one or two. Each afternoon she read us stories of Brer Rabbit from *Uncle Tom's Cabin*. I'm convinced that it was this as much as anything that awakened my childish mind to literature and storytelling. In later years another teacher read to us from *The Adventures of Tom Sawyer* and I recall waiting in anticipation each day to hear more about Tom Sawyer, Huck Finn, and maybe Injun Joe. Amazingly, discipline was directed by the pupils. If there was a rising buzz of noise, the teacher would stop reading and those pupils who were listening would shush the culprits to silence… the story would then continue.

Leaving Miss Horne's class and the infants years was a blow, since we went on to one of the older teachers: a complete nutcase, Miss Peacock, who had no control over us kids at all. One of her foibles was that if somebody farted in class, she would line the boys up (only the boys – apparently girls didn't fart!) and sniff their back ends before she punished the 'culprit' with a hard whack across the knuckles with a ruler. I seem to remember that when I was in Miss Peacock's class I became one of the unruly lot, being sent several times to see Madam, and risk the cane for some real or supposed insubordination in Miss Peacock's deranged mind.

I guess she was in her sixties; we kids knew nothing about menopause, or dementia or what she might have been going through at the time... Perhaps I'm being too cruel? Nah. She was just nuts.

Other memories from junior school concern the cruelty of children – myself included. A kid started school with us and he was obviously very poor and very weak. His name was Alan Spear and he had really bad asthma and had spent a good deal of time in hospital. We were warned of this and asked to treat him kindly... this did not happen; and at break times we used to chase him round the playground until he fell down, fighting for breath, exhausted. Amazingly, I don't recall any of us suffering any remorse or guilt about doing this – we just thought it was hilarious. Anyway, having a good memory for faces, I saw Alan Spear some thirty years later, still looking somewhat pasty but grown up... So, even with all our cruelty he made it.

In the junior school a momentous event occurred when I was ten. 'Madam' left... At the morning service the older teachers were crying, whereas the kids could hardly contain their joy. Who would replace her we wondered?

A few days later, I found that, unusually, both school gates were open... and through them came a bright red Hillman Minx. Then out stepped the new headmistress... a young woman – my guess is she was in her early thirties – a vision of loveliness: Miss Lovell. She had a winning smile, a beautiful figure, petite, with reddish hair and the brightest of scarlet red lipstick – she was like a bloody film star! I liked, loved, no, in my weird, sexually confused prepubescent mind, *desired* her! I became very close to Miss Lovell, the lady who brought air and light to the school, who made us proud of our achievements.

However, I felt a cloud of guilt too. I had several erotic dreams about Miss Lovell in which she was always naked – minus finer details in the pubic area which were unknown territory for me (I totally blame this omission on a certain girl who, for threepence, would show her 'bits' off to boys. I stood in the queue, my threepenny bit in sweaty hand... but she decided to shut up shop before I got to her – cow!). Anyway, the lovely Miss Lovell was naked and tied on a rope from the school rafters, swaying back and forth in front of me, and I would smack her ass as she went by... No sex (I didn't know what that was!), no kissing, just that... Having such dreams filled me with the most unimaginable guilt; when I went to school

I couldn't look at Miss Lovell for fear she knew what depraved thoughts I'd had about her.

Howsoever, when I reached eleven I became her firm favourite. As I was good at art, she'd single me out to paint pictures for the school. It was around this time that the class was asked to write a composition (essay) with the title 'Rain'. I remember that I suddenly shifted a gear in writing prose and I became quite philosophical for my young age. It was praised as much for its length as its content. 'Rain' broke the 'exercise book' single-page barrier, going a few lines on to a second page. Most pupils would only manage ten or twelve lines. I recall a feeling of pleasure and enjoyment at writing that essay, plus of course the accolades that came with it.

It was the year of the eleven-plus exam. I remember feeling worried, but not knowing quite why. I had mild encouragement from Mum and Dad to emulate my brother Roger and pass the eleven-plus and go to a grammar school; I sensed my mother wasn't so fussed if I did or not. I couldn't really understand the difference at that age. It's just that at grammar school, judging by my brother's evidence, you seemed to get a lot of homework. So, I surmised that if I failed I'd do less work; I wouldn't need to wear a uniform, or carry a satchel, or do homework.

I guess I didn't try that hard to pass the eleven-plus… and duly failed, along with most of my peers at junior school. So I would be going to the secondary modern next door and, unbeknownst to me then, doomed to be one of the majority of kids who had a limited range of occupation to aim for. Secondary modern schools were set up to cater for those looking to work in trades of some description. Top of the list was engineering – but only if you were very lucky! Then it went all the way down via shop and delivery work to general building and labouring. For boys the absolute height of ambition was to go into an apprenticeship in carpentry. For girls the outlook was pretty bleak: at the top end they could hope for a hairdressing apprenticeship, but it spiralled downward through children's nurse and shop assistant to mindless factory work – perhaps at the local bra and knicker factory – to fill the gap between leaving school and seemingly inevitable marriage and family. The school catered well for sports: physical training in the gym, football (no rugby), cricket and basketball. Athletics was confined to the school sports day held once a year.

In 1951 came the Festival of Britain. It was well advertised and it seemed unpatriotic not to go there, so Dad announced that we were to go to London on the train to see it. The exhibition came at a time of deep recession and, according to the then Chancellor, Stafford Cripps, grinding exchequer poverty. The Festival was supposed to somehow typify the hope of what might be, a strange and streamlined future, but without any real substance or even style. All I recall is being totally underwhelmed. (Exactly the way I later felt about the Millennium Dome.) I kept thinking, is this it? It seemed to me to be a collection of hopes and dreams among past achievements. An exhibit by the National Coal Board was as dull as it sounds. Plenty of balsa models depicting future atomic power stations and 'exploded cutaway drawings' of jet engines (claiming, erroneously, that it was a solely British invention). We all loved Rowland Emett's humorous mechanical sculpture contraption, all very British; but where were the fantastic inventions? The plans for a rocket to the moon which I'd assumed would be there? I needed to be excited, shocked, why not? However, shock and awe fifties style extended to the Skylon, a tall double-pointed structure resembling a rocket – but not. That was, in fact, totally pointless…

I seem to remember travelling to London quite often during this period. My Mum, and occasionally Dad as well, would take a special 'excursion' train to London. This was mostly an evening trip, starting at four P.M., with the return train being at eleven-thirty. Mum was terrified of the Underground and we quite often got on wrong trains and spent valuable time getting back to the right station. I recall that on one visit Mum got on the train but the doors closed on me, and there I was, left alone on the platform. I was cold with fear… what would happen to me? Then a station worker told me that they'd rung through from the next station and Mum was waiting for me there… phew!

On one 'excursion' we went to the London Zoo and Madame Tussaud's. We were with friends Bert and Lily and both Lily and Mum got horrendous blisters on their heels – they'd of course worn brand-new shoes for the visit and were now paying the price. That evening we dined at Lyons' Corner House ('down the bra-zairy' as Dad called it) where we had to queue for a table. It was ever so posh: my dad was completely overawed by having waiters in black ties and the silver service. He reverently pointed out that a couple at another table were drinking wine! It was served in one of those basket cradles.

I liked London. One memory is of an evening trip with Mum to the New Year celebrations in Piccadilly. I didn't feel too well; I remember feeling slightly sick. On our tube back to the station two young Americans were celebrating 'Noo Year!' and handing around a bottle of Bourbon. Mum allowed me a sip, but I took a gulp! Suddenly I felt great – all glowing inside and all feelings of nausea gone…

Certainly these trips to the Metropolis helped me, a bumpkin from the West Country, feel quite urbane, sophisticated even! When we visited my cousin who lived in Clapham, I was in my trainspotting phase and was allowed to travel by myself on the Underground to each of the great stations – Waterloo, Euston, Victoria and King's Cross – to watch and note down the numbers of strange, alien-looking engines from the Midland, Eastern and Southern regions. What a feast it was!

One special memory is of summer trips to Clevedon by bus. Mum had a close friend, Mrs Bishop, who lived at 138 Hillside Road with son Mervyn and daughter Maureen. Her husband had been in the ARP with Dad and worked at Spear's, the bacon wholesalers and makers of sausages and pies. So, first we'd go to the Spear's bakery in Old Market and pick up a family size pork pie from Mr Bishop, then walk to the nearby bus station and catch the Clevedon bus. An hour's journey took us about fifteen miles down the Bristol Channel. Clevedon has a pebble beach and rocks to climb. At that point the water is still a muddy grey brown and not particularly suitable for bathing. There was a pier where pleasure boats once landed to take people on trips across the channel to Barry Island or Cardiff on the Welsh coast, but it fell down whilst being stress-tested in the nineties; a new, exact replica is now in place after a huge and successful effort to raise the money to build it. The particular pleasure of Clevedon was the pebble beach where my friends and I threw endless amounts of pebbles at imaginary foes. We hunted for crabs in the muddy pools; then, if the tide should happen to be in, we'd try spinning flat pebbles across the water. All this combined with sunshine and the pork pie made it positively idyllic.

After complaints from Mum about paint smells in the house Dad decided to take his weekend work out of the house. The garden at 152 Hillside

Road was small but adequate, about ten metres by four. So, Dad built a large shed, big enough to hold a car or van (not for our car – we didn't have one – but for the weekend work which might be a van). It was the biggest shed in the street, brick-built with corrugated iron roof, second-hand Crittall windows and large wooden doors. It was nearly as big as our house! It was built by another man who worked at weekends – Mr Drinkwater, a builder friend of Dad's – so that it took a good year before it was finished. Amazingly, even with the new shed built, Dad still worked on things in the living room with posters propped up on chairs, still the smell of paint around.

The shed became my inclement-weather base for games with my friends, as imaginary fort, medieval castle or pretend laboratory; it also had a dartboard. Much later on it became the practice room for the traditional jazz band I'd helped form. That bare corrugated roof acted rather like a megaphone for the tortured sounds coming from the fledgling band, much to the chagrin of the neighbours. We had a car by then and the band members would have to push it out of the shed before practice could begin and back in again before we left. The shed was where I did my stuff too: model-making, and when I was around fourteen I attempted my first oil painting, and so it became my studio.

With the supershed and the Anderson shelter the growing space in our garden came down to a small onion patch before the tiny lawn outside the back window. So, we took one of the allotments out behind the back lane. I kept well away from it as it meant certain hard work. We grew spuds, carrots and cabbages – nothing exotic but it kept us in good stead during the cruel first postwar years.

In 1948 Dad set up a business with an old RAF buddy, Phil Legge, to form a signwriting and paint-spray business called Baker and Legge Ltd. They rented a sizeable workshop in Bedminster, on the south side of Bristol; it was large enough to hold furniture vans, so that Dad could do the signwriting and paintwork. Phil did spraying and upholstery, since this was his trade. Phil drove an enormous Wolseley convertible sports car which I was allowed to sit in and imagine driving… if I was lucky.

As a family, we were solidly working class; and Dad, I found out, was a bit of a leftie in the thirties. A card-carrying communist no less! He was a shop steward at one of his workplaces and when he stood up for a mate who was sacked he got the sack himself. My mother was that political anomaly, the working-class Tory: everything to gain from Labour but supporting the Conservative party. I think my gran was that way inclined too because she came from being in service as a maid in a grand house and my guess is she was convinced by her employers that Labour and socialism were evil. Gran had then passed it on to Mum. Anyway, Dad made that somewhat inevitable turnaround of views when he started his own business. Suddenly he was the boss, something that didn't sit happily with him.

I recall he had a job painting the logo on glass petrol-station pumps but he had to clean the old one off with sulphuric acid. The smell was horrendous, but the little bottle of acid was a fascination to me. It was kept on a high shelf in the shed and I recall several times when a scientifically inclined friend and I would use it in 'experiments'. This consisted mainly of corroding bits of metal and mixing it with stuff from the chemistry set he'd had for Christmas just to see the effect. All highly dangerous of course.

We didn't have a car or a TV; only the bloated plutocrats down the road in the big house had those... Dad eventually realised his dream of getting a motorcycle and sidecar, a 1929 Sunbeam with a registration number I still remember: YG 5507. Dad totally rebuilt the sidecar in the shed and painted it 'battleship grey' – of which more later. Once we had wheels, albeit only three, the world was our oyster – we were able to get out and about at weekends in summer for picnics or just a 'run out' as it was called. Mum would ride in the sidecar and I would take the pillion seat. For me it was exciting and informative to go through all the country lanes and back roads within twenty-five miles of home. It was definitely the origin of the now infamous 'Baker short cut', the phrase used by family and friends to refer to my practice of using my knowledge of back roads, allegedly to avoid traffic – back-way short cuts which often more likely backfired! Sometimes I'd get lost and those family or friends travelling with me would ask politely if I was taking a 'Baker short cut'? – which always took longer than going on the busy main road and quite often ended up in someone's back garden... it was much prettier though.

Longer journeys could prove more hazardous. Dad's Sunbeam had a propensity for breaking down – literally stopping for no apparent reason – usually on an embarrassingly shallow uphill slope. This meant any companions we were with, such as my cousin Ivor and his wife Mary, or our friends Ray and Joan, would double back and see what the trouble was. This usually meant much poring over the engine parts and making fruitless attempts at starting it. Then suddenly – again for no apparent reason – one kick and it would start... and we were off again!

One journey I will never forget is when we went to visit my cousin Enid in Clapham, London. It was planned with military precision and, taking into account the whims of our Sunbeam motorcycle, Dad tried to avoid very steep hills; so we chose to take the A420 which meets up with the main A4 London road at Chippenham, Dad preferring the idea of Tog Hill just north of Bath as opposed to the dreaded Box Hill, on the A4 on the south side of Bath (the hill that one I.K. Brunel chose to tunnel through for his railway). We started out in one of those summer downpours that progressively got worse and worse. I was wearing a flying suit we'd acquired: it was of thirties vintage, and was full of kapok. I looked like the Michelin Man, but it was warm. I'd never travelled to London by road before... this was my baptism of fire – or water...

As the journey wore on, the rain began to soak the flying suit and the kapok filling got saturated and began to build into lumps as it got pushed down the suit by the weight of water. By the time we reached Reading – a mere six hours after starting! – I was a huge lump of soaking wet kapok which had gravitated to my legs. I looked like I was suffering from elephantiasis! There was no choice to be made. Having nothing else to put on I had to continue wearing it until we got to Enid's house where I threw the huge soggy lump into the bin. Fortunately, on the return journey the weather was fine and without rain; even so the trek back to Bristol took eight hours with many stops for tea on the way. The old Sunbeam kept up a steady speed of thirty to thirty-five mph, the same speed as the trail of heavy lorries, so that overtaking was hazardous, especially remembering the bike's quirky behaviour when urged to accelerate. So we just slotted ourselves in to the lorry train.

The area on the outskirts of Bristol was the cradle of Methodism. St George was in the Methodist triangle of Hanham, Kingswood and St George – John Wesley's Bristol stamping ground. It was full of chapels: Wesleyan, primitive Methodist, Bethesda, Baptist and Presbyterian, showing up the schism within a schism after Wesley split from the C of E. It was where Wesley preached Hell, Fire and Damnation to poor miners coming up from the coal mine, knackered after twelve hours or so of gruelling work in the pit. He obviously held their attention. It's said that many a miner went home with streaks of white in the coal dust on their cheeks.

What a bastard he must have been! That Wesley? You work your bollocks off down the mine for twelve hours a day and here's this vicar threatening you with Hell! Because you are a 'sinner'. I can't imagine they had a lot of time to 'sin' anyway. The Rev Wesley's haranguing must have worked because it led to scores of Methodist chapels being built between about 1760 and 1900; in fact there are almost as many chapels as there are pubs! The Chapel I became attached to was Clowes Chapel, stricter than others perhaps since it enjoyed the title of 'Primitive' Methodist (Mr or Rev Clowes was another dissenter in the Methodist pack). I used to go to Sunday school there from the age of seven or so until I was fourteen or fifteen – until I got interested in girls that is.

Sunday school at Clowes was pretty ramshackle, run by two warm-hearted ex-servicemen just back from the war. I guess they must have been in their early thirties. They were Jack Venn and Albert Hillier. Jack did the Sunday school and Albert ran the Wednesday evening social club and concert party in which Jack sometimes played the drums – badly – for what was amusingly called 'The Swingtet' which featured a trumpet player called Leon Found who could hardly blow the notes and a clarinettist who held the instrument in his mouth but no sound came out! It made fascinating listening and could only be called a faint-hearted, jazz-ish music. They were only as good or bad as any others of the concert party, which occasionally did their show at hospitals… to further depress the patients I should think.

As a pre-teenager I was expected to go to Sunday school, as pretty well every other kid in the street went and they used to call for me at the house. Sunday afternoon was bath time; I'm ashamed to admit that the whole family bathed in the same water. Ugh! Being youngest I was last in and the water was nearly cold. That was pretty normal in the forties and fifties – not that you ever asked what your friends and neighbours' bathing arrangements were. Everything was private. You never told anybody anything about your home life.

My first 'best friend' was Phillip Tyler, who lived just down the road and once we'd established the pecking order – he could beat me up in a fight, so he was leader – enough said. The kids in the vicinity of the local grocery shop used to gather around the large house of Keith Harding, son of the owner of a successful chain of radio – and later television – shops. They lived in a spacious house with a large garden and a garage for the Jaguar car at the top of a drive. They were self-made, rich people, but they had been cursed by tragedy. Their first son had drowned in the swimming pool (used in wartime as a static water tank); Keith, their second son, caught polio and was paralysed from the neck down. Their third child Marilyn also caught polio, but happily she recovered fully.

Keith, though wheelchair-bound and with just limited movement in his right arm, could write, drink from a cup and hold a small cricket bat. Keith was of my brother's generation, so as a younger kid I was not too welcome to the games they played at first, but persistence paid off. Amazingly, the boy in the wheelchair was the boss of the gang, something way beyond sympathy: there was a loyalty towards him, a fealty even. Perhaps it was because he was the rich people's son? The fact that he was more intelligent than most of us may have helped! It was a matter of honour to push the wheelchair; Keith was always the stagecoach in our cowboy games and was never left out of anything. Another honour was helping Keith pee into a special bottle – one I didn't accede to! There's no doubt that Keith Harding was the leader of the pack, and he devised games and strategies from his wheelchair for his minions to carry out. As we got older, instead of war and cowboy games, we played cricket: stumps were chalk-drawn on the wall and the pitch was the road with all the hazards of back gardens to hit the ball into, but not particularly road traffic – a passing car or motorbike was rare. Keith could just about hold a bat in his atrophied arm and hand; bowlers were sympathetic, and bounced a gentle underhand ball at him. As time went by Keith took over his father's business and got married. The last I'd heard was that he'd started a family.

Sometimes I would tire of the Harding gang and make overtures to the bunch at the top of the road in the cul-de-sac of Batten Road. This lot had a chuff-chuff-train culture and spent time actually 'being' a train; with arms as cylinders, pumping away, they made stately chuff-chuff progress whistling and letting off steam from imaginary station to station, stopping at imaginary signals and puffing up imaginary inclines. Amazingly they did this without speaking. I was intrigued. One of these kids was Malcolm Windsor and a friendship forged then still exists today.

As I grew into adolescence, I found myself growing away from the Keith Harding bunch and attached myself to the top gang – they were hardly a gang, more a collection of individuals. Two of the older ones, David Tarr and Malcolm, had passed their eleven-plus and gone to separate grammar schools way across the city; they had to go by train or bus to get there every day. It is with these fellows that I got into trainspotting. At first I thought it laughable to collect numbers, but gradually the bug got me and led me into many an adventure. Like, for instance, experiencing the fear of creeping into the engine maintenance sheds in the evening. Spotters were strictly forbidden to be there: signs threatened huge fines if we were caught. But it was worth the risk for the sheer joy of seeing around twenty steam engines, like hissing steel giants bedded down for the night in a circle around the turntable. It was tremendous: the place was noisy, hot, smokey; the smell was a delightful fusion of coal, oil and soot… Wonderful! The whole atmosphere was lit in a sepia haze as dust cleaned from fireboxes filled the air, lit by sunlight from the opened roof above. The feeling of elation would be dispelled in a second when somebody shouted 'Foreman!' The Foreman would chase us out of the sheds.

The normal area for trainspotting was a place in Barton Hill called 'The Triangle', a piece of railway-owned waste ground tucked between the South Wales and Midland line to the front, just outside of Bristol's main station Temple Meads, the London line behind us, and, to the right, 'the loop', a line linking the Welsh line to the London line avoiding the station and mainly used by goods trains. The thing about trainspotting is that there's a hell of a lot of time waiting around for another train, so you get to talking; we used to tell jokes, argue, and occasionally plan a trip to some other maintenance shed – perhaps Cardiff – or even better Barry, which housed some very collectable engine numbers, including locomotive number '1' called 'Hercules', an ex-coal-mine engine. We schemed a visit to Gloucester, deciding to cycle the seventy-four miles there and back!

The Triangle was a male preserve; but I remember a girl who visited us now and then. Things inevitably got to being silly – she was pretty and we were all, I believe, interested in taking things further. Deep dark fears of making an approach to a girl and severe hang-ups about sex were exposed which were disguised in banter and pathetic attempts at being funny. This came to a head for me when I jokingly suggested that her newly formed pert breasts were in fact coconut halves shoved into her jumper. Her eyes narrowed as she looked at me with a half smile.

'No they ain't,' she said, which caused me to laugh nervously. She then delivered a thunderbolt. 'If that's what you think, why don't you come and feel 'em?'

God, I wanted to; but the trainspotters were all around me, waiting and hoping I would. I was scared and humiliated and felt compelled to make some slightly insulting remark to take the heat out of the situation.

Well, that was sex education! I must have been aged around twelve I suppose and, apart from my weird erotic dreams about the headmistress, I hadn't thought much about sex. I remember my first kiss: it was with the girl who lived two doors up from us, June ('Junie') Clarke. We actually hid in the bushes to 'do it'! I made the mistake of telling my mother, who thereafter seemed to have a special liking for Junie and urged me right up until I was married that 'you can't go far wrong with little Junie.' The thing is that as I grew older I couldn't stand dear Junie. Even when I divorced after sixteen years with my first wife, Vicki, my mother would say quietly: 'You'd've been better off marrying Junie Clarke, my son.'

Sex was never mentioned in the Baker household. For me it was an 'unknown unknown' as far as the physical act was concerned. However, I did become aware that my brother was doing something with his girlfriend, Margaret, that made my father query about the sleeping arrangements when they went camping together. There was a conspiratorial laugh when Roger retorted: 'We've even got a double bed in the tent!' I was so preoccupied with guilt in my early teens, like thinking that I was the only boy in the whole world who had nocturnal emissions and the only one to have pubic hair growing, which I had to carefully conceal when changing for sports or risk humiliation from the other boys. I finally got over the first when, one morning, I saw that my brother's pyjamas were in the same state as my own, and the second when I realised that all the boys had pubic hair. Duhh!

By the time I was thirteen, I began to worry a little less and actually fancy certain girls at school; but once more I was brought up short by a teacher who shouted: 'Baker! Stop making sheep's eyes at Mary Collins and get on with your work!' I'd quietly and very privately fallen in love with Mary from afar and couldn't keep my eyes off her. Apparently, she'd felt a similar thing toward me, so she sent a messenger, her best friend Beryl, to convey a spoken message that 'Mary likes you'. I was pole-axed. I didn't know where to put myself; but I gradually began to understand, through several messages from Beryl, that I might take her out sometime.

But there was a rival: she already had a sort of boyfriend – Mervyn, the son of my mother's best friend Mrs Bishop. Mary also went to Clowes Chapel and so I saw her there in the youth club, and on Sundays at the evening service.

One evening, I was idly scanning the road from our front room when there were Mary and Beryl walking home. I made a speedy decision to intercept them. I put on my father's sleek black overcoat and white evening scarf and made off to 'just happen to be' at the corner a little further up. Instead of a welcome I got some pretty peculiar looks and sharp replies to my questions. I began to back away, unable to take the flak. Then, when I was on my way back home, Beryl came with a message: 'Mary says you took her for granted,' and she stunned me with a final slash at my crumbling dignity – 'and she said you kisses wet!'

A new feeling had entered my emotional landscape – the blues, devastation and desolation! I went home and sat in the darkness wondering what the hell had hit me. Oh, the heartache and total despair; plus the nagging worry that there was a serious problem with my kissing technique! 'Kisses wet'? I resolved to correct my sloppy kissing. After this disastrous night, there was a rift between Mary Collins and me. For her part she became Mervyn Bishop's regular. They walked arm-in-arm wherever they went, almost as if they were conjoined Siamese twins. I always nodded to them and privately envied Mervyn, believing he must have mastered the secret of the dry kiss! Mary was fourteen then, and they continued walking arm-in-arm until they inevitably got married when Mary was twenty-one... I meanwhile secretly practised 'dry kissing' which called for a lot of sucking in of air before contact. This was until I realised what crap it all was and happily slipped into the glory of wet French kissing.

In my early life everything revolved around the houses east and west of number 152 Hillside Road. Up as far as 186 and down to number 75 ran the 'back lane' as we called it, dividing the gardens from the allotments.

This was my realm. I knew it intimately; it was my 'trail' where I was cowboy or cavalier or cavalryman, with my mac tied around my neck by the arms as a cloak *à la* Zorro. My range was beyond the allotments on the site of two derelict cottages; it was called 'The Piece' – piece of what I never knew. This small plot of land was used for everything: our bonfire, battleground games, picnics even! A fire was a must and potatoes cooked in the cinders until burnt black and crunchy were a delicacy. On one occasion, the girls from our road arrived with a frying pan and fried chips. Now that was a feast!

On one side of The Piece was an ivy-covered cottage wherein lived a nightmare of a man who would chase children, waving his walking stick at them and threatening them with indecipherable words of abuse. This was 'Old Man Blacker'. He lived alone in the cottage with no running water and no electricity, and a privy out in the garden – of which he left the door open when going about his 'business'! He seemed to us kids an unredeemable miserable old bastard. However, when my mates and I first started frequenting pubs some years later, there was Old Man Blacker in the corner sipping cider. Now he seemed a jolly soul who easily engaged us lads in conversation and talked with passion about his part in the First World War – then as 'Sapper Blacker'.

Another lane, Meg Thatcher's Lane, ran beside The Piece bounded by a high wall which guarded the orchards of the Cole family. One day, I discovered that a part of the wall had fallen down giving an opening into what was hitherto the secret orchard behind the wall. It seemed irresistible to my friend Phillip and I – and anyway Mr Cole was his uncle. We decided to pinch some apples and found beautiful sweet ones on one of the smaller trees. Suddenly Mr Cole ran out from behind a bush, clad in riding boots and spurs, and brandishing a shotgun! I was absolutely petrified. I assumed Phillip would claim that he was family, but he didn't and his uncle saw us off his land at gunpoint and then informed the police, which brought a visit to the house by a constable! Oh the shame of it! I was later informed that this was not Phill's 'nice uncle', this was his brother, the 'mad uncle'! That put paid to trespassing stealing apples in that garden. After our fright we gave the Coles' orchard a wide berth…

Beyond the high wall was the stable for the chimney-sweep's pony and trap. I clearly remember the odd smell of dung, straw and soot, which was no more when he bought a van. The lane followed round in a circle to meet up with Hillside Road via a cul-de-sac called Batten Road. Beyond this was uncharted territory, which had to be explored! The lane continued around the rim of a quarry with a deep pool in the bottom of it. All very sinister-looking. The lane then climbed up to stables and more smallholdings before coming out on the main Hanham road opposite the pub I was to frequent when I was older, the Horse and Jockey.

The back lanes and The Piece remained my haunt until older friends told us about the delights of Troopers Hill, which I could see from my bedroom window, with its stark derelict chimney on the summit; but my mother forbade me to go there since I would have to cross a main road.

I'm afraid I disobeyed my mother's edict and started to go there with friends who were not under the same ban. Troopers Hill was once a quarry, but was now totally abandoned. The hill builds up to a small plateau on which stands a tall chimney, built from black clinker around 1700, it being a defunct outlet for the noxious smoke from a copper mill by the riverside below. It required nerve to step inside the chimney and look up it as the wind funnelled through it with a howl like a banshee. There was a trench from the factory to the flue, which was at one time covered over but it had collapsed and was now what we kids believed to be a 'Roman wall'. The grass on Troopers Hill was a tough, long-stalked strain and on a hot summer day the grassy mounds swayed in the breeze like rolling waves. Elsewhere in this Eden there were old quarry workings that became ravines in which to ambush 'enemies', and dangerous rocks to climb: in particular one called 'the Lion's Head' for obvious reasons; climbing it was proof of one's prowess. There was even a flat bit where we played cricket. For kids, Troopers Hill was, quite simply, paradise. Happily it all still exists and is now a wildlife reserve.

When I entered the 'big school' – the secondary modern, next door to the junior school – I was extremely cautious, and kept quietly out of things. I had been told of an initiation ceremony called 'The Slab' which was meted out to newcomers by the older boys. (Strange how public school rituals filtered down to the lowly 'sec mod'.) The victim was put on a wall which was out of sight from the main playground, then tickled and punched by a gang of up to six boys; but the thing that scared me most was that they removed your trousers! I couldn't bear the thought of this and I managed to avoid being 'slabbed'.

The secondary modern syllabus included all the basics – English, maths, history and geography – but added on to this was woodwork for the boys and domestic science for the girls. There was science too, but only of a very basic kind; and the teacher didn't seem to have his heart in it. He normally spoke in a kind of mumbling monotone, but if crossed would go nuclear! He would throw anything that was at hand at the offending pupil, from chalk or the blackboard rubber to even, at one time, a set of delicate brass scales. Now, I think he was manic-depressive; but how were we to know?

Music lessons were enjoyable: we learned songs and sang them for half an hour. I remember that as I got interested in New Orleans jazz, courtesy of my brother, I asked the music teacher if I could talk about it and illustrate it with records. Totally unprecedented, listening to music at school, but he agreed; so I picked one of the stronger boys to help me carry our huge wind-up gramophone into school. I tried to interest my peers in the joy of jazz, but Jelly Roll Morton and Louis Armstrong only sounded old-fashioned to them – and knowing that a gramophone was available one girl brought her record of the leading hit-parade song, *Answer Me*. My claim that this was commercial crap was ignored and any attempt at converting others to jazz evaporated. How naïve I was.

I also took a book of Picasso paintings and started showing them to kids; I took up my father's view of 'modern art', claiming that children could do better. Then, at the picture called 'Lovers', which shows a couple embracing, one boy turned it sideways and said: 'Look – they're doin' it!' Before a minute had passed I had queues of boys, even the fourth years, wanting to see the couple 'shagging'. This lasted the whole day.

I did the first year in 'the Big School' and came out around the upper middle, helped by good marks in art and history, but at floor level or worse on maths, which I just couldn't fathom. The weeks and months went into a blur of repetitive days, high moments and low ones... Then one day, the world changed for Air Balloon Hill Secondary Modern School and for those in it, pupils and teachers alike.

One day – not the first day of term, but a few days after – three coaches turned up outside the school. They were full of children in grey uniforms. There was much conjecture among us kids about what they were doing there; maybe it was some sort of visit, or they'd come to take an exam. The children were debussed and marched into the school yard with military precision. There were about sixty boys and thirty girls. The most notable thing about the boys was their haircuts: highly unfashionable hacked-off short back and sides, whereas most of us with any sense of style had the Tony Curtis quiff and 'Duck's Ass'. On inspection, the grey uniforms were threadbare and ill-fitting; but the final shock revelation was that all the boys, aged from twelve up to fifteen, wore baggy short trousers. The girls were equally badly dressed and the poor things looked petrified.

We finally learned at morning assembly that the new arrivals were from Muller's Orphanage. Some liberal-thinking soul in the City Education Department decided that the orphans should be taught in state school alongside parented kids, instead of at the orphanage, so that the children, instead of spending their formative years in a closed, almost monastic community, might more easily become part of normal society.

The situation was quickly accepted by the school and most of the pupils almost bent over backwards to be nice to the new intake; but understandably they were nervous of us. They'd been thrown into the real world, with no idea how to cope with it… yet. They stayed in clumps of their own kind and were difficult to get to know. By this time I was an unprecedented third-year prefect and was one of those asked to show them around and try and make them feel at their ease.

Lunch hour for pupils was pretty straightforward: you either stayed for dinner, ate sandwiches or, if you lived near, you went home. Sometimes during the lunch break we would go to the nearby paper shop and buy sweets or comics. There was never any restriction of movement after lunch. It was about the third day after the Muller's kids arrived that I noticed they were clocking the fact that our kids could leave the school premises… First one… then another crept out of the school yard; and when they realised that nobody was watching them they started off down the road. They were free! Relishing this new-found freedom they all ran away! They just ran and ran and ran! I was one of a half-dozen search party of pupils and teachers sent to get them back. A kind of round-up. We eventually found the last pair walking the towpath of the river Avon towards Keynsham. Half way to Bath! They obediently came back with us, but I'll never forget the look on their faces as they ran. Sheer unadulterated joy!

Of course, after this episode they weren't allowed out of the school gates. I began to realise that these poor kids through no fault of their own were treated abominably at the orphanage, with strict rules for everything and harsh punishment if they were broken. I mistakenly thought that the kids were actually orphans, but of course most of them weren't – many were born 'out of wedlock' as they say, and a lot of others lost one parent and their second couldn't cope for some reason or other. The 'orphans' were subject to a harsh, very non-conformist regimen of prayer, piety and a pretty heavy dose of guilt laid on them too. I felt they were being blamed for circumstances totally beyond their control. Yes, Mr Muller was a philanthropist, but why turn these sad bereaved souls into prisoners? The Muller's kids had even developed their own language, a kind of amalgam of accents from all over the UK using old-fashioned words and even words they'd made up.

One of the Muller's boys, Malcolm, a pixie-like kid, made to look so by his unbelievably bad haircut which made his head look pointed, was put to sit next to me in class and we quickly formed a friendship, based mainly on the books about Dr Doolittle. I was told that he would be allowed to come to my house on Saturdays. I found out that outside visits were possible as long as it was set up in advance. So I used to go to the orphanage to pick him up. I had to wait in the huge dark corridor, where I saw children hurry past me – heads bowed – and if they uttered a word a voice would soon order them to be silent! Creepy isn't the word. I felt sorrow and anger at the same time. A place like that should not exist, and although things were moving to break Muller's up as an institution, as far as I was concerned it wasn't bloody moving fast enough. So there!

I made it a duty that I would lead Malcolm into the ways of the world. Mum made sure he was well fed, and I took him to the local fleapit to see 'X' rated films; one I remember was *Bitter Rice* starring the ravishing Silvana Mangano. I also gave him the odd sip of sherry, stolen from our sideboard. I hope it helped him get some kind of balance. However, all my subversive deeds were probably to no avail. When Malcolm left school he was put into a 'family home' with a family of religious maniacs. I went to tea to meet them and was practically ordered to kneel down and be 'saved'. When I refused they told me that they would prefer me not to see Malcolm again… So, I didn't – not because I didn't want to, but because he was moved on to another family of religious nutcases and, although I contacted him, he wasn't happy after the last debacle for me to visit him. It appears these were typical 'approved' families for the Muller children to be sent to.

The other cruel thing was that if a Muller boy or girl showed some kind of sporting or academic promise, all hopes of even trying to attain recognition for it were dashed to the ground. The edict from the Muller's hierarchy was that boys will be farm workers (and there was more than a suspicion that certain lucky 'Christian' farmers got a fantastic deal by having the boys working for them as virtual slaves on shockingly low wages). It was also decreed that girls would work in a factory or become children's nurses.

One boy was a fantastic footballer, and I mean in the George Best class; everyone at school knew it, and moves were made by the school sports teacher and the headmaster to get him a trial for Bristol City, but this was simply forbidden and he was sent off to work on a farm and sadly, was killed in a tractor roll-over accident. Another was brilliant at mathematics. He should have gone to university, but guess what? He too ended up working on a farm. Another, a girl, had amazing artistic and dramatic talent… she was made to become a children's nurse. What a sad, sad, waste! All ambition torn out of them by sheer ugly prejudice and oppression… just for the sake of it.

In the second year I made another close friend, John Gardiner, because of our mutual interest in science fiction and rocketry, mainly by way of the groundbreaking *Eagle* comic and its front page star: space pilot, Dan Dare. We spent hours at his house looking through magazines about astronomy. Also, John built himself a small telescope with which we looked at the moon. The craters were clearly visible and there was a tremendous excitement about looking at another world. The Gardiner household also had a television and we used to sit glued to it in the afternoon watching programmes aimed at infants! A strange thing happened whilst watching *The Flowerpot Men*: John put his hand on mine and said in a baby voice, ' 'Ickle me,' so being his friend I obliged – he wanted me to tickle the back of his hand, I had no qualms about it and did as instructed. Then he offered to ' 'ickle me' and he stroked the back of my hand. I didn't think about it until much later: there we were, two potential intrepid astronauts, sitting in front of a telly watching *Watch With Mother* and tickling the backs of each other's hands!

For some time, John Gardiner was my 'best friend'. Whenever I called on him, if he was having tea, his mother would insist I wait in the porch. I sat on the sisal mat bordered by the polished brass step. One summer evening I arrived at John's house to find another boy sitting on the mat... I suddenly felt hurt and wondered if I should go away and come another day. Anyway, John emerged from his house and introduced me to the 'interloper' as another John – John Wood.

We decided to walk to Troopers Hill. John Wood quickly started to stake his claim as being John Gardiner's long-standing best friend, and saying how highly intelligent he was: he attended the Bristol Cathedral School, one of the more prestigious grammar schools in Bristol. He also informed me that he was learning to box, and kept using me as a sort of punchbag, though claiming he was just showing me how to box clever. As we moved on, he showed me a right cross and clocked me one on the chin. I could stand no more and I hit him hard on the face, which to my horror brought blood gushing from his nose and mouth. I was highly aware of the fact that John Gardiner was silently laughing his head off at these two idiots fighting over him! I was shocked and remorseful for what I'd done and I walked home with him and confronted his mother. I was full of apologies, but, amazingly, she just smiled at me and said she hoped I hadn't broken his jaw. And so, as happens at that age, my friendship with John Gardiner waned as another one waxed. Of John Wood, more later.

It was around the end of my third year of secondary school that I realised I could run pretty fast. Again I was following in my brother Roger's footsteps. He was a member of an athletics club, and having seen him at various sports day events, I decided to join the Bristol Athletic Club too. I was a sprinter: hundred yards, two-twenty yards, but got into pain in the four-forty. At first it went well: I won third prize at the local police sports day, the prize being an alarm clock. I won the two-twenty yards at the Douglas Motorcycle sports day – this time a pendulum clock was the prize.

At the age of seventeen I was as fit as I'd ever be and decided to take athletics more seriously; and, despite enduring pain in the four hundred metres, I decided to go for that anyway. This meant that if I was to be any good or attain great heights of championship athletics I would have to train much, much, harder than I was at that time. I started doing road running throughout the winter months and, along with a couple of like-minded friends, began to build up my stamina – ready for the coming summer season of sports meetings.

Just to top off my winter road-running, as a stamina-building exercise, I entered a ten-mile cross-country handicap race. Since I'd never run a cross-country before, I was given the maximum handicap advantage of twenty minutes. It meant I launched myself into the race with a twenty-minute start on the rest! I was alone running the course for what seemed ages. Then, after about forty-five minutes, I heard pit-pat-pit-pat-pit-pat behind me. Somebody was gaining on me… Very soon the footsteps came up close to me and then passed me. To my utter horror and amazement I was being passed by a ten-year-old kid! Other, stronger, faster athletes passed me in droves. I finally finished last… And that, for me, was my last race. I gave up athletics and took up smoking!

One lesson that I grew to enjoy more was French, taught by Miss Willmott who was deeply in love with the headmaster, Mr Warren. He would find any excuse to come into the class and they would talk for ages, gazing lovingly into each other's eyes; the class would respond by a gradual rise in chatter until it reached pandemonium. Mr Warren would suddenly realise what had happened and yell at the class, and possibly pick out a few of 'the usual suspects' to deal with later – a stroke of the cane!

I'm glad to say Miss Willmott and I got on well. I was interested in French and was going through an early Ernest Hemingway idyll in my mind, all about Paris and his first lady, the fictional Cynthia in *The Snows of Kilimanjaro*. Came the day when I was asked to enter a painting competition set up by the twin-town Bristol-Bordeaux trust, or whatever. The painting was to be a sort of poster, to be titled 'La Douce France'. I decided to do it in (my father's) oil paint, a romantic French café scene with the Eiffel Tower in the background – even though at this stage of my life I'd not been there. Anyway, I won. Miss Willmott was beside herself with pride and excitement, suggesting that the prize could even be a trip to France. Imagine my French chagrin when I was presented with two pocket-size art books on Monet and Van Gogh. Boy did that cut me down to size. On the other hand, I think Miss Willmott must have had a word with the headmaster about me, because suddenly I became a 'trusty' as they say in nick. The head would call me to his office and ask me to go on errands, sometimes right across the city. (Happily I was familiar with all the City buses from the summer Sunday afternoons when Mum and I used to take a different bus to every destination going, just to see where they went).

I once had to take a key that she'd forgotten to the cookery and domestic science teacher, Miss Coombes: a peach of a lady, plump and ripe. She lived in Redland, some two bus rides away from the school. When I arrived, she asked me into her house and offered coffee, then talked to me as if I was an adult, about news, current affairs, ambitions; and all the while she blew smoke into my face from her black and gold Balkan Sobranie cigarettes which she seemed to chain-smoke. I was stricken and fell in love with the beautiful Miss Coombes there and then.

It so happened that I was so bad at woodwork the teacher told me to get out of his class and not come back. So, I decided to visit Miss Coombes' domestic science class. She welcomed me and asked me for ideas on redecorating 'The Flat', the place where her girl pupils practised housework. I became the only male member of the domestic science department, though I was only there more or less as an observer. Very pleasant it was too.

Mr Warren had me get him his tins of Meggezones – cough pastilles which he chewed constantly; when you were near him you could smell the menthol… I wondered what Miss Willmott must have thought of that? Another time I was asked to accompany a young first year to the clinic to make sure he saw the doctor. The headmaster thought the lad might be malingering – a new word I learned that day. These were halcyon days of my secondary school life; coming up fast was… what the hell was I going to do for a living? This brought me to a head-on confrontation with my mother.

My brother had finished grammar school with a complement of O and A levels; he was a tremendously talented artist. I looked with indrawn breath at his art folio when he brought it home after finishing school. He wanted to go to art school, and Dad saw Roger fulfilling his wish to become a 'proper' artist. So grants were applied for, and obtained; Roger then studied at the West of England College of Art, and soon became aloof from the family and descended into what Mum called the 'Bohemian lifestyle' – jazz, long hair, the obligatory duffel coat and worst of all… girls. My mother used to say to me with utter disgust, 'Oh, you don't want to muck about with girls.' I wasn't quite sure what she had in mind, since I had 'mucked about' with some already.

So, when it came to my time to talk about what I wanted to do with my life I said I'd like to go to art school too. My mother suddenly changed from closest friend to wicked witch and told my father, who was at least considering my plea, that if he let me go to art school she would leave him!

I was utterly dumbstruck.

It took me a long time to realise that she felt she was protecting me from the Bohemian, louche lifestyle. She liked everything to be 'little', and 'only', so she could at least face the neighbours and say: 'Bob? He's got a nice little job, only down the Co-op.' I could bloody hear her saying it.

It was time to leave school. The Youth Employment Officer weighed up my case and could only suggest some kind of clerical work. That was not for me; so I consulted Roger, now a kind of mentor on everything from athletics and jazz to modern artists. He had decided to specialise in sculpture, and suggested that I try monumental sculpture: at least it was to do with art – wasn't it…? So I did.

CHAPTER THREE
Bob the Obscure?

MY APPRENTICESHIP AT THE Co-op started in September 1954. The Co-op monumental department was housed in what had previously been the stables for the horses of the Co-op milk department when milk was delivered in horse-drawn carts. When it was changed to electric vans, the stable was redundant and taken over as the monumental department. It still had the divided stable doors and a forge where the horses were shod. Inside, there were several concrete 'bankers' or work stations, like tables, only made of one-foot-thick reinforced concrete so that they were able to take any size of headstone. The workshop was pleasantly cool in summer but freezing cold in winter, the only heating being from an open coke fire that only threw out heat to a radius of three feet. The classic dilemma: if you were close you burned down one side, if you were out of the three-foot radius you froze...

I was introduced to the foreman, Wally Chinn: a man with staring eyes, a truly fanatical socialist as it turned out, who couldn't believe there hadn't been a revolution in 1926.

Wally started me off on 'ends'. I was given a piece of York stone ashlar, to be put on a grave as a stone surround (a sawn piece of stone three inches by six inches in cross section and three feet long) and told to square off the end. Oh God, I thought, shades of bloody woodwork again! But now my tools were steel chisels and a huge heavy applewood mallet (the heaviest mallet in the place; I was later told, 'If you can use that, you can use any mallet!'). First a set square was used to mark out the 'end'. A pitcher or snub-nosed chisel was used to crack the stone down to within a quarter inch of the line; a one-inch, very sharp chisel was then used to cut all around the edge to the line, leaving a high bit in the middle. This lump was taken down using a 'punch', or pointed chisel. When it was close to the desired level, a claw, or ten-pointed, comb-like chisel was used to take the rough off and square off the end; it was then smoothed off with a block of carborundum.

I soon began to get a feel and rhythm of it. Wally showed me how to lighten the blows as I got to the edge, so that the corner wouldn't chip off. When I started thumping the chisel too hard, Wally said of the mallet: 'All you 'ave to do is lift 'n up. God almighty'll bring 'n down!'

Wally was a strange character. As mentioned, he was a staunch socialist; but as foreman he was very much the boss's man, always urging you to work faster and stop talking. He had some pretty awful habits too. He never used a handkerchief and just blew out of his nose, his finger holding the other nostril. He often used to eat pig's trotter for lunch – nothing wrong with that, but the knife he used was really filthy and I'd seen him previously cleaning his nails with it! By far his worst habit was to leave the lavatory door open when he was crapping, so that he could still keep an eye on things. Bless him. One other memorable tale I was told was that when Wally was younger and had quite a big beer belly, some wag had said to him, when they were talking about sex, something along the lines of, 'I don't know how you do's it with a gut like that Wally?'

Wally retorted with a wink: 'There ain't no bones in bellies my sonner.' A quip I used later in a TV film, *Thick as Thieves*, uttered by a very portly George Woodbridge.

I did 'ends' for weeks, and gradually got to know the rest of the workforce. There was Alec Griffin, whose father had been in the trade too; he was about fifty-five, a very skilful carver and letter-cutter who had a vast understanding of the trade. As a person, he was a depressive sort of guy who always expected the worst and loved to tell self-deprecating tales about himself. Personally, I found Alec to be a gentle soul who had a massive knowledge of Bristol history. He kindled the interest I still have. It was Alec who taught me how to make my own chisels in the forge, how to draw out the metal by hammering and shaping it on the anvil, then hardening and tempering it. The hot chisel was dipped briefly in water for about two seconds, then taken out to watch as the metallic colours that denote the hardening process spread from the chisel base to its point. Purple, blue, straw, and lastly almost white. Then you select the temper you require. Blue for stone, straw for marble and light straw for granite. When the appropriate colour was at the chisel point, it was dropped into cold water to set the temper.

Of course the smithing of tools was obsoleted during my time at the Co-op by the introduction of the tungsten steel-tipped chisel; although I'm glad I learned even a small range of forging skills.

Then there was Graham, only twenty-five, hardly out of his own apprenticeship. He was the foreman-in-waiting, as Wally was about to retire in the following spring. Graham was from Sennybridge in Wales and was eloquent and full of exciting-sounding ideas; we became immediate friends. He was married to a stunning chick, called Zara – Chick, as it happens – who taught dance, according to the plaque outside her house. Zara was beautiful and a fair bit older and taller than Graham and was the source of much gossip, perhaps because of her dyed blonde hair and heavy make-up. Jealous people claimed she was a bit of a tart. Zara was a lovely woman, but the last thing you expected to come from her luscious ruby-red lips was a strong Bristol accent...

The rest of the team were the 'fixers' who drove out to the churchyards and cemeteries to fix the headstones and surround kerb sets that had been lettered. The skill of the team was centred on Jack Mutch, an amazing character, who sported a very military moustache and spoke in a strained, affected, upper-class accent, all heaped in irony... until something went wrong. Then, out came: 'Bloody-fucking-bastarding-fucking-bollocks and cunt on it!' It was a tirade that could last up to a minute. Then came silence... and Jack was his other self again.

To learn all aspects of my new trade I often went out to fix gravestones with Jack. Apart from his verbal explosions, he was an interesting bloke, always very defensive and quick to make sarcastic comments, which were often very funny. Jack was a creature of habit, and perhaps a tiny bit on the mean side. He smoked five Players Navy Cut cigarettes a day, no more no less; and kept them in a silver cigarette-case, the fags having been taken from the fifty tin he bought each month. When he took his two-week summer holiday, he and his wife only ever cycled within ten or twenty miles of their home. The others at work used to joke about Jack's holidays 'on the cheap'; but one day, a long time after I'd left the Co-op, I met Jack and his wife on their summer holiday. They'd cycled to Slimbridge wildfowl reserve and were wonderfully happy enjoying the countryside. I suddenly realised how you could enjoy yourself perfectly well – perhaps even more – by keeping things simple. I suddenly envied Jack.

The thing I will never forget is how Jack showed me how to move a four-hundredweight headstone from the back of the lorry to sit on its base stone, a distance of ten yards or so, without lifting an ounce. It was achieved with an iron bar, planks, rollers and tough wooden boxes. It was an object lesson in management of heavy weights.

Jack's usual labourer was Ted Rowe, who I got to know more when he worked with us inside the workshop. He was one of the best mates a person could have; we were total confidants in all matters. Ted was an ex-Paratrooper who had taken part in the D-Day landings; parachuted into Normandy the night before, he along with many others got completely lost when higher than expected winds spilled the parachutists over a wide area. He found shelter in a farm and was hidden from searching German troops. Ted was a fund of good stories, and not just about the war, and had a philosophy of life born of hard knocks along with humorous, very apt but earthy sayings like 'He shit and fell back in it' and 'Never shit on your own doorstep.'

Once Graham became the foreman, things changed; obviously, that was the idea. Firstly, the best move he made was to headhunt his instructor from his previous employer, a marvellous guy called Tom Aliband. He was a fund of knowledge in many areas, but Tom was first and foremost a naturalist. He studied and had acquired great knowledge of flora and fauna and painted pretty mean watercolour landscapes. Most importantly, Tom was the best letter-cutter I'd come across; his style was unmistakable, almost perfect deep-cut Roman and Gill sans-serif lettering. What a craftsman! With Tom, as with Ted, I could discuss all manner of things in an intelligent adult manner, including art, music, religion and – yes – 'life, and everything, and nothing'! Occasionally I was the butt of a joke; though I did mind it, I didn't show it. I remember Alec remarking: 'That's what I like about Bob. He can take a joke.'

The worst thing about Graham's stewardship of the monumental department was that we had to listen to him. What were obvious exaggerations about Graham's life in Wales, and now in Bristol, built up into gigantic whoppers! I remember looking past Graham, when he was on one of his fantasies, and seeing Tom gesture with a silent tut – 'Oh Christ, not again.' It seems that Graham's father had been a huge fighting-type constable in the South Wales Police and was responsible for quelling notorious riots single-handed and flattening football hooligans by the dozen. All criminals were beaten soundly and regularly! It was strange, too, that you'd read something in the paper about some heroic act by a copper, then Graham would trot out a story about his dad doing the exact same thing. As time went by the exaggerations got bigger and bigger. His younger brother was just coming up to O levels; according to Graham, he was doing ten subjects! In the exams, he passed every one with over ninety per cent. It wouldn't have been so bad, but you had to say, 'Wow Graham, how fantastic!' because he was the boss. I remarked that my brother had got into the Slade School of Fine Art at University College London. Next morning, Graham confided in me that his wife Zara had gone to the Slade too. Again I smiled warmly and remarked on how wonderful that was. I got beyond being annoyed about this and eventually felt very sorry for him. Sadly it was obviously something that Graham needed to do.

As I came into my second year of the apprenticeship I was informed that I was to do a 'day release' to Bristol Technical College, housed in the very same Muller's Orphanage, now emptied of those poor souls condemned to live there. I was mixed in with about ten apprentices from building firms in Bristol, and there were some interesting characters. One, called Ginger, was set to work as a mason by Bristol City Football Club. This was a regular thing for City to do whilst the player was on trial: he would work as an apprentice mason so that in case he didn't make the squad, he still had a trade. Anyway, Ginger was pretty cool and was a bit of a card sharp, so in any spare time, three-card brag was played. I watched, but was hopeless at most card games, so stayed out. The youngest apprentice was a spotty kid called Colin, who always insisted on being in on the game. Every Thursday lunchtime the wages were brought in for the lads. (Not mine – mine would be waiting for me back at the Co-op.) Young Colin would take out his wages, a precious white fiver, and every week, without fail, lose the lot at brag. I often wondered how Colin coped in later life.

The thing about my day release was that it was intended for building masons, that magnificent trade in existence since the days of Gothic cathedrals. I have to say, it was most interesting trying to work out what shape stones you'd have to carve to build a circle-on-circle arch; that is, a curved arch on a round building, like a castle turret perhaps, that is itself curving. It was more mathematics than carving. The stone used in the class was Bath stone which was a bit like cutting cake, rather than the stone I was used to. Also, it had nothing to do with sculptural carving or letter-cutting which was my particular trade.

So, happily – and I'll always be thankful to Graham for this – he suggested I do my day release at the West of England College of Art. There I was, an art student, exactly where I'd wanted to be, but for only one day a week; and I was getting paid for it! It didn't take long before I made lots of friends, all of whom thought I was a full-time student, but one who took a lot of days off or something. I was in my element, going to art school parties – and unbeknownst to the Co-op I was doing life drawing, not lettering as was specified in the curriculum for my day release. The lovely thing was that, because of the connection with my brother, no one at art school knew or cared what I did. I was in the Thursday all-day sculpture life class. Fantastic. I began to learn pretty quickly that I needed, not formal education, but to find something else. Something to do with self-expression… I got some help when the very Mancunian, very workin'-class head of the Sculpture School suggested: 'Go and buy yourself a set of fookin' values shag!'…

I pondered on this for some time, and then over a couple of years it began to sink in. It was just what was needed: not only for art, or music – it could be the equipment for the whole of life. My brain was beginning to lock on to something. It was fairly insubstantial to begin with, but was hardened and tempered by the time I finished being at art school 'officially'. I realised that what I'd believed to be wasted years at the Co-op in fact became an important and valuable part of my life and being; that everything, any experience, is important. I began to feel less of a failure and more confident about myself, so that instead of concealing my lack of academic achievements, I could actually boast about *not* getting any GCEs or A levels!

One particular cringe-making memory I have of the Co-op was when I saw Graham talking to a lady who was showing him pictures from an art book on the abstract sculptor Barbara Hepworth. I was intrigued. He was being very reassuring to her and kept looking over at me and winking. When the lady had gone he took me aside and told me that the lady would like a bird bath and that she wanted it 'modern', sort of after Barbara Hepworth. The picture she'd shown him was of an oval kind of shell with wires through the hole in the middle. I began to get very excited about it. Graham pointed out that I was to do it in my own time. That was fine by me. I was delighted. At last a chance to be involved in something interesting! I did loads of drawings and came up with a kind of abstract angel-like figure enfolding the 'bath' and felt very pleased with myself.

Then came the terrible truth. The stone I was instructed to use was from the existing bird-baths which were held in the Co-op stock. They were three feet tall and tapered up from a foot square to around six inches with a square 'bath' placed on the top. I found out from Alec that these so-called 'pedestal bird baths' were a job lot purchased during WWII when, apparently, it was difficult to get hold of any stone at all. The stone was called Elland Edge, a soft red sandstone that had the consistency of a freshly cooked meringue! So, for my 'modern sculpture' not only was I restricted to the stone shape given to me, but to my horror I found it was impossible to touch this fragile stone without it crumbling. I was reduced from hammer and chisel to scraping it with files; but as I chipped away at it, the sculpture cracked and broke... It got smaller and smaller. I soon had to abandon the first idea after the top twelve inches crumbled away. Then, after more fracturing, the second foot of stone disappeared... It kept on crumbling until there was barely one foot of stone left and, instead of the ethereal modern-looking angel I'd imagined, I was left with a twelve-inch high, ugly, fat dwarf! I could do no more. I pronounced it 'finished'.

It was given to Jack, our fixer, to take it to the house and cement the base and bird bath together. When he returned, I asked him what the customer had said about the 'work'. 'I don't know,' he said, 'I just put it in the garden and ran away!'

It was during my years as an apprentice that I became an avid jazz fan, and began playing first trombone, then clarinet in the Hillside Stompers – even getting the odd gig for real money! An important part of the jazz thing was listening to 78rpm records. The potential band listened to these records in each other's houses each weekend, into the small hours. We were in the middle of what was called a 'jazz revival'. Bandleaders like Humphrey Lyttelton and Chris Barber faithfully copied the music that developed in

New Orleans, by mainly black musicians, and labelled it traditional – or 'trad' – jazz. Jazz-minded young Britons would put themselves in one of two camps: 'trad' or 'mod'. The followers of trad wore their hair long and an ex-army duffel coat was an absolute must!

The 'mod' (meaning modern) contemporary jazz had developed over the years from the first World War. Modern jazz fiends had short smart crew-cut hair, wore suits, and older fans might sport a pork-pie hat or similar. French berets were popular too, since the 'modern' bebop trumpeter Dizzy Gillespie wore one.

At the beginning of my musical exploits I was a firm traditionalist and the band we formed was of the regular trumpet/cornet, clarinet and trombone front line backed by bass, drums and banjo – it had to be a banjo. The records we listened to were all recorded either in the nineteen-twenties or thirties, or by contemporary European or American bands copying the style of that time. The band practised as mentioned in the shed in our garden. We'd have devoted fans come to visit. One man was a piano player, a brilliant musician called John Shirley, who said he'd like to join us… only problem being, we didn't have a piano! So we searched around and bought a piano from a house about a quarter of a mile away. None of us could drive and we couldn't afford a van, so we pushed the damn thing on its castors all the way down the road to the shed!

The crazy thing about it all was that, fuelled by just having the desire to play jazz, we went out and bought instruments knowing nothing whatsoever about music! We thought, quite erroneously, that all New Orleans musicians would scorn arrangements and musical dots; after all they played from the heart and that was enough, wasn't it? So we had an uphill struggle to learn how to stay in tune, about chord structures, keys and modulation. I stuck to the motto that if I could improvise on a melody I'd be okay, but it took a while to realise that it didn't just come to you. You had to work at it. Some of the band members, inevitably, fell by the wayside.

We had loads of like-minded kids who would listen to our rehearsals, and sometimes budding musicians who would sit in with us. At this point I was playing trombone – badly. A visitor came along with the pianist one night and he was carrying a trombone case… I recognised him immediately: it was John Wood, who I'd had the fight with. He played his trombone in the band and I knew immediately he was miles better than me. At a band meeting I agreed that John Wood should replace me.

As it happened, at that very time, our clarinet player, Roger Tucker, was not doing too well with the clarinet and had decided to give up trying. So, I bought his clarinet and started learning how to play it. It took up every spare minute of my time; and soon I loved the instrument and was playing well enough to be back in the line-up, playing the clarinet. From here on John Wood and I became the best of friends, and the fight thing was completely forgotten.

CHAPTER FOUR
Love, a Many Splendoured Thing... in E Flat...

IN THE SUMMER OF 1956, my cousin Brian was staying with us for a few days. We went to the Park Cinema to see something in Cinemascope (the Park was possibly the smallest cinema in Bristol but was the first one to have the gigantic wide Cinemascope screen). Behind us in the audience was a beautiful girl; I'd seen her a couple of times before somewhere, so I nodded to her. When we got outside she was with her girlfriends and she came over to me and suggested in a roundabout way that I take her home. Brian was very understanding and left me with her.

I held her willing hand and we walked very slowly back to her house. This was Dianne; I fell in love with her immediately. However, Dianne was a mass of complications and a very difficult girl to love. To wit, when we arrived at her house, her 'regular' boyfriend was in the front room with her parents, whilst I was in the back room petting with Dianne. I thought it odd, but didn't question anything since I was enjoying myself too much. Occasionally her mother would call from the hallway: 'Di? Richard is still waiting to see you.'

I gradually found out, and had to accept, that Dianne was not content to have one boyfriend, but had to have several. At first I was too stricken by her to worry too much about this; but then I became really serious about her, so not unnaturally I began to get jealous of her seeing other boys. I kept seeing her as a possession and feeling that she should only be with me; but she couldn't be tamed. She – or rather the mad house she lived in – became the subject of a play I wrote called *Offspring* which charted a typical evening at Dianne's house. Her mother had married a man she hated (why, one wondered?); and, like *Long Day's Journey into Night*, things would build to a frightful climax where Mrs Read would threaten to kill her bus-conductor husband. She would take up a knife on some occasions, but he'd just chuckle at her and say, 'Go on then.' Mrs Read would then start crying, much to his amusement. This melodrama would be played out on a regular basis to Dianne and me – or any other boyfriend she happened to be with.

Mr Read was a huge man and always wore an enormous Bristol Tramways issue black waterproof mackintosh, with capacious pockets big enough to conceal a flagon bottle of Worthington E in each one. He was a strange, cruel man, who would think it funny that he'd murdered the cat next door that had been pissing on his garden plants.

With Dianne, I had gigantic mood swings from glorious happiness to the darkest depression, all because of her predilection for multiple boyfriends; I realised inside that our relationship was doomed. It came to a head when I returned unexpectedly from a holiday and found she was with another boy, someone I knew and disliked. So that was it. At work, I'd written 'I love Dianne' in the alcove where I made the tea. I solemnly crossed it out.

As far as girls were concerned, I now had the college to pick from as well as girls around where I lived. I found myself getting to like a shy girl at college called Sally. She lived in a big house in the country and, when I was going out with her, I many times walked her the five miles from St George to where she lived in Bitton, half way to Bath. It's funny: though I told her I loved her, I somehow didn't really believe it myself. But she fitted perfectly with the criteria set by my friends for the perfect girl and possible future wife – that she be good-looking and live in a big country house and have rich parents. So perhaps it wasn't that I loved her? Only when she dumped me – then, ours was the greatest love ever! What a mawkish prat I was…

I took bad advice from a friend on how to put things right, and I recall with shame the pathetic melodrama I became involved in. I was instructed to ignore her and not answer when she spoke, be rude, poke my tongue out at her, but mostly not even look at her. Well, it sort of worked; and we were together again. She invited me to meet her parents. Her father was an eminent skin surgeon and, as is usual, continued to use his army rank. He was Colonel Jones, a very calm and gentle man, as you might expect. Mother, however, was from the world of riding, 'the season' and debutantes; I guessed she found me coarse and well beneath her in the class rankings, definitely not someone she would want her daughter to get mixed up with. I'd met them, on a warm autumn day; we sat and talked outside in the garden and when the time came for me to go she said: 'You must come again Bob… in the spring.' Sally was definitely upper class and I'm sure her parents might have had a hand in choosing just the right military type for her to marry. (I found out later that she married a sailor, a navy lieutenant.)

The thing about art school is that it was – at the coalface – a great leveller. Girls and boys from a stratospherically high class were brought down to earth by art: to be good at it didn't require breeding, or wealth, or connections. One had simply to keep asking questions and hope they were the right ones. It's possible that some of the girls quite fancied 'a bit of rough'. I remember another friend, an eloquent, highly educated but very Bristol-accented young student, who told me how he had a desultory affair with a girl called Beth, just out of a girls' public school. Twice a week, they went to her flat and screwed all day, hardly a word spoken between them; then as he left she'd say, 'Shall I see you next week?' I must say I was rather amused and touched by that.

Meanwile, back at the Co-op, by the time I was sixteen or seventeen I was regularly cutting letters: mostly what were called 'also ofs' or an additional inscription of a family member to an existing one. It was more convenient and cheaper for the Co-op to have me go to the stone, rather than bring the stone into the workshop. This outside work took me to all the cemeteries in Bristol and its surrounds: the giant rambling old ones and the newer ones with 'lawn cemeteries' along American lines.

I particularly enjoyed going to do jobs in country churchyards. I began to take notice of the architecture of the churches I saw. There was nothing better on a sunny afternoon than to be at one with nature, as it were. And of course, if near enough, one could take lunch at the village pub and maybe chat to some local people. It was quite a different matter if the weather was inclement; then a kind of tent was erected, made from an essential piece of outside-work kit, a tarpaulin. This, and a few sticks that were begged, borrowed or stolen to hold it up with, definitely ensured a miserable day…

As I became more proficient I worked on new stones, beginning with kerbs – that's an eight-inch-high stone or marble surround to the grave. I then graduated through tablets and finally to headstones.

Letter-cutting in the fifties was done, as it had always been, by a craftsman wielding a hammer and chisel tapping away at the stone. It was always possible to recognise another letter-cutter's work by their style and little idiosyncrasies. Graham did incredibly thin letters and we used to comment that his inscriptions looked like spiders crawling over the stone. Tom Aliband, my mentor, cut well rounded, warm and generous, almost perfect lettering. Alec's work was, like Alec, good solid craftsmanship, without flair. From the very beginning I had trouble with Rs. The lower half of an R looks a bit like legs; I always seemed to manage to get them wrong. I was famous for the 'running R'. Cut at the start of the word 'Resting' the R looked as if it was running away at speed from the 'esting'!

In the workshop, when we weren't putting the world to rights and no one was using the power tools, we listened to the BBC afternoon play which was accompanied by the tip-tapping of hammers on chisels. I remember hearing plays by Ibsen, Chekov, Shaw and some of the up-and-coming British writers like Arnold Wesker.

I found that when I was letter-cutting I drifted off into a kind of dream trance; only ten percent of my mind was on the cutting, the rest was thinking about things. And anyway there was always an interesting conversation to be had with my workmates, Tom and Graham. So I chipped stone, talked and thought. As Graham's grip on the power of being foreman took hold, he tended to spend less time in the workshop and was always popping out on some urgent mission in the 'dodgem' as we called it – one of those Co-op electric-powered delivery vans we'd inherited from the milk department, customised for us as a flatbed truck. It was a brilliant piece of kit as long as it was kept charged up. I well remember going in the 'dodgem' to a cemetery the other side of Bristol, some six miles away; we realised on the way there that the charge was low, but there was nothing we could do but hope for the best. We staggered back reasonably well until we got to the last mile from base, when our dodgem began slowing down noticeably… Suddenly we were only travelling at around one to two miles per hour. Mums pushing prams were sailing past us. We felt so stupid and dared not look at the irate faces of overtaking drivers. It was highly embarrassing... but funny too.

I was now seventeen, still hanging on to some of the old things from the past 'me'. I was still doing athletics, training twice a week, even doing cross country in winter evenings. I got out of running and jumping by taking up smoking, thinking, stupidly, that it made me look cool.

I was still in the Air Training Corps, but found it difficult to keep an interest in aircraft when we were deep into the Cold War and the only use for my beautiful flying machines was to drop a nuclear bomb on somebody. I was increasingly turning towards CND, though I hadn't ventured onto one of the Aldermaston Marches; but it was a subject that came up often, the morality of 'The Bomb' and the mess that was British policy toward a possible World War III, and the anachronism of such things as Civil Defence. My dad, having been an Air Raid Warden, felt sort of obliged to join the Civil Defence Corps and was issued with the same stirrup pump he'd had in 1940! To put out fires from nuclear bombs? It was so absurd we could even laugh at it.

I felt no remorse at being thrown out of the Air Training Corps for appearing at a ceremonial guard of honour with dirty shoes. However, unbeknownst to my squadron leader, I immediately joined the ATC Silver Wing Band so I could learn to play the alto sax and use it in the band I was hoping to form. Sadly, the CO of my previous squadron recognised me when I was performing at an air show and put me on a charge (which actually meant nothing). He gave me a dressing down and said: 'How dare you? We kick you out the front door and you simply walk around and come in the back door! I won't have it.' He ended with an ultimatum: I could stay in the Silver Wing Band if I ran for the squadron in the group sports. I agreed and went to the British finals at RAF Uxbridge, where I came last in the final of the four hundred and forty yards... Soon after I bought my own saxophone and handed back the ATC band one, thus bidding goodbye to the military life.

Looking back on the Air Training Corps, I joined it because of my love of aircraft, but the meetings – twice a week in a damp condemned building – seemed to get more and more tedious. The two things I appreciated about it were firstly learning to march, which I found made me confident and proud even; and secondly, I took my first flight. It was only half an hour in an old Avro Anson training plane, but it was fantastic to me.

It was around this time that the band members not only listened to jazz but started listening to classical music. This was something quite new for me, but a few of my friends were pretty keen on it, and as we listened we kept a respectful silence until the very last note. I began to enjoy the classics and appreciate what it was all about. For me it was like looking at a painting but, instead of image, colour and drawing, going into patterns of sound. I achieved this revelation while listening to Beethoven's Sixth Symphony, the *Pastoral*. I went on to rave about Bach's Double Violin Concerto, then on to Stravinsky and Prokofiev and Haydn. All this led my friends and me to go and listen to classical music concerts.

At the same time we hardly ever missed each new production at the Bristol Old Vic. We sat in the 'gods' or upper circle, gladly suffering aching butts to see Peter O'Toole in plays such as *Look Back in Anger*, *Hamlet* and *Brighton Rock*, and particularly *Waiting for Godot* which had a profound effect on me. This was of course before O'Toole went on to Hollywood stardom.

The exploration of theatre and music combined to form an enormous inrush of information, making it a time of huge emotional and educational expansion for me. The band became more than a group of musicians; we used to go out for long walks, usually ending up in a pub, but all the time talking and always questioning everything, including, of course, changing the world for the better – and wanting, to use that awful present day cliché, 'to make a difference'.

The fascinating thing is, all these friends of mine were receiving a high-grade grammar school education; meanwhile I, as a lowly 'sec. mod.' bod, listened and tried to join in at their level, but it took a while – at first I only supplied the jokes. Within a year or so, by joining in discussions with them I was, without realising it, gaining an education. We entered into deep philosophical discussions; and, perhaps, one might have detected the first buds of satire from John Wood, who would later gain fame as John Fortune, at the Establishment Club and then on TV with Eleanor Bron and (with John Bird) as one of 'The Two Johns' in the Rory Bremner show. The great thing was that, through our music, I was appreciated as an equal; and the band members were gentle with me if I made the occasional howler in the intellectual stakes.

I remember one specific thing that might have spurred me on, not just to make something of myself, but to go a good deal further than that. We were playing a gig at the Pro Cathedral Hall in Bristol. I came across one of the drummer's friends, a handsome, tall, rugger-playing type, Max. I suddenly realised that we were making a play for the same girl, so it came down to him claiming all sorts of wondrous assets to impress her. He'd obviously been told about my job as a monumental mason, so he made the usual joke about graveyards. I defended myself, talking of the wonders of working with stone; but he looked at me and said, 'Well, I think you're a moron!' At this, all background noise stopped. I was stunned, angry and humiliated and left him with the girl… It could be that Max inadvertently gave me the impetus to continue expanding my horizons so that such comments would bring a smile instead of humiliation.

The band members began to look at our material: all pretty run-of-the-mill trad fodder. I think we all realised that our attitudes and tastes were changing. With only one exception, we were leaning toward what was called 'mainstream jazz' and were able to appreciate a much wider selection of musical styles, musicians and bands. My first move was to get a saxophone, which was anathema to the one dissenter, our cornet player, Bev Pitman. He stood firmly for 'purist' jazz – the jazz of New Orleans – and would hear of nothing that came after 1929, which he deemed to be commercialised crap!

The only way to go was to start a new band. We scouted around for a trumpeter and came up with a genius: a lean, pensive guy called 'Bonce' Archard, whose solos of impassioned flurries were quite literally stunning. I could hardly believe we'd got him to play with us since he was much in demand. We recruited a close friend of mine, Ron Caines, who I'd met at art school; he too played clarinet and both of us had ambitions to graduate to the saxophone. We also got ourselves a double bass player, a tall wisecracking individual, Basil Dark. Malcolm, who'd played drums in the former band, realised he couldn't match the line-up as drummer; then, and quite surprisingly, took up playing piano and was more than adequate. We acquired a new drummer, Alan Rich, who was (as all drummers) pleasantly mad. Lastly, we were able to get rid of the banjo and replace it with an amplified guitar which was played by Tony Vann, a student doing physics at Bristol University before going on to work in optics at British Aircraft Corporation, as it was then… Something to do with guided missiles… shhh!

A new band, a new name. We could no longer rehearse in my garden shed and so we rented pub function rooms, mainly the Earl Russell at Lawrence Hill; so that became our new name – The Earl Russell Jazz Unit. The 'Earl' we felt might put people in mind of the greats like 'Count' Basie and 'Duke' Ellington and 'King' Oliver. Of course, inevitably, some people would ask which one of us was 'Earl Russell'!

We frequented the Avon Cities Jazz Club every week. My first visit made my neck hair stand on end. It was fantastic: there I was, listening to an otherwise unpopular kind of music in a converted summerhouse in the garden of a bombed-out Georgian house. I felt it was 'cool man'; maybe a little dangerous, but certainly subversive. Perfect!

It was at the Avon Cities Jazz Club that I met and became friends with Bill Stair, an amazing man: the perfect example of what we now call bipolar behaviour. Bill was certainly the funniest person I've ever met. He could make you laugh and laugh, adding more Goon-like humour on top of any comic situation. However, for the joy of knowing Bill, you had to take the down side. He was also, perhaps, the most depressing man I ever met; man, could he bring you down. Again, Bill was a really clever guy who would build word pictures, not just humorous ones, but of any situation whether it be attempting to deal with girlfriends, the way the busses ran or world politics.

Bill soon became part of the band's inner sanctum – what you might call the 'other activities' section. It included John Wood (Fortune), Malcolm Windsor, Tony Vann, Bill and myself. He also joined us on our peregrinations and visits to theatre and cinema. We were all interested in film-making; and John, who was doing drama at school, was extremely keen on directing. So, we decided to make one. To begin with, since Tony Vann owned a projector, we chose to take a look at some film classics hired from the BFI to give us inspiration. We saw the Dadaist *Entr'acte* by René Clair; *The Great Train Robbery*, which was the very first film drama ever made; and D.W. Griffith's *Intolerance*. These, along with our respect and liking for Buñuel, the French 'New Wave' directors and Ingmar Bergman, led us to make a film with a title suggested by Malcolm, who was by now studying physics at Bristol University. *Entropy* was a kind of allegorical visualisation of the Third Law of Thermodynamics which states that things universally move from order to disorder and that when the universe ends there will only be one element left… Lead. Apparently.

Writing was put in the hands of Bill Stair and myself. After many script sessions where everyone chipped in, Bill and I came up with a crazy story of two men, to be played by Bill and me, rushing around various locations chasing each other. The film was shot on out-of-date RAF 16mm gun-camera film stock, so old that it quite often shattered in the camera: a 16mm box Brownie, holding around two minutes of film. *Entropy* was a silent film lasting around eight minutes; putting sound on it was way out of our price bracket.

Seeing it after some fifty years I am struck by how good it is. It tells a simple, understandable and visually exciting story and has some pretty adventurous camerawork. It complies with all the established filming techniques: master shots, close ups, tracking and panning shots, plus one incredible chaotic final shot where the camera twirls around from a high shot, slowly spinning and circling as it goes. So there it was. *Entropy*. A serious subject matter with quite a few laughs on the way.

We were desperate to make more films, and managed an 'epic' lasting twenty minutes which we shot in sand dunes over an Easter weekend in North Devon – the time limit set by the fact that Tony Vann and I had to get back to work. Again Bill Stair and I provided the script guidelines and John directed. Soon after this our group had to break up. John went to Cambridge, Malcolm studied at Bristol University for a PhD. Bill Stair was at art school… The band too gave up, but Ron Caines and I continued to play; he played alto and by now I was playing tenor sax. We now played a version of so-called modern jazz in a combo we called 'Soul Brothers' at one of the oldest pubs in the city, the Bear and Rugged Staff.

I met Vicki Hollis at an art college dance. She was studying at St Martin's School of Art in London and had come to Bristol to visit a friend. We got on very well; and then I found she lived in Colchester! To a young Bristol apprentice, it seemed light years away. However, we had clicked and things began to get serious; but the sheer distance made courting extremely difficult. I kept phoning her at her London digs, desperately wanting to see her again – though I recall one time, after a long gap between calls, being distraught because I couldn't remember what she looked like. I decided to take the train to London and meet her on

Paddington station. We then for some daft reason took the Underground one station, to Royal Oak, and walked dark streets in the freezing cold until it was time to catch my train back to Bristol.

I began to write to her and some while later realised we must be in love… to quote HRH: 'whatever that means!' I have asked myself many times, was it absence that made the heart etc etc? Or was it a deeper, genuine love? Anyway, I had all the recognisable symptoms of love – and, believe me, I was loving it.

After several perishing cold meetings in London she asked me if I'd like to go to her home in Essex and meet her parents. I was fine with that, but didn't then realise it was to become the beginning of a regular fortnightly dash: finishing work at the Co-op at five P.M. and taking a bus to the station to get the first available London train to Paddington; then on the Underground to Liverpool Street station to catch the Ipswich train to Colchester. The memory of that slow, stopping train still stays with me. Hearing the guard calling out each point along the route: 'Chelmsford!' then Hatfield Peverell, then Whitham, Marks Tey and finally Colchester. Arriving at around nine-thirty, I had to run pretty sharpish from the railway station to the bus station in order to catch the ten P.M. last bus to Little Bentley Corner on the Clacton road. I then faced a walk of a mile to the village of Little Bentley itself…

The Hollises lived in a neat Georgian house, 'Mill House', converted from two cottages and a former mill. It was surrounded by Mr Hollis's market garden where the money crop was greenhouse-grown tomatoes, of the Moneymaker variety; but he kept going in the winter and spring with spuds and broccoli, then expanded into growing Christmas trees not long after I met Vicki.

Bernard Christian Hollis lived up to his middle name: he was an honest man – too honest perhaps – of deep humanity. I took to him immediately. He was always one to engage in conversation that went just that little bit deeper than pleasantries and delved into more philosophical areas. His one drawback was his wife Enid, who was petrified of dealing with anything she was unsure of. She would warn Bernard, usually at the dinner table, to get off certain subjects which might possibly lead to discussion, or even worse open disagreement. For Enid, everything had to be smooth and laid out as it always was, the way she wanted things. I soon learned to duck and weave or simply retreat from conversation that was 'forbidden!' This meant politics was out, as was religion – and woe betide anything philosophical. Everything had to be ordered and nice. Sadly Bernard was trained and drilled into strict obedience by his wife, and crumbled at the sound of her voice.

In fact they were a strange couple to be married to each other, a very strong woman and a very gentle man, and now with three daughters they hoped would follow the path laid out for them… by Enid of course. Already one daughter had gotten out of line. The oldest, Elizabeth, had married a quirky Canadian theoretical mathematician she met in Cambridge, John Valleau. He was quite weird: he had a high-pitched hee-haw bray of a laugh you could hear throughout the house. He also suffered from some kind of claustrophobia and insisted on leaving the toilet door open when he was crapping… There was other strange behavior. Liz and John would be completely sealed off in 'their world', hardly speaking to anyone and going hand in hand everywhere. When forced to be with the family in the lounge, they'd read the newspaper together, holding it high up in front of themselves; then we'd hear John's shrieking laughter at some article he thought funny. Liz would of course share the joke… all behind the paper. Vicki and I, along with the middle sister Joanna, found their behaviour very odd.

I recall, on my first visit to the house, meeting Liz alone on the stairs and she said: 'Are you Vicki's stonemason?' I smiled a yes, expecting some kind of patronising remark; but no. She said: 'How wonderful it must be to work in stone.'

I could see she really meant it and thereafter I began to care about her and actually worry for her, believing she had maybe married the wrong guy? But that was her business, even though it was still like being in a house with two ghosts, beings you rarely saw but heard through the woodwork now and then. I could tell that Enid didn't particularly like John: not because of his manners, which I'm sure she deplored, but the fact that he was going to take Liz far away, to Canada, to live. Too far away and right out of her life and out of her control and influence.

Enid Hollis, née Livingstone, was a chuck from Leicester, all very *nouveau riche*; her father had been in the shoe business, but cleverly moved from making footwear to designing the machines that made shoes. (Bernard too was from a *nouveau riche* background in Hull; his father had started a timber importing business, Hollis Brothers, which had done

71

rather well.) Judging by the photograph albums, Enid had led a charmed life in a mansion of a house with summer tennis, winter skating, frilly dresses for dancing, playing the piano, a youth filled with music and laughter and song. It seems hard to fathom how a very serious man like Bernard met and courted, and then married her. Enid was an archetypal example of what we now term a control freak. A frantic cougar of a woman; Bernard resembled a slow loris by comparison.

Enid was from the outside a committed Church of England Christian: she sang in the choir at church and did the flowers, plus any other jobs she could do. She must have been a godsend to any vicar. As I gradually got to know her I noted that she was something of a snob – very condescending to the working-class village people, farm workers and their families around the village.

In her domain, only her opinions were true! Things would only be done in her way! I believe this was entirely due to her upbringing during the last fling of Empire, thinking that we Brits were the best people in the world and that money and class meant everything. Yet Enid was something of an enigma. Here she was, bucking the trend by marrying a timber salesman (though of the required social/financial level) whose ambition was to be a market gardener! There was a darker side to things though, obviously so shocking to Enid that she erased it from history. When World War II began, they'd had Elizabeth, Joanna and the baby Vicki. Like many people at the outbreak of hostilities, they expected bombing to begin immediately; so they arranged for Enid and the kids to go to America, to a small town in New Hampshire, for the duration. Bernard stayed behind, expecting to be called up for service, which he duly was.

Again, I may be surmising this a bit, but some time during his basic training Bernard had a mental breakdown. He'd tried, but failed, to reconcile the evil that Hitler posed with killing another human being. So Bernard became one of a comparatively few conscientious objectors in that conflict. This meant some time in an army prison with some pretty unpleasant treatment from those around him. How long he was incarcerated, or how bad his breakdown might have been, was never discussed. Eventually in 1942 he was posted to Belfast to work as a fireman. He once spoke to me about it (in the garden of course). His clearest memories were of his dismay at the deep hatred between

Protestants and Catholics. During the five years of war, he corresponded regularly with Enid and I imagine she kept him informed of the girls' progress in letters full of bright chatty news and information from the sunny, safe US of A. There was no mention of what was in his letters to her. The thing is, after discussing it with all three sisters, they agreed that something happened that changed the relationship between Enid and Bernard when they were reunited after the war. My feeling is that it was the stigma of mental illness that had slightly skewed Enid's attitude toward him. Anyway, it empowered her to rule the roost with an iron hand; and she talked him down, with what can only be described as a kind of bitter resentment, whenever he tried to interject.

It was all grist to the mill for me: I was packing these facts away, not knowing they would all be part of a drama to be written some twenty years hence – *Murder at the Wedding*, my last work with Dave as a partner. We used Enid and Bernard as inspiration for the central characters.

After visiting Mill House for nearly a year, something happened which pulled me up sharp. Vicki was pregnant. I knew I'd been absolutely stupid. 'Why?' friends asked incredulously, 'didn't you use something?' I suppose the truth was that in my airy-fairy romantic notion of love, you couldn't interrupt the flow of passion by stopping to put on a 'joey' as we called them then. And so I had to accept the consequences.

Vicki and I had already decided to get married and talked vaguely of some time in the spring of 1959. Then when I visited them in the November of '58, Mrs Hollis suddenly suggested we get married in January… why wait? We both thought it odd; but later, when I found out that Vicki had been throwing up every morning, I wasn't that surprised. They knew of course.

So, it was full steam ahead for the wedding which took place on 21st January 1959.

It all went reasonably well and, apart from feeling a bit of a prat in a topper, I actually enjoyed it. A short January honeymoon in a surprisingly warm Mevagissey ended with a sharp slap of reality… Husband and expectant mother require place to live. Prenatal visits to clinic to be set up. My mother reacted badly: oh, the shame of it! She was devastated by what the neighbours would think, and told Dad to put the house on the market immediately. A wild overreaction, we'd think nowadays; and in a way it was a way of putting the shame back on me. 'We're so ashamed, we have to move house!' It was all very emotionally complicated, but I had no time to get entangled in it. I had to get a move on with the most important thing which was finding a place for us to live.

We found a flat to rent on the second floor of a Victorian house right next to a church in a tree-lined road in the St Andrew's district of Bristol. My friend and fellow musician, Ron, had helped me to secure it as he and his wife Sue and their new baby, Mark, lived on the ground floor. I was still working at the Co-op and, having finished my indentured apprenticeship, was now earning a princely ten pounds a week.

On the face of it we were poor; ah, but we was 'appy. I cycled to work every day and on each trip I tried to break the record of the day before. I was on a high! Married life was good and I didn't think much beyond the next few weeks. The summer came and Catherine was born in the July. There I was, a father at nineteen years young – for a couple of weeks until my twentieth birthday.

Around then, several events occurred that were to change my life completely. The first was at work. As mentioned, I was very close to Tom and Ted and was a bit shocked when one day they both started haranguing me. Tom said, 'What are you doing here Bob? You've got to get out now!'

Ted came in hard. 'Look,' he said. 'I'm telling you: if you don't get out of this place now, you never will! So fuck off!'

In the coming days, particularly on my bike ride home, I began to see what they meant; but there was fear in my belly – where do I go? I was scared, because I knew how right they were. I could see myself at sixty, leaving the Co-op every evening, exactly like I'd done for the last five years. Bless Tom and Ted. I was still frightened of taking the step but I knew now I had to do it.

The second thing was that Vicki knew that she'd been left some money by her Aunt Bertha, but lawyers were still working the sums out. We had no idea what the amount might be; I gathered that it was substantial, but that meant nothing – could it have been five hundred pounds, even a thousand? There were no figures. We discussed the possibility that it might be enough to sustain us whilst I went to art college… When mooted to Enid, we were surprised to find that she was all in favour. 'Education is the most important thing in getting a good job,' etc etc. After all, hadn't she done the same for Bernard when he went to agricultural college after the war? (Which was news to me!) So it was agreed that I go to college with a view to becoming an art teacher at the end of it. In the event the inheritance was enough for me to start college.

The third, oddly enough, was metatarsalgia. I suddenly started feeling an unpleasant pain in my right foot, every time I set it down. The doctor told me that the constant lifting of heavy weights had caused the metatarsal bone and immediate area in my foot to become bruised. I would have to keep off it for at least three weeks! It was amazing: this was longer than I'd ever been off work before, and I used the time sitting around at home painting pictures of everything around me in the flat. I arranged an interview with the principal of the West of England College of Art, Jack Chalker, and took the paintings along, with the view of starting college in the following September. Happily I was accepted.

The course in those days was four years, the first two being intermediate studies in which students experienced a range of disciplines after obligatory drawing, painting and sculpture and on to etching, stone carving or illustration and fabric design. Third and fourth years were when a student specialised in one of the studies they'd done in intermediate up to the NDD – National Diploma in Design… Not quite a degree. But that was about to change.

CHAPTER FIVE
Art for Art's Sake

IT WAS DECIDED THAT because of my day-release time at college and the standard of my work, I could miss out the first year of intermediate and start straight in at the second year.

So there I was, in my own mind about to set out to be a famous artist and eager to learn about everything I could. In the classes I was a bit of a sore thumb, since I was a good five years older than most of the students and was treated with a bit of awkward respect. I set about being a student with a vengeance. I worked harder and longer than most of the kids in my year; of course, I was used to working from eight A.M. till five P.M. every day, so it seemed easy to me. Plus, there was never anything I didn't want to do. By the time the intermediate examination came up, our second child, Paul, had been born. We moved to a new flat in Clifton, within easy walking distance from the college. We now had a maisonette, the top two floors of the house. By now some of Vicki's inheritance money was coming through by way of dividends from shares, so we began to live quite decently. We even had our groceries delivered from a quaint old-fashioned emporium called Lock and Barrel; each week our grocery box contained our booze order of four pint-bottles of screw-top, Usher's Amber Ale... We felt very sophisticated.

One of the students in my class was a restless character called Al. Al's only interest was his guitar. He brought it into all the classes and tended to it as if it were a child. Al, along with a few other like-minded students, formed a rock band called Alan G. Read and the Statesmen. Musically, at this time, I was playing what I hoped was 'modern jazz' at a pub in town. Al felt his band needed something to make it stand out from all the other three-guitar line-up rock groups – of which there were scores – and asked me if I'd like to join his band.

This demanded a great deal of thought and was no easy choice, since rock and roll was anathema to me: it was noisy, simplistic and – to my mind then – utterly banal compared to the kind of thing I was trying to do, which was art of course… in other words I was a musical snob. I joined the Statesmen, for better or for worse. I was also making more money from playing with the Statesmen than I ever did playing jazz…

As I started into the third year, I had selected painting as my specialist subject for the years up to final exams. I remember being totally sent the wrong way before my interview to join the painting school with Head of Painting, George Sweet. One helpful adviser insisted, 'The college really only exists to create teachers, not fuckin' artists, so emphasise how much you want to teach.' This I duly did and got a sharp condescending answer.

'Well it sounds to me, Mr Baker, as if you're much more interested in teaching than in painting.'

I was stunned and angry. That's all I wanted to do. Paint! But I'd scuppered any chance of backtracking on what I'd already said.

Anyway, I got into the painting school. It was housed in what was called the annexe, a three-storey Georgian house on the street at the back of the main college building. The canteen occupied the ground floor and the painting school had the first and second floors. The top floor had George Sweet's office and a couple of studio rooms. There was a rather quaint, old-fashioned feel to the school. Sweet was in his sixties and close to retirement; he'd run it for years and promoted his 'Euston Road' style of art. This style could not be accomplished without the use of a brush called a 'rigger', a thin, pointed brush with which one drew initially on the canvas and then left it showing through as a kind of under-structure to the painting.

George Sweet used to, very occasionally, give lessons to individuals, although if you didn't have a rigger at hand he would pass you over. His main thrust (which I now heartily agree with, but didn't then) was: keep your brushes clean! The only memorable thing I remember him saying in his rather art-patrician style was: 'Constable told Turner, and Turner told

Sickert, and Sickert told me, that the world was one pudding basin inside another.' Yes… of course it is.

The star of the painting school lecturers was Paul Feiler, a known, professional and collected painter. He has several paintings in the Bristol Museum and Art Gallery. Feiler was a German Jew, who'd escaped his homeland and possibly the Holocaust, only to be interned in Canada during World War Two. He spoke to students in parables. It took a while to figure out what he meant, but once cottoned on to it was sound advice. To one student who was using some newfangled swanky coloured pens, I remember him commenting something like: 'If your problem is that you want to get to London, it doesn't matter if you travel by Austin Seven or a Rolls Royce; what is most important is that you get there.' I must say I always found him fascinating to listen to.

I was set to finish my last year in much the same way as all the other students; the seemingly inevitable prospect after NDD was ATD – the Art Teaching Degree. I felt I was on a belt moving inexorably toward doing something I wasn't sure I wanted to do. Then something quite unexpected came to pass. There was change in the air around art education. Gossip abounded that we were to leave our Victorian building bang in the centre of Clifton and the university campus and go to a new 'green field' site outside the city. A new examination had been decreed to give the equivalent of a university degree, to be called DipAD – Diploma in Art and Design. Hordes of government inspectors were sent to see what we were doing. They occasionally asked questions. One of them asked me what I wanted to do when I finished. I was vague and said something honest: I wanted to be a painter.

'What about teaching?' she said. 'Aren't you going to be a teacher?'

I hummed and hawed and told her I didn't necessarily want to be a teacher. She glared at me then asked directly, 'What are your qualifications?'

I was embarrassed and 'fessed up' to being entirely without O or A levels. She immediately asked what I thought I was doing there without any qualifications. The sculpture head, Ernie Pascoe, came to my rescue, telling her I was a special case and – after surreptitiously winking at me – that I was taking all necessary exams at evening class. She was placated. But then I was obliged to enrol for evening class to do English language and English literature at O level.

Amazingly, the very thing I was most embarrassed about came to my rescue. I actually managed to fail English. There was then no possibility whatsoever of becoming a bloody teacher.

A revolution happened in my last year at college. The old edifices were crumbling; the college was awash with new, mostly young lecturers, fresh from the London colleges.

Everyone was encouraged to do something exciting and modern, something dangerous. For some it was liberation, for others it was pure hell and they just couldn't cope with it. The powers that be were out to break down and obliterate what they saw as the dusty, old, stolid, antiquated ways and create a revolution by causing artistic mayhem.

The casts of the Parthenon and famous Greek and Roman sculptures that had graced the corridors and Life Room were all removed. 'Art' was going on all over the place; in every room, students started some construction or other. It was for a while like Dante's *Inferno*! I, along with a few fellow students of like mind, decided to make a huge, joint, scrap-metal sculpture imagined from the airflow of a jet engine. It was based on the Bristol Olympus 593, the Concorde engine – and it was the size of it too! We decided to weld together three different sculptures: (one) intake and compressor, (two) combustion chambers, and (three) afterburner, which then fitted together. We raided metal scrapyards for likely shapes to put into the mix.

The existing staff had to play catch-up with the new boys, otherwise they'd be out. George Sweet was the first victim; near retirement anyway, he was quietly allowed to resign.

Once stripped of the old, it was a crazy world, full of crazy people. My co-sculptors and I, for fun and recreation, devised a 'War Game' which took over the entire Life Room (the largest room in the building). We built fleets of balsa wood warships and made tiny aircraft replicas no more than two centimetres in span. Battle was decided by broadsides from each fleet guessing, to the exact centimetre, the distance or range between the ships to score a hit. The range was measured with a pull-out tape measure (the air component was more complicated, so much so that I can't remember how it worked!) It was daft but it was really fun and some of the new lecturers who came across us whilst we were playing the game really believed, as we believed, that in the very playing of it we were a work of art. Shades of things to come...

Among my contemporaries at the time were Richard Long and Nigel Hall, both of whom gained giddy heights of fame in the world of art. Initially in Richard Long's story things looked pretty bleak. I believe that through no fault of his own he'd made enemies in the sculpture school and they were determined to get him thrown out – which they did. I hope they were kicking themselves when he became a highly successful and respected artist known and appreciated throughout the world. So, what's the best way to success? Get kicked out of the West of England College of Art! I didn't know what happened to Nigel Hall after college, apart from the fact that he went to America for some time. I was surprised and delighted recently to see some of his massive sculptures on display in the Yorkshire Sculpture Park.

Whilst on the final two-year diploma a student of one discipline, painting or sculpture, was invited to take a subsidiary course so that the mind was broadened as to different aspects of art. There was a fledgling film department and I immediately plumped for that. It was run by a prissy photographer who refused to let the students use the 16mm Bolex camera – it was much too precious! Having already made a few films I was rather miffed that the guy was being so stupid about it. He was soon replaced by a recruit from the film industry, Jack Daniel. His background was in animation, having worked for many years in perhaps one of a very few successful British animation companies: Halas and Batchelor who made commercials and cinema shorts, but were most well known for their feature-film cartoon of Orwell's *Animal Farm*. They also did cartoons for the BBC including the Gerard Hoffnung orchestral comedies.

Jack quickly built a simple animation rostrum and I began to take note of the possibilities of using this method to make bigger and better things, but using less. I began to think of using collages as backgrounds – stuff from magazines to create a streetscape. I was also allowed to use the Bolex movie camera after showing the films I'd made earlier. Very soon, in my final year, film began to take a bigger place in my ambition than painting; but there was no qualification in film-making at that time, so I limped through the painting course, completing an awful, wordy and totally crappy thesis on the Pre-Raphaelites.

I passed my exam. Now at twenty-four, a father of three lovely children with a keen interest in film and clutching a useless National Diploma in Design, I had no idea what I wanted to do. Fortunately, the inheritance money was enough to keep us going; but my frustration as to the career I wanted to pursue took on a strange bent. I went through a second childhood.

At college I'd met with a really great bloke: a proud Cornishman from Liskeard, Ron Fuller. A contemporary of Peter Blake and David Hockney, he'd come from the Royal College to Bristol Art School to teach printmaking. Ron was, for me, the consummate artist craftsman, a printmaker who had a very quirky, pop-art-influenced style of work. Ron was interested in everything I was – aeroplanes, racing cars and war games – but the difference was, he was a toymaker and he taught me how to build models that flew and then added radio control! I was flying! He always did things with a flourish and after seeing a set of Scalextric racing track and cars, he set about making a twenty-foot-square track that fitted on his huge worktable; then we built cars to run on it. He made fantastic cardboard soldiers and cavalrymen from folded card and painted them all in suitable Napoleonic period uniforms. The game was played with all the 'troops' divided between players and each side had a pair of one-inch-nail firing Britain's toy cannons; you just kept firing and knocking down cardboard cannon-fodder until you were out of nails or soldiers. It was an amazing pastime after a few glasses of wine, each side getting more and more frantic as the game progressed and usually ending in wild laughter.

I spent three years in this 'wilderness', now and then getting worried about the cash situation. One time, I got a job as a taxi driver for 'Silver Sails'. I was stupid enough not to realise that I had become an employee not of a taxi firm, but a private-hire company. This meant that I couldn't be 'hailed' on the street and had to return to base after every trip to collect my next call, so that if you went at normal speeds on the most obvious routes you got hardly any work at all and therefore less money. During this period, my already sharpened senses for a short cut went ballistic. At rush hours, I would devise routes that kept well off the main roads.

The main bill of fare at 'Silver Sails' was taking remand prisoners and their escorts from Bristol's Horfield prison to the magistrates' court and back again. Occasionally I got a trip to a more distant court; one was in Dorchester. The prisoner got out with his two escorts and I then settled down to read the paper and waited for them to return. The prisoner came back and sat in the car with me, all very nonchalantly, and began telling me amusing stories of the 'nicks' he'd been in. I was rather worried that the escorts hadn't returned and was uncertain what to do, expecting him any second to turn nasty and tell me to drive somewhere of his bidding 'or else!' The escorts finally returned after having been for an 'Indian' with a few pints as well. Afterwards they assured me that that particular prisoner wouldn't harm a fly; he was an 'old lag' who was looking forward to spending Christmas in the nick, but he only got six weeks – just missing the festive season by a week!

One other memory is of picking up 'trusties' and taking them back to the prison. One evening, as I was about to go home, I was told to pick a prisoner up from a house nearby. The car I usually drove had been taken by another driver, so I was given the key to the London taxi which was hardly used. I drove to the house and saw my man waiting for me in the garden at the bottom of a long sloping drive. I drove down and then, to my acute embarrassment, could not get the gearstick into reverse. After several minutes of scraping and scrunching, the prisoner offered to help; so I let him take over driving the cab back up the slope. Only when I walked up to the road did I realise what I'd done. There was a prisoner in charge of a vehicle and I'd let him have it!

Vicki and I heard of a property going in Clifton and decided to buy it. The house was in Windsor Terrace, a Georgian house with stunning aspects: the Avon Gorge and Brunel's magnificent suspension bridge at the back, and over the docks and the countryside beyond at the front. As we'd dreamed of in our liberal-minded youth, we made Windsor Terrace into a commune house; my friend from childhood, Malcolm, and his wife Georgeanne were 'tenants in common' with us. The commune idea worked well at first, but I began to realise that such a romantic ideal was destined not to work in the long term. We were saved by Malcolm getting a research fellowship at UCLA. He and Georgeanne went to America for five years and didn't return to Bristol. As if to prove my misgivings, a similar idea of community living took hold in a house three doors further up the terrace. Three couples lived communally: they bought food in bulk and shared the chores, cooked for all and ate together at a big table. All went very happily for about two years. Beyond that they stopped speaking to each other; except for essential things, they stored all food separately under lock and key, and ate in their own rooms. They all hated each other and it dragged on like this, a bitter house of horror, for another six or seven years...

CHAPTER SIX
Writing for a Living

AFTER THREE YEARS OF being in the wilderness of not knowing precisely what I wanted to do, I was on the road to thirty with very little to show. Then came the meeting with Dave Martin and the events which led to the commissioning of a *Doctor Who* adventure, *The Claws of Axos*, as described in the opening chapter. There followed a whirlwind of work for BBC, ATV, Thames, but mostly from HTV.

We delivered our first completed *Who* script in April 1970. It began life as *Doctor Who and The Gift*, a seven-part show; then changed from that to a six-parter, *The Friendly Invasion*; then to a four-part series, *Vampire From Space*, which was finally transmitted as *The Claws of Axos*.

I recall the naughty pleasure I felt at putting in the names of some people I knew, like my old foreman at the Co-op, Wally Chinn, and the builder I was currently refurbishing houses with, Bill Filer. Dave and I found writing the scripts pretty easy after the toil of doing the outline; it was sort of like going downhill, or plain sailing after the storm of 'outlines'. However, as well as tightening the story ourselves, there were also requests for revisions by script editor Terrance Dicks. At the last minute, after we thought all was right, Terrance rang us and asked for an amendment, something that could only be for *Doctor Who*: 'Can you put a six-foot rat in episode one?'!

When I saw the programme on TV, I was pleased with the way it had been made. The gold-faced Axons looked good and sounded totally convincing; and from Pigbin Josh up to the Chinn character the show was very well cast. In fact, apart from a few dodgy SFX moments, both Dave and I felt very well served by the director and the production team; plus there was the fact that it was, after all, our first one. Dave and I were invited to the recordings where we met the wonderful Jon Pertwee and his then companion, the delightful Katy Manning. All very nice, but we couldn't hang around – there was more work to do.

For having worked so hard on HTV's *Pretenders*, the Monmouth Rebellion serial, Programme Controller Patrick Dromgoole gave Dave and me a sort of bonus. He simply said: 'Write me a thriller set in Bristol.' Patrick was to direct it. He was hoping that somehow we might pull off something that was distinctly about us, the people who lived in the West Country, not some rural idyll but something gritty, about the big city – Bristol. There was already the Liverpool genre, tough working-class dramas, and Salford was awash with directors trying to better *Saturday Night and Sunday Morning*. Setting it in Bristol was a godsend for me, as it was a chance to use all the fantastic locations I'd discovered when I made films as a teenager. I remember stunning Dave with how amazing they were; he'd not lived in Bristol for very long and was unaware of the atmospheric nooks and crannies of the city.

And here was an opportunity to do something that would be ours alone – perhaps the start of a writing style? Would Dave be happy about this? And why not? After all, *Likely Lads* writers Clement and La Frenais had achieved it.

We decided to make it into a simple robbery story carried out by a motley and totally incompetent crew, recruited just for that particular 'pop' (the colloquial thieves' word for a safe-blowing). We decided that a little research was in order. Dave just happened to know a local boxer who'd been involved in a bit of crime – though only, he insisted, as a 'fixer'. This man offered to introduce us to a 'peterman' (safe-blower) who might, for the price of a couple of pints of Bass, be willing to give us the detailed information we required so as to make the safe-blowing scene in our film totally authentic.

We were to meet this certain gentleman in a pub in Bedminster, a fairly rough sort of district at that time. After introductions, a long silence… Then our man, Grant, said: 'Where's this safe you want blowin' then?'

We were very alarmed and said, 'No, no, no, no, no! Didn't he tell you? We're writing a film about a robbery... What we need to know is exactly how it's done.'

He began to relax and tell us his life story. How he'd learned how to crack safes in the army when he was recruited for MI6. (We later learned that all safe-blowers say that.) He talked about jobs he'd done. 'I did ten cinemas on the way back from London one night.' Then: 'My latest? Well, I've done eighty-seven egg-packing stations in the last six months'...! And of humorous incidents like putting a little too much gelignite in one safe – inevitably at an egg-packing station – and being blown through the tiles, leaving his head and shoulders in the cold moonlight... Subcontracting a couple of his mates to do a job because the heat was on him, and sending these two idiots to crack a safe at a car dealership and steal the plans of a new model before it went to press, and then getting a phone call – from inside the car dealers – informing him they'd managed to lock themselves in! Could he possibly pop down and let them out? All his cover was then blown and he was picked up by a passing copper as he was trying to get in, to let the would-be thieves out!

Grant went on to tell us in every minute detail of how a safe is blown: how a fingernail-sized dob of 'jelly' (gelignite) with a wired-up detonator (usually a 2.2 bullet) pressed into it is placed into the 'receiving end' of a condom, and pushed in through the keyhole with the aid of a wooden spatula (ice lolly stick) until it rests on the locking bar of the safe; then it's wired up to a battery. The peterman piles as many bits of carpet or curtain around the safe as he can, and then sits on top of the safe! After holding his nose and opening his mouth wide, he 'pops' the jelly by touching the two wires together on the battery. The resulting explosion, he assured us, is no louder than two thick books being slapped together. And so we listened through quite a few pints. The more he talked the more excited he became, and he began to display a high-pitched manic laugh with each story.

We started to discover what this was all about. The thief gets a tremendous rush of excitement taking part in a robbery; he takes drugs sometimes, but he's already 'high' on the thrill of it all. As Grant said: 'Doin' the job! Greatest thrill you'll ever get!' It's all about 'bottle'... from the cockney rhyming slang, bottle and glass – ass – in other words doing a scary job without shitting yourself. People in Grant's world had either 'got a lot o' bottle' or were 'not a lot o' bottle' or they'd 'lost their bottle'.

We said goodbye to Grant and remarked what a skilled job safe-blowing was; and he replied: 'That's it, see, too much fuckin' trouble these days innit? It's a bloody sight easier snatchin' 'andbags… Night then.'

Dave and I realised that he took much more pleasure in telling us stories about when he was doing 'bird'; and afterwards we deduced that Grant, married with a couple of kids, had spent at least twenty of his forty-odd years inside. It was then we decided to call our story *Thick as Thieves…*

So, armed with our research, Dave and I began to build our characters around the main one. We called him Eddie: a man who lived to steal, who knows no other world than being free, or being caught and doing time. All kept together with the pride and esteem he was held in by his fellows for having 'bottle' and being able to do time. 'That's where you learn it all…' Prison, the academy for crime.

We were thrilled to learn from our director, Patrick Dromgoole, that Leonard Rossiter had agreed to play the part of Eddie. We introduced him to Grant, and Len picked up the inner violence of the man and the manic laugh and put it in his portrayal of 'Eddie'. We also wanted to introduce a black character, and make him really a part of the structure; we'd seen too many 'token black' small parts, and so we wrote in strong parts for Horace James and Nina Baden-Semper as his girlfriend. We were surprised and delighted to get Corin Redgrave to play the 'Mr Big' who plans the job; and George Woodbridge, who'd played the pub landlord in umpteen vampire films, played a fine drunken wastrel who surprises us with his bravery at the end.

The shooting went well and again Dave and I were occasional 'extras'. The only thing that did make things a bit temperamental was that Corin Redgrave was at the height of his 'Socialist Worker' phase – much to Len Rossiter's annoyance, since Corin was given to lecturing the other actors on their politics and making daily collections for the postal workers, who were on strike at the time.

Otherwise everything went well, and *Thick as Thieves* was transmitted on the ITV network on 26th February 1971. It gained some very flattering and encouraging crits from the national newspapers including the Sundays. One particular quote worth mentioning was from the *Sunday*

Telgraph's TV critic, Philip Purser, who wrote: 'Rossiter's shifty, insecure, peg-toothed grin was like the locale: absolutely specific and therefore universal.'

Thick as Thieves won the Pye 'Oscar' for best regional production at the British Film and Television Awards in 1972. Also, a copy was obtained to be kept in the National Film Archive. We made sure all the crew and all those who helped make the film shared in these honours.

Writing and being involved in making *Thick as Thieves* was a tremendous experience. We again managed to get location catering done for the crew by our mate Keith Floyd at his new bistro – of which more later. All in all, the whole experience was nothing less than idyllic. In addition to having great respect for his work, Dave and I seemed to hit it off with Len Rossiter and we talked of other possible ideas for the future... even a series based on Eddie the thick thief. There were tons more sad yet hilarious stories that came from Grant.

No sooner had we finished filming *Thieves* when *Doctor Who* loomed once more. We'd been contacted and asked to put in an idea for a six-part *Who*. Dave and I were both keenly interested in the postwar British Raj and the retreat from India and Empire... Make the country a planet and it's been colonised by Earth people, who'd rather stay there if they could. It's just that there's all those inconvenient bloody natives... How nice if the planet could be without them! However, to stay there they must chemically change the atmosphere... A concept since echoed by stories such as *Total Recall* and more recently and specifically *Avatar*.

This story, *The Mutants*, was in my opinion the best *Doctor Who* we did. All the elements seemed to come together. We managed, just – with excellent guidance from Terrance Dicks – to avoid the dip that happens around the middle of a six-part *Who* by introducing what's called a 'dog leg'. At the end of episode three, a totally new aspect was introduced to the story which brought in a new character, Sondergaard – who'd been already 'signposted' – to keep the show moving. For their part the BBC got the special effects working well and the designer came up with some terrific monsters... 'the mutants'. The show was particularly well directed and the monster scenes kept to a minimum and often shot in darkness which made them seem more sinister. With this show, there were loads of special effects and most of them came off well; unfortunately, technology hadn't managed to cure the 'silver outline' on the CSO (Colour Separation Overlay) and sometimes Jon Pertwee seemed not to be walking in the same direction as the special-effect tunnels! We couldn't blame the BBC for that, knowing full well that they were doing their best with the technology available at that time. *The Mutants* was a show to be proud of.

After doing *Thick as Thieves*, Dave and I seemed to be working on several things at once, and between *The Mutants* and *The Three Doctors* in 1973 we devised a thirteen-part series called *Arthur of the Britons*. This deserves a bit of background.

The Arthur legend: is King Arthur fairy story? Or is he based on a real person? This was something I'd begun working on with Bill Stair when we were making stuff for John Boorman. I'd been contacted by the Camelot Research Committee, a strange amalgam of amateur archaeologists, historians and students led by a relentless old lady called Jess Foster. She'd contacted me as being a person who had a movie camera, and who might film an upcoming 'dig'. After a few hours of chatting with her I suddenly contracted what might be called the Arthur 'bug'. It was a subject after my own heart; I'd discussed it many times at the Co-op with Tom and Graham: 'Was there ever a real King Arthur?'

Jess introduced me to the books *King Arthur's Avalon* and *From Caesar to Arthur* by Geoffrey Ashe, a firm believer in an authentic Arthur, who sets out the thesis that 'King' Arthur was perhaps a soldier, or a general in a Romano-British army just after the Romans left. Drilled in Roman cavalry tactics, he defeats the foot-soldiers of the Saxon armies and saves Britain from pagan Saxon rule for long enough so that, when they do defeat the Britons, they are by that time converted to Christianity. As Winston Churchill wrote of such a theory in his *History of the English Speaking Peoples*: 'It's all true! Or it ought to be. And more and better besides!'

The Camelot Research Committee, whose patron was the amazing diminutive ninety-year-old archaeologist, Ralegh Radford, were proposing a 'dig' at the place they were convinced was the ancient 'Camelot', namely the Iron Age Hill Fort at South Cadbury in Somerset.

With Jess's connivance, rather than just film the 'dig', they were proposing I was to make a film in support of the views the Research Committee held about Arthur and Camelot. The idea was turned down because, at five hundred pounds, the film was deemed too costly. However, Bill Stair and I had done quite a bit of work on a script and had taken pictures of actors in costume for an animated section. I showed the script to Dave and told him all about Arthur and Camelot. Dave duly caught the 'bug' and we started an epic film script called *Ardur*, the Welsh or Celtic way of writing Arthur. It turned out to be a whacking great screenplay of two hundred and forty pages or so; a huge weight to put in the post, but we duly sent it to all our contacts. We met up with Clive Donner to see if it was something he might do; but he'd just finished filming *Alfred the Great* starring David Hemmings as Alfred, and was about fed up with epics. We had kind words from many agents and producers, but nobody was willing to take it on. We decided to turn it into a book and commissioned a fellow writer who lived in Clifton, Ivan Benbrook, to rewrite it as a novel; sadly, Ivan wasn't as fired up about historical greats as we were and it was never properly finished. But it was still a great story. So, we suggested it to HTV as a series…

It was somehow cursed and turned into a sad tale. It was something Patrick Dromgoole was keen to do; but HTV was only a regional station and couldn't afford the costs of an 'epic'. His only resort was to search around for a co-producer with money. He met an American producer at the Cannes TV market who said he loved the idea and would be keen to become involved, and that he had investors who would put in cash. His name was Skip Steloff, and he always wore vaguely nautical clothes. He was, apparently, a veteran film producer and fixer of co-productions; he was always seen at the film and TV markets around the world. He told us – confidentially – that all film and TV deals are done in the New York Yacht Club… where he was a member.

So, HTV had found a co-producer to help with the costs. As far as Dave and I were concerned we were most anxious to get close to the feeling of a 'British hero'… Arthur, who was not a king, but a trained war leader, who outfought the mighty Saxons at a time when Britain was in mortal danger. This, in place of the romantic 'Round Table' version: Malory's *Morte D'Arthur* which was how King Arthur was known to most people.

Sadly, when the new producer was put onto the show, we were dealing with a man who'd just finished doing what was, in my opinion, a rather lugubrious series of *Black Beauty*. We disagreed on practically everything and it soon came to the point where we had stand-up rows.

Something had to go and unfortunately it was Dave and I. We'd fouled up our very special relationship with Patrick and HTV. If that wasn't bad enough, feelings got worse when our promised 'series creators' credit disappeared (even though it was specified in our contract). HTV covered themselves by putting it, handwritten, on the 'end board' (the HTV house emblem). Then, to sour things even further, after we'd written our one and only episode in the series, the producer asked us in a letter if we wanted our names 'emblazoned on the telly screen'? Or were we happy to have it credited to one 'Emilio Dungheap, a lesser known Afghanistan writer with one leg'? However insulting, we didn't rise to this and sent an extremely polite reply saying it would probably be simpler if the episode had our names on it.

When we looked at the series afterwards, it didn't seem so bad, but it had none of the powerful images we'd hoped for. It was helped by a great lead, the redoubtable Oliver Tobias, an energetic and charismatic actor. Unfortunately the series was beset by cloth-cutting to make it affordable and Arthur's Camelot became a circle of huts on waste ground. So unlike what we'd had in mind. We didn't want nor expect Disneyesque pointed towers, but some semblance of an authentic hill-fort dwelling. In fact, the 'Camelot' village looked so unkempt and scrappy, we felt the series should have been titled *Arthur in the Stinging Nettles*. However, it was for a children's slot with a five-thirty showing and it obviously went down well, earning a deserved Writer's Guild Award for Best Children's Series in 1973.

So, after this disaster, we learned that you cannot expect to get exactly what you want every time; and that when co-producers are involved, who hold the purse strings, 'temperamental writers' get kicked out! Our only real option was to have pulled out at an early stage and let them get on with it. That is hard to do when you feel passionately about a subject. As it was, we'd gained nothing, and had lost our close relationship with Patrick and HTV.

The final irony, though, was that the vaunted Skip Steloff who spoke of 'American money' and the 'American showing of *Arthur*' had conned HTV completely. It became clear that Steloff had no money whatsoever and his 'deal with an American network' was total fantasy. HTV paid up for the lot! *Arthur of the Britons* was shown in the States… on the TV screens of McDonald's hamburger restaurants throughout the north eastern states, and nowhere else…

We started mending fences with Patrick and after a ridiculous, bizarre, drunken exchange between Dave and Patrick at the *Arthur* end-of-shoot party, feelings were running high. I noticed too, that there was a difference from the unit and crew we'd known on *Pretenders* and *Thick as Thieves*. The 'family feeling' seemed to be breaking up. One young aspiring director started in on Patrick, threatening to beat him up, and I stepped between them, risking a punch in the nose.

It was nothing much, but we all suddenly saw the stupidity of our rift. It was all about quality and integrity, and that was what we all desired above everything else. There was no real enmity. We both found ourselves in positions we had little control over: Patrick trying to convince his board at HTV that an overspend on *Arthur* was worth it; us wanting to give something to the legend that was new, innovative, exciting and reasonably accurate.

It was around this time that I met with Adge Cutler, the originator of Somerset-based band 'The Wurzels', who shared the same agency as the band I was playing in. Adge knew my brother from the days when Acker Bilk had a club in Bristol at the Crown and Dove Hotel; he and Roger were doormen on alternate weeks. I remember Roger mentioning him. Now I got to know him when we occasionally met at the agency; we'd always have lunch together and choose somewhere different each time. These lunches became a regular feature and Adge christened it 'germittin''. Adge was in fact a gourmet, but a gourmet with rather rustic table manners. We'd assess each meal on a points system, rather as if we were from the *Good Food Guide*! He told me incredible stories of how he'd once been Acker Bilk's road manager, driving the coach from gig to gig, and the adventures he got into. This is when he'd started 'germitting' all over the country and all on his own as he waited for Acker and the band to do their performance. When I met Acker some time later I reminded him of Adge's 'roadie' days and he remarked, alluding to Adge's digestive processes: 'Aah, 'course we had to put a canary in the coach before we could get on board.'

I remained a good friend of Adge after the early success of the Wurzels and we kept up our 'germitting' for quite a while. I realised that Adge, far from being the coarse figure he'd created on stage, was a lover of the countryside and felt elated to drive 'up on Mendip' in his MGB convertible. He was a poet with a special feeling for the villages around the place he grew up in, Nailsea in Somerset; the songs he wrote were ballads of a bygone time and were full of real imagination, passion and understanding of specific places in his world. Aside from being a country poet, Adge spoke fluent Spanish, learned the hard way…

When Acker Bilk's brother, Dave Bilk, sent Adge to Spain to buy land for the opening of a new departure for the burgeoning Bilk empire – building holiday villas – he was given a few hundred pesetas and drove his beloved Fiat 600 to Alicante. After six months, he'd completed all the land deals necessary and had, moneywise, been running on empty for quite a while. Phone calls to the Bilk office in London requesting money resulted in promises, but no money. Over the next six months, Adge had to use each bar in the town he was staying in and run up a small bill in each one to spread his debt. His poor car was a filthy heap of dusty metal with all the tyres flat as pancakes. He was trapped in a Kafkaesque nightmare in the town: penniless, his clothes literally in rags. He was then forced to vacate his hotel and decided to live in a wooden beach hut; but one night on his way back there he saw a glow in the distance. The hut had caught fire… He managed to live in the spare room of a British ex-pat for a time. Then finally, after spending a year totally on his own, Dave Bilk arrived and ended his misery.

It had been a bleak year… but he had learned to speak Spanish.

It was a terrible shock when I heard that Adge had been killed in a car accident while returning alone one night from a gig with the Wurzels in Hereford.

By this time Dave Martin and I were working full pelt, with hardly time to relax. Looking at our working relationship, I was happy with the way things were going and so, I believe, was Dave. I was beginning to get hold of the way he thought – and he me; it was as if we were one schizophrenic mind which was held in delicate balance.

On the outside, Dave was very much attuned to the Ernest Hemingway lifestyle and held the same kind of wish to put himself in harm's way: something I might have appreciated from afar, but didn't wholeheartedly share. I suppose I'd led a pretty exciting life but I don't think I'd tried doing anything particularly dangerous. This was about to change.

CHAPTER SEVEN
Enter Mr Floyd... and Others

THE CHANGE WAS BROUGHT about by a third person who became fixed in our firmament. Dave and I had met Keith Floyd quite separately. They'd met in a Clifton pub called the Greyhound, a place where the arty folk of Clifton met, including some pretty weird eccentrics. It was Dave's watering hole and he often met with Keith and they had long, often drunken conversations about what they wanted from life.

Keith wanted firstly to be famous, and had fantastic ideas about changing the face of British gastronomy, his background in this being a summer working in a hotel in Cornwall. He'd subsequently worked as a cub reporter on the *Bristol Evening Post*; then, bizarrely, as a second lieutenant in the Royal Tank Corps where, apparently, he often cooked for his fellow officers when they were in battle training on Salisbury Plain and later on Luneburg Heath in Germany. He went on about how he'd felt about the army and realising with deep regret that he couldn't be the sabre-wielding cavalry officer galloping toward the enemy that he'd hoped to be. Dave listened to his story and decided it was tremendous material for a film.

It was amazing how Dave had an almost photographic memory, and even after a night's drinking he would sit down and write out, longhand, all that was said during that session! When I saw the story, I thought it was fantastic too. So we called the ensuing script *A Man's Life*. This was, of course, the story that attracted the people from *Doctor Who*. However, it was never made as a film.

My own first encounter with Keith was on a memorable evening when the band I was playing in – The Franklyn Big Six, a group that had evolved from The Statesmen – were the support group at the Bristol University Union to none other than The Cream (later known simply as 'Cream')... Wow! What a night that was! Our roadie came up on stage just as we were finishing our set and told me, 'There's a bloke down in the audience says he wants to manage you.' I went to see this 'bloke' and met a charming man in spotted bow tie and immaculate blazer who introduced himself as Keith Floyd. Without further ado he went into a spiel about record contracts, gigs he could get us in London – we'd heard it all before but there was something about this guy I liked; and anyway he really did love the band. Thereafter I met Keith on my occasional visits to the Greyhound to see Dave and a friendship sprang up between the three of us.

Dave was very much into sailing: something that, apart from on the local park lake, I'd never done; and there was somehow a fusion of things and people that pulled me into the area of boatbuilding. Firstly, through Dave, I met an amazing man called Hywel Price, whom Dave had met when he was on a stint working at the Bristol Old Vic – Hywel was the enigmatic propmaker/designer when Dave was a flyman. Formerly Hywel had been a racing driver of cars and motorbikes; he'd managed a touring seaside show of underwater escapology and a troupe of lady formation swimmers called the 'Aqua Lovelies'! He'd fished professionally from ports in Wales as well as Newlyn and Brixham. Above all, Hywel was a boat builder, and thought of little else; an obsession which he claimed came from being lost at sea off his home town of Rhyl at the age of ten. He was always thinking of the next boat. So, deep in the bowels of the Bristol Old Vic alongside the props for the coming pantomime were the ribs of a thirty-foot sailing boat. There is a fantastic story attached to that particular craft.

When finished, Hywel intended to sail the boat to America; but, as usual, he didn't have the money, so he advertised for 'passengers' to sail with him to the Caribbean and share the costs. He was joined by two young men anxious for adventure. All went well, until they reached Bermuda. It should be mentioned that, at the start of the voyage, for some reason, perhaps with sharks (or even pirates?) in mind, Hywel had taken along a .303 Lee Enfield rifle and ammunition for it... It was hidden down in the scuppers.

They moored in the smart Bermuda Yacht Club. The two lads went ashore leaving Hywel on board. It was very hot, so Hywel decided to swim ashore and go to the club bar for a drink. After a few Bacardis someone on the balcony commented that a boat was on fire in the harbour. To his horror Hywel saw that it was his boat, and it was well ablaze. Police and emergency services, both land and waterborne, were closing on it. Hywel ran out and went to see what he could do. Then he suddenly remembered the rifle and ammunition. It could explode! Police and firemen were approaching the burning hulk trying to put the fire out. Hywel was waving his arms frantically, shouting and screaming at them, 'Go away! Keep off!' The fire burned down to the yacht's waterline. Fortunately the ammo didn't explode. But Hywel had lost everything: his boat, all his cash, all his clothes; and he was now standing in all he possessed – a swimming costume! Then the Bermudan police arrested him… They accused him of burning his own boat for insurance purposes. He was in the depths of despair when one of his 'passengers' turned up, got him released and handed him some cash for clothes and a first-class air ticket to London. This young adventurer just happened to be the son of the then Governor of the Bank of England!

It was stories like these that turned me on to the sea and the idea of maybe taking a trip on a boat, experiencing something different. Dave was always urging me to 'have a go, at something or other'. When we were in the early stages of *Arthur of the Britons* (i.e. still on friendly terms with HTV) he suggested we take riding lessons so that we could be 'riding extras' on the upcoming series. Despite my fear of large four-legged beasts, I agreed – and duly got thrown off a huge mare that suddenly got frisky when a colt galloped by in the next field! No more riding for me! Of sailing, more later.

We had a call from *Doctor Who* script editor Terrance Dicks who asked us if we would like to write a special tenth anniversary edition of *Doctor Who*. We felt this was quite an accolade, being relatively new to the series. The difference in this show was that the three Doctors would be together at one time. The premise was that the Time Lords faced a threat too great for just one of them to handle.

Terrance Dicks told us that he was working late in the *Who* office one evening when an old man popped his head around the door and, half-joking, said 'Any chance of a job?' It was William Hartnell. It got Terrance thinking about the tenth anniversary edition; and he put forward the idea of using three Doctors, and chose us to write it. We got working on it during the summer of 1973.

That summer turned out to be a busy one. Having made our peace with HTV we were asked to write a drama-documentary about Bristol history, since the city was about to lose its charter of 1373 granting it city and county status (which provided for it to hold assizes). The whole area twenty-five miles around was to be in a new county called Avon. This apparently presented fantastic opportunities to all involved.

As a Bristolian, stored away in my brain were loads of historical details that came from my gran, from Mum and Dad and the guys at the Co-op. 'Scratch a Bristolian,' it is said, 'and underneath you'll find a historian.' Here was a chance to use up all the stuff I already knew about and a chance to learn even more!

We used a Bristol pilot cutter, a beautifully preserved boat named the *Peggy*, to travel from Pill, a village at the mouth of the Bristol Avon – where the craft was built in 1903 by Rolls of Pill – into the city, picking up on all the historical facts and figures from the point of view of three passengers for whom the boat represented a kind of time capsule. The first of these was the Lord Mayor when the charter was granted to Bristol in 1373, William Canynges, played by Norman Tyrrell. Robert Lang played a writer and journalist, William Matthews, from the heyday of the Clifton Spa and the slave trade, author of *The New History, Survey and Description of the City and Suburbs of Bristol, or Complete Guide* (a real sizzler!); and Tony Adams played a whizz-kid in fashionable bell-bottom suit, an entrepreneur of the 1970s.

The Bristol charter had run for six hundred years; so the title of the piece was *Bristol 600*. I had wanted to call it – in the Bristol dialect, with its predilection for putting 'L' on the end of words – *End of an Earole* which would have been fun, but our producer Leonard White would have none of it. One amazing thing we came up with in an old book on Bristol was a theory that America was not named after Amerigo Vespucci, as generally accepted by history, but after someone else. In those times it was the custom for a new land to be named either after a monarch, where the Christian name was used, or after the surname of the discovery expedition's sponsor. In Vespucci's case, the new land would seem to have taken his Christian name, Amerigo. But Vespucci was no king. Who then?

John Cabot sailed from Bristol in 1497 to discover new lands across the seas. Henry VII, the king at that time, was all for the voyage but was a little short on cash, so he asked the local Bristol customs man to put up the money on his behalf. This he did, and so became sponsor for the voyage.

That man's name was John ap Merryck… or John Amerrick.

Think about it.

I was delighted to hear this very theory put forward on the TV show *QI*… so it must be true!

We got *The Three Doctors* finished by September of that year. It was provisionally titled *The Black Hole*, being a new discovery at the time which filled us with ideas about 'singularity' and 'event horizons'. I think we felt that we'd got the characters of the three super-egos satisfactorily with a good exchange of cynical or disparaging quips: 'So you're my replacements? A dandy and a clown.' We'd originally wanted it to be 'a hairdresser and a clown' but it was thought by the producer to be going a little too far.

Omega was one of the best megalomaniacs we'd written. 'A hero? I could have been a god!' He was based on an idea in a book by Aldous Huxley called *Time Must Have a Stop* about a being who existed only by his own willpower. He was only 'an awareness of an awareness'. Omega was an outrageous and rather sad figure who has certainly made his mark on the series, being used in some later stories and still appearing on independent *Doctor Who* DVDs and CDs.

The Three Doctors episode topped the viewing figures for children's series that year. However there was no stopping us. 1973 was a very busy year. Dave and I had by now left the entertainment agent's offices and were encamped in a room above what was to become Keith Floyd's signature restaurant, simply called 'Floyd's Restaurant'.

After *The Three Doctors*, we managed to fit another job into '73: an episode of *Public Eye*, a super private-eye series starring Alfie Burke as Frank Marker, a sort of hangdog gumshoe, set in Chertsey. We did a story called *Lifer*, a story about a father whose child had been murdered, twenty-five years previously, who finds out that the killer has been released from prison. He hires Marker to find him, lying that he was a long-lost relative; but when it comes to dealing out death, and even with the murderer inviting him to kill him, he cannot do it. A pretty heavy story in a fairly dark series. Dave and I always felt that even the darkest tale needed a few jokes. Or rather, humorous moments. We had a few in *Lifer* but when we read the shooting script sent by the producer, we found that he'd cut them out – or even worse, turned them into something else.

A case in point: after a session at a BBC recording, Dave, Trevor Ray who worked in the *Who* office at that time and I had a meal in an Italian restaurant in Charlotte Street. We were served by a gorgeous, suntanned, London Italian lady who wore a very low-cut blouse. Dave ordered the salade Niçoise; and after a while I could see he was a little unhappy with his choice. When we'd finished, the waitress asked us if we'd enjoyed our meal. Dave piped up to say he wasn't pleased with his 'Niçoise'. She looked at him with a winning smile and said, 'Oh, didn't you know? We do the worst Niçoise in London;' then, emphasising her ample bosom, continued: 'Must be somethin' brings 'em in'… What can you do but smile. We put that into *Lifer* verbatim – and our producer changed the word 'worst' for 'best', which made it totally unfunny. It makes the mind boggle sometimes. When we pointed this out to him he got a bit shirty… Won't be working for him again, we thought.

The Three Doctors aired in the summer of 1973 and pulled a huge viewing audience, a record for the show. Dave and I were very happy with the result in terms of the story and the acting; as is well known, William Hartnell's appearance was cut severely when it was sadly realised that he was very ill. I'm afraid we were not overly impressed by the 'Gel Guards'. After the superb *Mutants* monsters, these looked a bit like escaped Christmas decorations that wobbled! You can't win 'em all! Powerful performances by Patrick Troughton, Katy Manning and Jon Pertwee and Stephen Thorne as Omega ensured a really good series.

At this time I was still doing up houses, and playing tenor sax in The Franklyn Big Six – now with up to three gigs a week. The band was asked to appear in a Bristol University production of *Marat/Sade* as the asylum orchestra, acting and playing in it at the same time. It was a most fantastic experience, going to rehearsals and getting to know the play from the inside as it were. It remains one of my favourite plays. It was directed by a completely mad genius called Michael Kullman, He and his slightly hippy lady lived in a couple of rooms in Hotwells, but I realised during one night of heavy boozing that they didn't have a toilet; one was supposed to, as his lady informed me, piss in the sink. Michael owned a souped-up mini van and drove at seventy mph even through the centre of town. I only went in that van once. Never again! There was talk of another musical play, Brecht's *Mahagonny*, but unfortunately it never came off.

Enter 1974. Derrick Sherwin had been the producer of *Doctor Who* when we first went to see them, but he'd subsequently gone on to do *Paul Temple*, still at the Beeb. Again Dave and I presented loads and loads of storylines, but in the end they were all rejected.

Derrick then left the BBC to set up in Soho to do a German/Swiss co-production called *Ski Boy* with partner Martin Hall. We were to write the series outline and do episodes one and two to set new writers on the right path. We in fact ended up doing four episodes. *Ski Boy* was eventually shown on the ITV network, but there wasn't a second series. Finance problems were at the root of that; and it led to us coining a phrase from the indefatigable Derrick Sherwin who regularly assured us that 'the Germans were still there', as meaning that the programme had no hope whatsoever of being resurrected.

We had a call from Richard Harris – the writer (*Stepping Out, Outside Edge*), not the actor. He was script editor of a series suggested by *Z Cars* creator Ted Willis who'd come up with an idea for a rural police series, set in Rushden, Northamptonshire. We went to see Richard at ATV in Borehamwood and developed a rather tense relationship with him: interestingly, for some reason he seemed to see us, or rather Dave in particular, as a threat. This, however, did finally pass and Richard, and his wife Hilary, became good friends.

We were taken to Rushden to see the empty police station that had been chosen as the main location and met some of the actors. Dave had already met Ewan Hooper, who was to play the lead, at Bristol Old Vic and was impressed by his work. We also met with Duncan Preston, who played the 'rookie' PC Pooley. We rather enjoyed writing for *Hunter's Walk* and felt it could have been among the greats, but I suppose the very 'ruralness' of it was both its strength and its downfall. I remember commenting: 'Chases don't seem the same in tractors!' The stories we came up with had a sort of quiet Englishness, and tackled subject matters such as male chauvinism, childbirth/abortion, as well as sheep rustling and crop stealing and one about sudden violence at a gentle church wedding, which featured a brilliant new actor as guest star, who was to go on to greater things: John Rhys-Davies. This episode was struck on the anvil of truth. Dave had had a run-in with somebody at a party, and this strong young rugger type thumped Dave and pushed him over some pointed railings, piercing Dave's stomach in the area of the appendix. Dave went through several months of pain, before the – perhaps cathartic? – exercise of putting it all into a script.

After this came an invitation from producer Leonard White, who was working at HTV. He wanted us to present some ideas for a late-night drama, an experimental series of half-hour plays under the umbrella title of *Through a Glass Darkly*. The one and only premise was that the plays had to be about television. 'TV looking up its own ass you mean?' said Dave. We learned that every regional ITV station that made drama had been asked to contribute, of which six eventually did. We were asked to submit two ideas.

Patrick Dromgoole was to direct the first one. It was good to be back in harness with him again and at our first script meeting he pointed out that our first draft, which was full of conspiracy and news editor machinations over content, was totally in the wrong direction. News is at the mercy of events; things happen. It's all in the process of what is doable and what isn't. It was called *Item* and in it we show the news editor seeing 'rushes' with the editor and complaining at not being able to see the face of a distraught, crying mother of a dispossessed family forced into squatting, and how much effort should be put into this one story; then finally deciding to cast aside the squatter-family-in-poverty story in favour of breaking news of a fire aboard a ship in the harbour. The father in the family story is being made up ready for his piece to camera, but the make-up girls stops when she gets the shake of a head from the floor manager and she tells him: 'You're not needed.' After all the film shot for his tragic tale, he watches a ten-second clip that has been hastily slotted into the main news. *Item* was well received by the critics and was chosen as the ITV entry at the Monte Carlo TV festival.

For the second play, Dave and I chose to move into the sci-fi area and used a simple TV family game show, *Mr & Mrs*, as a vehicle. It was directed by Derek Clark who did the regular *Mr & Mrs* show. It begins with the normal show and presenter Alan Taylor, then skids off to the

Me with my brother
Roger in 1941. I was
two, Roger was five

Louisa, our Gran:
'I'm only an old Bristol d'oman'

My father, Stanley

Roma, our Mum, with Roger and me.
A photo taken to send to Dad while he
was serving in the RAF during the war

1947: my eighth birthday

Me aged ten

The Baker brothers
in 1953

1954: going for the flamboyant look

Lettering a
headstone at
the Co-op
Monumental
Department

With Dianne, my first
girlfriend, in 1954

In my Air Training Corps uniform, 1956

Playing clarinet in my first band,
the Hillside Stompers, with
John Fortune on trombone

Attempting to look studious

Getting married to Vicki at
Little Bentley in Essex,
January 1959

Roger was best man at
my wedding to Vicki

At Mill House (Vicki's
parents' home) with our
three children: Catherine,
Paul and Martin

Hexagon Films
L TO R: Tony Vann, Malcolm Windsor,
me and Bill Stair

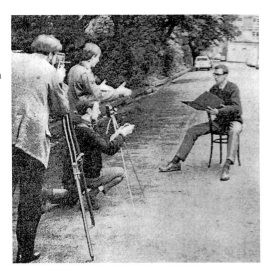

On location making our first film

Directing
*Search and
Destroy* with
my brother
Roger as
an extra

On location in Bristol for *Thick as Thieves*. In those early days the HTV unit became like a family

Marc Harrison wearing blue contact lenses as the title character in *Sky*, first transmitted in 1975 and now a cult show

Leonard Rossiter and Nina Baden-Semper
in *Machinegunner*

A page of rehearsal script
for *The Invisible Enemy*,
the first *Doctor Who* story
to feature K9

Rehearsal Script   PROJECT NO: 02347/2204
BBC 1 - COLOUR

THE SENDING OF THIS SCRIPT DOES NOT CONSTITUTE
AN OFFER OF A CONTRACT FOR ANY PART IN IT.

'DOCTOR WHO'

SERIAL 4T

by

Bob Baker & Dave Martin

EPISODE FOUR   'The Invisible Enemy'

PRODUCER.............GRAHAM WILLIAMS
DIRECTOR.............DERRICK GOODWIN
DESIGNER.............BARRY NEWBERY
SCRIPT EDITOR........ROBERT HOLMES
P.U.M...............JOHN NATHAN-TURNER
P.A.................NORMAN STEWART
A.F.M...............TONY GARRICK
ASSISTANT...........PAT HARRINGTON

COSTUME SUPERVISOR...RAYMOND HUGHES
MAKE-UP SUPERVISOR...MAUREEN WINSLADE

FILMING: Week 12

OUTSIDE REHEARSAL: 15tn April - 23rd April

CAMERA REHEARSAL AND RECORDING: 24th, 25th, 26th April

TRANSMISSION:

- 1 -

Milton Johns as Ergon
in *King of the Castle*

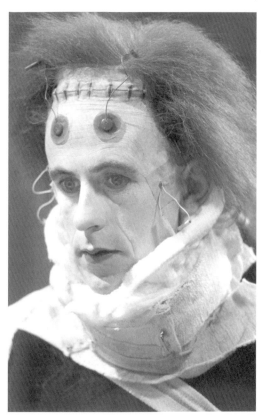

7 P.M. 7/7/77: Dave and me at the
Northcott Theatre, Exeter, for the
opening night of *Rat Trap*

Playing sax at a gig

MFV *Solon*: the calm before the storm

Murder at the Wedding, Dave's and my critically mauled swansong

Dave and me doing extra work on *Robin Hood*

Ron Moody as Rothgo in
Into the Labyrinth

Bobby Gee in the *Dramarama*
episode *Purple Passion Video* –
my first outing as producer

Script editing at HTV in the 1980s (notice K9 engrossed in one of the books on the shelf!)

Pie Noon, the *Function Room* episode written by John Collee who went on to a hugely successful writing career

Rula Lenska in the *Function Room* episode *Cary Grant's Nose*

Mel Martin in *Frontier*

A Harvey's wine
company photoshoot
for the series *Vintage*

Roger Crago and I looking
through some stills for
Cthulhu Mansion

All at sea

Marrying my third wife, Marie, in 1991 after being pushed up the aisle in a wheelchair

Starting work on *A Close Shave* with Nick Park at the Aardman offices in Clifton, watched over by the Oscar for *The Wrong Trousers*

Nick and I sharing a joke with HRH Prince Charles on a visit to the Aardman studios

With my treasured BAFTA award. On the wall behind me, a souvenir prop from *A Close Shave*

K9 regenerated

future in a sort of time slip… It then becomes *M+M* now hosted by Robert Stephens, described thus by one TV critic: 'Robert Stephens made an excellently odious ringmaster; "host" implies a measure of courtesy entirely foreign to this monster's nature.' It is only the questions asked that help us learn, by hints and entirely oblique references, of regimented citizens living like battery hens rationed to the back teeth and beyond, with many future Britons being hunted, killed, or imprisoned for the good of the rest. *M+M* was a play that came 'nearly there', perhaps because the director didn't have the sharpness to deal with the new situation. However, the play got a lot of good crits, and both plays won accolades for what was then perceived as 'little regional HTV'.

Chapter Eight
Sky High!

MOST REGIONAL TELEVISION COMPANIES, if they were interested in doing drama, would have to submit their work to the 'Committee' – a board of senior executives from the larger network companies, who decided if a work was good enough to go on the network. However, in the area of children's drama, most regional stations could expect to get fourteen half-hour network slots for the five 'til six o'clock period. With the difficulties of getting adult drama on the network, the children's option seemed a fruitful way to go, since it kept original drama coming in the pipeline. Patrick Dromgoole commissioned Dave and I to do a seven-part children's drama; we were given no brief, we just had to come up with an idea. Again, happily, Leonard White was to produce.

The sixties and early seventies were awash with drug-taking, alternative lifestyles, a hotch-potch of beliefs both heartwarming and sometimes sinister; sex, mysticism, hippy culture, protests, and wildly contrasting extremes, such as flower-power love-ins and the Manson gang who murdered the pregnant Sharon Tate.

Dave and I thought to take a look at some of these through the eyes of a sci-fi character we called 'Sky', a time traveller destined for a future time on earth to try and avert a disaster of some kind. He is hit by the blast of a supernova and blown off his intended course so that Sky is deposited in the right place at the wrong time... the (then) present day.

Sky was a chance to put together a lot of the ideas we'd had for *Who* and been unable to use, plus a new concept to do with conservation. The character Sky represented an entity that was out of place and out of time; indeed completely out of tune with the Earth and who was, therefore, like a virus that had to be eradicated by the Earth's defensive mechanism – kind of like antibodies attacking a foreign virus… you get the idea. This force was called 'the Animus', personified as Goodchild, Sky's dark enemy who controlled living vegetation and used it to attack him.

Sky was studio-based, but with filmed inserts; again we were able to use some of the fantastic locations I'd come across in my travels with mates in the fifties – not least the disued tunnel of a very early (circa 1780) tram line which once conveyed coal from a mine some miles away to waiting barges in the river Avon. It was a very atmospheric location which set the tone for the serial. When we used other evocative locations such as Glastonbury Tor and Stonehenge, we hoped to point up a possible link between ancient sites and time travel. We were, of course, in the years of von Daniken's book *Chariots of the Gods*; everyone seemed fascinated by the prospect and tended to believe that some kind of 'spaceman/men' had landed on Earth, long, long ago and helped the Egyptians build the pyramids, the Incas Machu Picchu and the ancient Brits build Stonehenge.

The story of *Sky* itself has elements of *E.T.* as a bunch of kids try and help an alien escape the earth and get back on track to his destiny.

This particular serial again had the HTV 'regulars' working in concert to produce a highly competent show with loads of special effects and techniques which were totally new to them. It didn't always come off, but happily the most important ones did – in particular, Sky's eyes. Actor Marc Harrison, a talented newcomer straight from drama school, wore blue contact lenses, allowing the studio to superimpose images on them so that, as we come into close-up, we see the universe of stars in his eyes… Script conferences with Leonard White and Patrick Dromgoole were fascinating as they took on board what a leap forward this was for them, both in technical terms and in content and subject matter. Dave, in a press interview, said of the show: 'I suppose the story has ended up with a religious aspect; but we think our *Doctor Who* experience has shown us how to be entertaining, with suspense hooks and cliffhanger endings, while still retaining deeper levels.'

Sky was well received by its audience, and has since become something of a cult show. When I was working in Australia recently, I did a radio interview and the DJ kept asking me things about *Sky*. Of course I could hardly remember a thing about it! A DVD of the series has recently been released, for those who might like to refresh their memory of it.

By the mid seventies, my life was changing. By now I was earning enough to pay the bills. I'd got out of buildings and refurbishment of old houses and from the unpleasant situation of being a 'landlord', since my tenants tended to do a moonlight flit after running up huge rent arrears! My kids were now teenagers and my marriage was beginning to break up. Furthermore I (along with practically every other male at that time) had long hair and sported a 'Zapata' moustache.

Dave had introduced me to sailing and Keith Floyd had introduced me to terrible danger along with a pretty good idea of good living, good food and wine…

On the danger side of things, I had not known Keith for very long when I became involved in a crazy 'lost weekend' with him and Dave. The reason for this 'celebration' was ostensibly to celebrate the birth of Keith's son Patrick. (I was later to find out that there were other factors at work here.) We met in the Greyhound pub for an early evening drink to 'wet the baby's head' as they say… Keith, with sudden incredible enthusiasm, suggested going fishing in a pond he knew of. It seemed like a suitably daft thing to do. Dave was all for it. I had concerns, but put them behind me and joined this merry jape.

Keith picked up a fishing rod and we got into the new Fiat van Keith had just bought to take supplies to his restaurant. He then informed us that the pond he had in mind was in Wiveliscombe, in Somerset where Keith grew up, some fifty miles away. I'd not experienced Keith's driving… I was in for a baptism of fire!

There was no M5 going south then, and the only way was by the A38 Bristol to Plymouth main road. It was packed with traffic moving at around ten to twenty miles per hour in both directions. Not us though. Floyd had turned into a suicidal maniac. He overtook on hills, blind bends and took the centre 'overtaking' lane when it was full of traffic coming in the opposite direction at a closing speed of around a hundred miles an hour! Keith had two driving mainstays: the accelerator and the horn. He overtook at any time, clear or not, and blew the horn and willed the other drivers into saving themselves rather than end in a heap of twisted metal.

We finally got to Wiveliscombe and Keith drove up a track to a pond where he was supposed to be going to catch trout. Unfortunately the track was winding and rutted; when we got out of the van it was at such a steep angle that it began to fall over on us and it was only by quick reaction that we managed to manhandle it upright so that Keith could drive it to flatter ground.

After about an hour of unproductive fishing it was decided to repair to the local pub for food and more drink. It was about time we left anyway, since the pond was a private one and the owner had set his dogs on us!

We all, including some locals, got totally pie-eyed and ended up taking rooms and staying the night at the inn.

That was my introduction to Keith's wild side. I should have known better, since when we talked to him about his army life story, the signs were there of what Dave called a kind of death wish.

On the other hand, Keith's life seemed fairly settled. He'd opened his 'Bistro' in Clifton, Bristol's equivalent of Hampstead, about a hundred yards from the Suspension Bridge. I remember helping out on opening night and was still tacking the sisal carpet down as the customers came in. His bistro soon found national acclaim.

The premises were owned by a potter, Paula Hubner, a good friend of Keith's who used the basement as a kiln room to fire her pots. It turned out to be a bit of a mixed blessing. In winter, if Paula was firing pots, the Bistro was very warm and cosy, but in summer the floor felt as if it was on fire and customers were stifling hot.

The food at the Bistro was like a breath of fresh air. Previously, the height of gastronomic delight was either a very expensive hotel restaurant, or at the other end of the scale it was a meal at a Berni Inn: the infamous trio of prawn cocktail, steak, chips and peas with ice cream and a flake to finish. Oh, and Irish coffee – a brilliant innovation for its time. Not since the thirties had families gone out to eat. Now they did. It was 1970... At last the war was over!

Floyd's Bistro served starters such as whitebait; once I remember having black pudding and apple, followed by *coq au vin*; or perhaps I could have chosen Keith's favourite, duck *a l'orange* – that was a mallard, very rare, with orange sauce – or *boeuf bourgignon* as main; then some fruit concoction, a sorbet or tart as pudding. It was all incredibly new to me, to Bristol and to Britain! An affordable gastronomic feast! Customers came from far and wide to eat at Floyd's Bistro. With more and more praise heaped on the place, including a mention in the *Good Food Guide*, things seemed to be set fair for him. But Keith had more grandiose plans…

The Bistro all went swimmingly for about a year, then Keith met wheeler-dealers who wanted to make him rich. He was a sucker for this and borrowed heavily to open two more restaurants in quick succession. 'Floyd's Chop House' was a cheery, hearty type of eatery serving perfectly cooked English dishes, with a roast joint and three veg on Sundays. It was a place I took my parents to several times and they were amazed and delighted by it.

In tandem with the Chop House, Keith bought an empty chemist's shop and turned it into simply 'Floyd's'. This was his restaurant targeted at people who wanted to spend a bit of money and drink expensive wine – his *pièce de résistance*, where he would emulate the best French cuisine. He soon had a fantastic menu that changed practically every day. Again it was the apple of the food writer's eye and it quickly got into the *Good Food Guide*. Keith was now famous in the world of new and exciting cooking that was beginning to take hold in Britain. It was Keith's special pleasure to drive down to Cornwall after closing time and pick up lobsters and fish for the following day or two. By now he had his favourite Triumph TR5, as well as a weird Italian 'Noddy' car and the aforementioned Fiat van. I feel especially blessed never to have accepted a ride in the TR5, given the mad drive to Wiveliscombe that time!

Keith had let the top half of the restaurant, and Dave and I took the first floor rooms for our office. This put us perilously near temptation after we finished work for the evening, and in danger of launching into a Floyd evening.

It wasn't worth asking Keith what was going on in his life, but as bystanders in the flat above we guessed it was turbulent. There were stories of mayhem, of theft by the staff, of rows between Keith and his wife Jesmond. Anyway, one day in 1974 it all came to an end. He sold up everything and was left with just enough money to buy… a yacht. What else?

Flirty was a forty-foot Bermudan sloop built in Sweden around 1910, a beautiful craft with a counter stern and tiller steering. Inside she was done out in dark red leather with four bunks around a table. She was powered, unusually, by a Ford V8 petrol engine adapted for marine use. I took one trip – my first taste of the sea – in *Flirty*, which I will deal with later.

Keith disappeared in his yacht. To Spain, or Portugal; we didn't know.

By now, Dave had a family too: his son Leo and daughter Thea. We often went on holidays together; and on one memorable occasion, in a deal set up by a good friend of ours, the composer Edward Williams (best known perhaps for his theme music to the David Attenborough series *Life on Earth*), I agreed to use my by now rather rusty masonic skills to build a set of stone steps at a holiday farmhouse in the Lot area of France near Cahors, in return for three weeks' free holiday there.

The reason for making the flight of steps from the front door to the toilet on a lower floor was because the owner – Richard, a navy man and Edward William's brother-in-law – had lost a foot in the war and every time he got up in the night to go to the toilet he fell down the grassy slope, describing it thus: 'Ass over tit to the bottom!'

We were joined by another Clifton family, the Stokes and their two kids. Paddy Stokes and her husband Mike had been incredibly kind to us when we were neighbours during the 1962 freeze-up. They kept us supplied with water for six weeks! Thereafter we all babysat for each other and became good friends.

We all arrived and found a dark and creepy house with an outside water supply worked by a very noisy pump engine in the garden. The kids weren't at all happy sleeping near the rafters, made even worse by a handwritten message on the wall with an arrow: 'Rats here!' We finally got them settled and managed to spend a very pleasant holiday.

Everyone did their own thing. I got down to the step-building while the others went off to swim in the *piscine* or even the river. The Lot is fairly peaceful at that point. I did manage to see the amazing cave drawings at Lascaux before they were closed to the public.

I rather enjoyed getting my hands dirty doing the building work. After finally getting hold of the materials (sand, aggregate and cement) – not easy with my schoolboy French! – I did my level best and succeeded in building a set of steps very much in keeping with the house itself; they had a kind of rambling rustic (*rustique* even!) feel to them. Doing that manual work somehow made everything on that holiday more precious; I felt the landscape and the whole ambience of that part of France. It brought back memories of working for the Co-op, and in my father-in-law's market garden.

As I worked, I found that I was constantly under surveillance by our French neighbour there, who muttered (probably derisory) remarks through his ever-present drooping Gauloises fag.

When finished, I found time to do a couple of drawings and crayon sketches in the country nearby. All in all, a terrific time, each doing our own thing. After dinner, our evenings were spent with all the kids playing the card game 'Knock' (which, because there were so many of us, we called 'Monster Knock)', during which the adults got a bit sozzled on a drink given to us by our caring, sharing neighbour. It had the slightly misleading appellation *eau de vie pruneau* which sounded as if it might be quite delicious… It wasn't, and I renamed it 'aviation fuel'!

Some months later I met with Richard, the owner of the French house, and asked him how he'd fared with the new stone steps.

'Wonderful,' he said. 'First night I was there I went out for a pee and fell ass over tit and broke my good bloody ankle!'

You can't please everybody!

Dave and I returned to our office and had calls from the new *Doctor Who* script editor, Robert Holmes. They had a slight problem; could we help them out? They'd commissioned a great story called *The Ark in Space* but had gone a teeny-weeny bit over budget. The new producer was Philip Hinchcliffe, a chap we'd met and got on well with at ATV, where he was a sort of trainee producer, so we were very pleased to find he'd fetched up on *Doctor Who*.

We discussed various ways of getting around the problem; but the simplest was to make *Ark in Space*, which was a four-part story, then do an ultra-low-budget brand-new story, a two-parter, which would link with *Ark*'s last episodes. Our story was to be something new for *Doctor Who*: it was to be done all on film, on location. This way, the Ark's costs could be spread over ten episodes and they would reuse the ark set in a future story that would bring costs down even further – or something like that.

Dave and I somehow clicked with Robert Holmes, a dedicated writer and editor and an ex-policeman whose reminiscences about life in 'the force' provided us with some ideas for *Hunter's Walk*. There was an air of, not panic exactly, but things seemed more rushed than usual, so we were perfectly happy to use the Sontaran monster character Bob Holmes had created for a previous story; we understood that this was to cut costs, since the mask and costume were already in existence. However, we felt Bob Holmes went a bit over the top when he began to give us background information about the Sontaran race, to help us in the writing of the Sontaran warrior Styre. He'd obviously gone deeply into this subject, and started to explain the species' lifestyle – even telling us in detail about their method of reproduction! All a bit too much information since we knew that Styre was no more than a cruel, fascist, megalomaniac! The usual type that was a regular feature in *Doctor Who*.

The location for *The Sontaran Experiment* was on Dartmoor and, for once, the show seemed to have breathing space. There was, however a problem. Our Sontaran had brought a surveillance robot with him; and whilst the BBC props department made an excellent job of this contraption, problems arose when it was realised that it would only run on a flat surface. This meant laying a track over the rough Devon terrain, but the robot was only able to work on the twelve-metre tracking area. The terrain caused other problems, too, for Tom Baker when he fell on the rocks and broke his collarbone.

We managed to get the story done quickly and were pleased with the result, but we'd had little time to stop and think about it, On seeing it again recently, I was quite surprised at the dialogue given to the Earth 'survivors'. It sounded really deep and profound (perhaps unnecessarily so?) amid all the action-adventure going on around them; but heartwarming all the same.

Slap bang in the middle of *Sontaran Experiment* we received a commission to do two stories for the evergreen police series *Z Cars*. It was still a good show of the genre, but after about ten years it was coming to an inevitable close. For our first episode (entitled *Quiet as the Grave*) we turned to our 'safe-blower' format, and the resulting script was based on a true story of a robbery that had taken place in Bristol some years before when a gang took over an empty paper shop that just happened to be one of two empty premises right next door to a bank. Over three consecutive nights the gang knocked through the basement walls of both shops and got into the bank. The Bristol robbers felt this fantastic 'pop' needed something, or someone, special to blow the bank strongroom safe, so London villains were invited in on the job – one a specialist in thermic lance work. There was some tension between the London boys and the locals, but everything went spectacularly well, the logistics ran smoothly – even catering was organized… They got into the bank and got the money, but unfortunately by the time they shared the cash out it had become light… a bright sunny Sunday morning. The London villains insisted that they all stay there until dark, a whole day; the local boys were distraught and wanted to go out spending their ill-gotten gains as fast as they could. They couldn't stay cooped up there for a whole day with cash burning a hole in their pockets. After a bizarre series of votes, the democratic decision was taken that they should leave the shop in ones or twos. The London guys had no choice but to agree, but gave the stern warning: 'Whatever you do, don't fuckin' run!'

Of course, as soon as they got outside, the first two ran like rabbits dragging huge holdalls with them. By sheer mischance an off-duty police officer on his way home noticed this… Within four hours the whole gang was caught along with every scrap of money they'd taken.

At the end of the trial, the London boys got much heavier sentences than the Bristol boys. After that, the word went out among London villains – 'never work in the provinces!'

We managed to weave that story into a slightly more introspective *Z Cars*, perhaps taking a closer look at both police and villains, having the slightly more sophisticated London boys discussing their marriages and the private education of their kids against the bravado of the locals. We had the police station have a 'quiet night' so the cops had more time to talk about real concerns, like pensions and police conditions, instead of plot all the time. We also had some terrific guest stars acting in it, namely Harry Landis, John Junkin, Norman Beaton and Patrick Durkin.

Our second script was of a more familiar kind of police story titled *House to House* which starred the regulars including Alan Slater. For the BBC, *Z Cars* was getting a bit 'old hat' considering the infinitely more robust offerings from ITV like *The Sweeney*, along with more fanciful kind of stuff like *Dempsey and Makepeace* and the superb, reality-based *Hill Street Blues*. Soon after, the series came to an end. It had been a groundbreaking series and I felt it an honour to be part of it.

During these very busy writing years, things were happening in my other life too. As I mentioned, many of my friends were keen on yachting and sailing. Dave was particularly fascinated by the sea; he encouraged me to read books by single-handed sailors describing their voyages. I began to understand the thrill of the dangers in sailing, but still had a certain amount of built-in fear of the sea.

When Keith Floyd asked me to go with him on his new yacht *Flirty*, I hesitated but then agreed. We were going to sail from the Hamble in Southampton to see the start of the *Observer* single-handed transatlantic race. We were going to wish 'bon voyage' to a boat called *Strongbow* built by another friend of ours, boat designer/builder Paul Weychan.

Hywel Price was to skipper us; that made me feel more confident about the trip. I was totally bemused by all the ropes and lines and did my best to keep well out of the way, but Hywel kept telling me to do things, using the proper sailing terms for the tasks: 'Bob, pull in the sheet!' It all sounded like double Dutch to me.

After a day getting out of the Solent we decided to put in at Newport on the Isle of Wight. It was here I had my first experience of 'boat bashing'. As we sailed in to moor at Newport, I found myself holding a piece of rope – I knew not what for. Then Dave told me I was to jump onto the jetty with it and tie the boat off... Mmm. 'Okay,' I murmured. As we came closer to the pier, there were several other boats moored there and there was only a small space to get *Flirty* in. Keith leapt off with the bow line, I had the stern line. I jumped ashore, but didn't know what to do with the rope. The consequence was that *Flirty* scraped along the boat in front. Hywel did his best to manoeuvre away from it, but the motor died.

I've never seen anyone move as fast as Hywel did at that point: he was off the boat, snatched the rope from my fingers and did what seemed an instant bowline and threw it over a bollard; then raced to Keith who had the bow rope, took it and manoeuvred *Flirty* into the space between the two yachts. He was livid. A man of his reputation just doesn't do that sort of thing. He then inspected the other boats and found with relief that the only real damage was to *Flirty* and the wooden pier we were now moored against, and that was very little. It had sounded worse than it actually was. Even so, Hywel got all of us on deck and taught us how to tie a bowline – by rote, following his instructions, tying the knot in short lengths of rope. 'Here's the tree, here's the rabbit hole, out comes the rabbit, runs around the back of the tree and back down the hole again.' Four grown men reciting that as they tied the knot for about an hour… this knot class must have seemed bizarre to any onlooker! Thing is, after that, I've never forgotten how to do a bowline!

Next day, we sailed on down channel, a fine sunny day with a following wind. I was allowed to steer for a while; I got used to it and began to enjoy it, of course under the watchful eye of our skipper. Keith was all for sailing straight to Plymouth, day and night, but Hywel had a holiday in mind and insisted we stop off in Weymouth. We moored in the town, right next to a pub, and witnessed a 'run' of mackerel, the river Wey literally turned silver. It was alive with them. Keith fished a few out for our lunch next day. This brought out one of Hywel's arcane maxims for sailing: 'Never eat fish at sea,' 'Never wash down dry decks,' and on a passage, 'Don't whistle'… (up a wind)!

We woke to hear Hywel consulting the harbour master as to the best time to go through the notoriously dangerous Portland Race. He advised us to go at 'slack water', the hour between ebb and tidal flow. Hywel liked to keep a mystery about him and when at sea he always chose to wear a hacking jacket, corduroy trousers and desert boots. Naturally we would dress casually as well, then sometimes you'd go out on deck on a perfectly fine sunny day and find him dressed in sea boots, full weatherproofs and a life jacket! Sure enough, a little later cloud would build up and a storm would arrive. Not so much Hywel having premonitions as him listening to the BBC shipping forecast on his transistor radio, as they were called then.

As usual, we were just about to go into Weymouth to get food and supplies when Hywel said: 'We're going!' We had no alternative but to obey the skipper. Off we sailed. He decided that we had missed the 'slack water' window and sailed south for about ten miles into the channel to go around the dreaded Portland Race. When we finally turned west for Plymouth, the wind dropped and the engine took over. I could just see the Portland Bill lighthouse in the far distance. We chugged on for hours, then the engine started overheating; this was alleviated when Hywel decided that all of us should take turns to pour glasses of cold water over the engine block! It worked; and on we motored. After a sleep below in the cabin, I came up and sat on deck. I looked for and found the lighthouse; to my horror it was way off to the west of where it had been before… we were going backwards! The channel tide was carrying us away from our destination.

Not long afterward, a slight breeze blew up, enough to fill the mainsail and we began to move again, and in the right direction. I stayed on deck as the weather changed to a grey overcast. Dave was on watch and the others went into the cabin. I moved to the bowsprit and leaned out and over the bow, *Titanic* style. I spent hours there as the entire world around me became a monochrome bubble amid the flip-flap sound from waves slapping the bow. As I peered out into the emptiness, I suddenly said to myself, 'What the fuck am I doing out here in this terrible place? I can't just get off, I'm stuck!' It was later that I realised that this was the beginning of the sailing bug... You just put up with it... and wait for something more exciting.

We were making course for Brixham now, and I realised that Keith was getting a bit pissed off with Hywel, but he bit back his feelings. He didn't want too many stops because he had no money and couldn't be generous in buying rounds of drinks and treating us to food, which was his style of living. But it required finance...

It was closing time when we reached Brixham. I was surprised when Hywel moored *Flirty* right on the end of a line of six working fishing boats, especially as there was a sign telling private owners not to tie-up there. When we left the café after eating supper, I noticed that two more fishing boats had moored outside of us. I was expecting some angry exchanges when the fishermen came to cast off in the morning. However, when we woke up next day, all the fishing boats had gone and we were moored snugly against the jetty. The fishermen had moved their boats and gone out fishing without a sound and didn't disturb us at all, then tied us alongside the jetty. Hywel of course knew some of them, having once fished out of Brixham.

Out of Torbay, we rounded Berry Head and on a bright breezy morning we found we had a huge following sea: giant twenty-foot rollers that moved us forward, nosing us down into the next wave. I was steering at the time and found it truly exhilarating, if a little frightening at first. By evening we found ourselves in Dartmouth, where Hywel looked up a few old friends – yet another boozy night.

Tides and hangovers conspired to keep us until nearly midnight when we left for the last leg of our journey to Plymouth. Early next morning we crossed another 'Race' off Start Point. This time it was in full spate and it was like going through a witch's cauldron, the boat being pushed in all

115

directions. Once through it, the wind came up and we 'goosewinged' (with both foresail and mainsail wide open to the wind) all the way to Plymouth. As we approached Plymouth Sound, Hywel decided to see what *Flirty* could do. With a stiff south-easterly breeze, we entered Plymouth Sound on a broad reach, heeled right over going like the clappers and screamed up to the docks. What an entrance! Only to be greeted by a man with scrambled egg on his hat who told us we couldn't go into the docks and had to moor over in the yacht club. Bugger! But we had to comply.

Next day we sailed out to see the start of the *Observer* single-handed race: around forty hopeful sailors in yachts that varied from a huge 138-foot French entry, the three-masted schooner *Vendredi Treize*, Sir Francis Chichester's *Gypsy Moth V* (the race he had to be rescued from) down to a tiny, twenty-foot junk-sailed yacht. The race was won by the French trimaran *Pen Duick III* in twenty-one days. Our friend's boat *Strongbow*, skippered by Martin Minter Kemp, came seventh, making the crossing in twenty-eight days.

As a footnote to this: some months later Dave Martin took the opportunity to sail back to the UK from America in *Strongbow*; Hywel was skipper and a couple of other people were included as crew. After an uneventful first thousand miles, in the middle of the night all hell broke loose. *Strongbow* had lost her rudder! Fortunately the sea was calm, so at daylight Hywel went over the side to look at the damage. There was a small replacement rudder on board and Hywel toiled away to fit it. With jury-rig rudder in place they had a choice to continue to England or head the three hundred miles or so to the Azores. They chose the Azores, to mend the boat properly and then come home. Dave told me he had the time of his life in the Azores and took part in the Pamplona-style running with the bulls on the island, and got propelled over a wall by the horns of one of the beasts.

The seventies was a time when the nation's tastes were changing. Pubs were in a gentle decline and wine bars were seemingly springing up everywhere. The only problem with many of them was that the wine they sold was usually crap; that is, the basic glass of white or red wine. The white could often be of Austrian origin, and the red a really rough Spanish rotgut called 'Rocamar', which I remember with loathing: it was a sharp, almost rancid liquid which we actually used to put up with!

Keith Floyd was not a man to put up with this either; and he arranged with Richard Hawkins, a friend of his now living in Provence, to stay with him at his farm while Keith bought some decent wine from the lower Rhone area to take back to Bristol, where he'd obtained assurances from several wine-bar proprietors that they'd take his wine. All he needed now was transport...

To my shock and surprise, by the next weekend, Keith had purchased an obsolete Post Office Telephones line-repair vehicle from an auction. It was a three-ton Leyland lorry with a double cab. That would be handy for sharing driving: someone could sleep as the other drove. Behind that was a sort of box filled with trays and metal cupboards. He worked furiously taking them all out... Over a drink, Keith outlined his idea to me and asked me if I'd go with him on the inaugural trip; I of course agreed.

Keith picked me up from my house and drove to Southampton, and we caught the ferry to Le Havre, where we stopped to take lunch of *fruits de mer* at a quayside café before driving off toward Paris. As we hurtled across France (at sometimes up to fifty miles an hour!) Keith warned me that the lorry's gears were double-declutch, something I'd heard of but never come across when driving. Keith decided to hand the lorry over to me for the first time just as we approached Paris... in the rush hour! I found it excruciatingly difficult to double-declutch, and with screaming gears I drove onto the Paris *peripherique* which has *priorité à droite*. It was absolute murder! I was in a three-lane flow of traffic and cars came hurtling down slip roads to my right which made me want to move to my left to avoid. Keith kept screaming at me, 'Don't go left! Don't go left!' After an agonising hour we reached the *Autoroute de Soleil*... The long road south, as Keith called it.

It took another day and night driving four-hour shifts to get to our destination: a place called St Didier, near L'Isle-sur-la-Sorgue, which is about ten miles from Avignon. We arrived at Richard Hawkins' farm in the dead of night, scaring the occupants out of their wits. There were four young men staying there, all of them gay, so in the absence of what is now known as 'political correctness' we dubbed the farm *Palais des Pouffes*.

Next day we got down to the business of ordering the wine. We had considerable help from the mayor of St Didier, Claude, who I met at the town bar called Dédé's. He was a charming man with a stunning wife, Aurore, and together they ran a drying-out clinic in a chateau that belonged to Aurore's family. Claude had done all the introductions at the wine *caves*, so now all we had to do was go and collect the stuff – simple! Oh no, nothing could ever be that simple…

We took the lorry to the huge wine co-operative; everything was fine: several hundred one-litre bottles of red, white and rosé were waiting for us. However, Keith had requested that they were packed into cardboard boxes. This consignment of wine was in ten-bottle wooden crates with handles, much too cumbersome for the limited space in the lorry. Even worse, there was a hefty deposit on each crate. The proprietor told us, sadly, that the cardboard-box factory had had a strike and there were none available. There was no alternative but to load the wooden crates onto the lorry. Worryingly, by the time they were loaded they filled the entire loading space and the cab as well!

We decided to go to the industrial estate where the boxes were made and see what was available. We were shown a few alternatives and decided on flat apple-boxes. We found we could get ten of the litre wine bottles into each box lying flat, but we would need packing of some kind. On return to the farm, with the help of some friends from St Didier, we unloaded all the bottles from the crates and loaded the wine into the apple boxes, using newspaper as packing; as we were doing this Keith drove back to the wine supplier and redeemed the deposit from the crates. Meanwhile, we soon ran out of newspaper and started using grass and leaves. When Keith returned we loaded the boxes into the lorry – they practically filled it. In my innocence I thought that was it: that we'd be driving back to the UK the next day. 'Oh no,' said Keith, 'there's a lot more to get from another supplier – some quality wine and some "cubitainers".' These were ten-litre plastic containers. I didn't dare ask how many…

Carpentras sits at the bottom of Mont Ventoux, the famous killer hill on the Tour de France cycle race. (It's difficult enough to drive up, let alone cycle!) It is a bustling little town and has an adjoining wine area of Vacquras. We called at a *cave* for the cubitainers of wine. The proprietor was a jolly sort of bloke who made jokes – so I'm told – in the local dialect.

He showed us into his *cave* – a sort of cavern in a wall – pointed to a pile of empty cubitainers… and then went to a petrol pump, unhooked the nozzle and filled one of the containers with red wine! Wow! Wine from a petrol pump, whatever next? He invited us to fill our own containers, so Keith brought them to me and I was filling them under the eye of the proprietor when his phone rang and he ran to answer it. I could see him through a glass partition having a heated conversation. I soon got pretty adept at filling the containers; but when I got to the last one, I pulled the pump nozzle out but found I couldn't turn it off! I called and called to the man on the phone, but he was too engrossed in his conversation. *'Monsieur! Monsieur!'* I cried, but he couldn't hear me. The red wine by now had made a puddle on the floor, and was running out into the street where it began to flow like blood down the gutter… Finally the proprietor came to my rescue and exploded in French invective after he saw the 'river' outside. 'You mad bloody English idiots fuck off out of my *cave!*' is only a very rough translation of his parting words!

At Vacquras we bought a few cases of the 'special reserve' Vieux Clocher and some of that delicious Baume de Venise pudding wine, plus of course some of the Marc de Provence made especially for the owner. Fire water, in other words.

I don't know if it was a saint's day, or simply a special event, but we got invited to a dance in L'Isle-sur-la-Sorgue, a charming village criss-crossed by mill streams. It was held in the boules park. All the tables had been cleared and a small band played in a kind of barn with open doors. Everyone danced to sort of polka-type tunes; but later came the highlight – a competition where a prize was awarded to the man who could throw his partner highest in the air. The music played for this was *Ta-ra-ra Boom-de-ay*, the tune building up to a crescendo when the partner-lifting took place. It was a chance for all the young people of the town to show off a bit. One insisted on doing a kind of Russian spin; another couple tore round in true *Come Dancing* style. Shy teenage boys sometimes bumped into girls as a kind of embarrassed introduction. I began to get whirled along by the sheer wild drunken exuberance of it all.

I met up with Keith, who was sitting on a wall. He looked at the sky and said: 'Amazing… This is what everybody wants, if they had the guts. Sunshine and flowers and music and laughter and song… A good time before dying and a little something to ease the pain.' He sipped his *pastis*. 'Well, they can have it – only they'll have to bloody pay for it!'

I later found that Keith had decided to buy a gigantic empty monastery near St Didier, with the idea of turning it into a country club cum 'fun palace'. It didn't happen of course, but Dave Martin and I took the idea to write a movie script called *Succubus* – yet another screenplay that came very near to being made, but wasn't. It did, however, finally get made long after Dave and I had ceased writing as a partnership. It was the old firm back together again: Patrick Dromgoole directed it as a TV film co-production.

After the dance I went out into the farmyard to sober up, since we were making the trek back home the next day. In the moonlight I looked at the lorry from the back and saw that there was a noticeable lean to the left. The whole thing was over on its axles! It was carrying at least double the weight it should have. It was stacked full: even the precious rear-cab bed was taken up with boxes of wine.

Before departing the following day, we decided to stop at Dédé's café and say goodbye to Claude and Aurore and thank them for their help with our enterprise. This was to be the inaugural trip of many more to come. After the goodbyes we clambered into the lorry; Claude then said – seemingly as an afterthought – 'You are going to England aren't you?'

Keith frowned. 'Well of course.'

Claude then said: 'Good; would you mind taking my daughter with you?'

How could we refuse? Sophie was a lovely, chubby girl of seventeen who'd found a job in Bristol, as it happened, as an *au pair*. She got into the lorry along with three large cases! We had to move the load to find even a tiny space for her. Sophie turned out to be charming, but there was an unforeseen drawback.

It being our first trip, we had been warned that the British customs service would be very fussy about our load and would most likely insist on it being unloaded in front of them by specially hired dockers; they also might use sniffer dogs as well, to make sure nothing untoward was being carried.

Out on the *autoroute*, our lorry would barely do 35mph. We were in for a long trip, and we had a boat to catch; there was no time for long stops, or meals that couldn't be eaten in the cab. I began to notice that Sophie was, without fail, at all times, happy and giggly. I began to wonder why; then I noticed that she would go to the back of the lorry out of sight now and then, like when we stopped for toilets. I confronted her one time and saw that she was dipping her finger into a jam jar full of... 'What?' I asked.

'It is my *confiture*,' came the reply – jam…? She smiled at me and proffered the jar for me to try it. I realised immediately by the smell that it was a cannabis confection. No wonder she was bloody cheerful!

I warned Keith and he immediately realised the serious risk we would be taking with the British Customs. We spoke with her and persuaded her to dump her cannabis 'jam'. As an added precaution I suggested I go as a foot-passenger with her on the ferry.

We headed toward Le Havre against a strong headwind (at a cool 25mph!) arriving just in time to board the boat. Sophie insisted on having a full English meal of egg, chips, sausages and beans. As she was carrying her tray from the café to the table, the boat edged out of the port into the Channel, meeting a force eight gale. The ferry dipped into the first trough and the whole boat sounded like a percussion section: plates crashing, cutlery tinkling and drinks spilling. Sophie's tray flew through the air and landed somewhere in the front of the café… and she creased herself with laughter.

We had arranged for Keith's then girlfriend, Paddy, to pick Sophie up from the docks. I was to wait for Keith and the lorry to clear customs and meet up with him on the outside of the dock. We managed to get a message to Keith and he told Paddy to take Sophie back to their place, as he might be some time yet. I waited, and waited… and waited. The ferry had arrived at around three in the afternoon; I was still there at three in the morning. Finally, Keith emerged from the dock, smashing his way through a poster! He'd been left locked inside the docks. He then told me what had happened.

As expected, customs wanted to search the whole load and dockers were found to unload it. Now and then a case would drop and you might hear, after a shattering of glass, an 'Oh dear!' from the loaders. Once one bottle was broken, the rest of the contents of the box were taken as 'perks' by the dockers. Keith then found out he had to pay for this 'service'! Even worse, Keith was locked in a room for hours before being interviewed by the chief landing officer and another tough customs officer. They asked – and knew the answers to – questions about his school life, his early jobs, his army record and some rather worrying facts about his private life, including former girlfriends. Keith, however, had done interviews like these many times in the army to see if the 'Russians' (Intelligence Corps) could crack him and they hadn't. Finally, after many hours, the officer flashed a card in front of him and said, 'Will you please read this sir?' It looked like the usual blurb you were confronted with, but actually read like this.

Her Majesty's Customs and Excise
apologise for any delays our interview
may have caused you.
Now will you please fuck off!

We waited around till morning and then found the lorry with its slightly depleted load and drove it back to Bristol. It seems they didn't mind us importing wine, but wished we would do so by the tanker-load instead of in bottles, all of which had to be checked.

The wine bars bought the wine and begged for more. There were to be other trips to L'Isle-sur-la-Sorgue, where Keith was destined to settle for a while and open a restaurant. However, on further trips we made sure to exit and enter the country by any port except Southampton, which we avoided like the plague, using Poole–Cherbourg, Newhaven–Dieppe, Plymouth–Roscoff and even Weymouth–St Malo as alternatives.

Elsewhere my life was changing. My marriage broke up after sixteen years. Sadly, my wife was very ill and diagnosed as a schizophrenic and after trying hard to tame the tiger, I gave up. There is nothing you can do to cure, or even help in this kind of illness. She had the three children and I rented a place in Thornbury, nearby where Dave and Celia lived in a rather grand but run down grange house that was formerly a girl's school. We refurbished the 'girl's club room', a barn, into our office. We mostly lunched in nearby Oldbury-on-Severn where there was an idyllic pub in an idyllic village and nearby an idyllic nuclear power station!

When asked to do our fourth *Doctor Who*, our script editor was Robert Holmes, whom we'd first met on *The Sontaran Experiment*. We had a long session with him bashing out a story. Bob Holmes was very fond of thirties horror movies and we discussed, among others, *The Invisible Man*, *Frankenstein* and a slightly more obscure one about a severed hand called *The Beast with Five Fingers*. We finally settled on this last story as a theme. I cautioned Bob Holmes that it might be a bit too scary for children's TV. He simply said: 'Yes it is... so let's frighten the little buggers to death!' Dave and I thought about it and then wholeheartedly agreed.

We called it *The Hand of Fear* and chose to set part of it around a nuclear power station and, surprisingly, when we asked our friendly neighbourhood nuclear power station if we could look around to research our script, they welcomed us with open arms! Not only us, but the whole BBC *Doctor Who* production team, actors and film crew when they shot the location film sequences there.

It was great PR for the nuclear industry, showing how sure they were that nuclear power was totally safe. We spent some time in the main operating room and I was curious why a sign in red letters came up at regular intervals saying 'Danger'. When I asked about it, one of the technicians said, 'Oh, it always does that'… Well that explains it then, doesn't it, I thought to myself…

All went well and the show garnered over ten million viewers. It was also, sadly, the story in which Lis Sladen, who played Sarah Jane Smith, left the show. We let Robert Holmes do the 'writing out scene' since he had already written one for a previous show in which she didn't leave… Mad isn't it?

We received a call from HTV asking if we could do a children's series, another seven-parter like *Sky*. Yet again we were simply asked to come up with a story, and found ourselves working with Leonard White once more as our producer and Patrick Dromgoole as executive producer.

We decided to do a story about the horror of being a child: how school and pre-adult life can prove a rocky journey, especially if you don't quite fit in. We wanted to explore emotions, social and domestic environments, and with a comment on the dilemma of those who feel 'out of it' in some way.

Dave quoted from Browning's poem, 'Childe Roland to the Dark Tower Came…': a good starting point, we felt, to enable us to explore our 'Roland' whose dark tower is represented by the tower block of flats he lives in – on the top floor. We also chose to make him 'out of place' in his school, as a scholarship boy who attends a smart private school because of his singing abilities. Roland has to return from this rarified atmosphere to his dwelling in the 'dark tower' where he is forced to ascend the stairs because the lift, as usual, is broken. On his way up he is set upon by the rough types who lie in wait for him on the stairs like vagabonds.

Both Dave and I were keen admirers of contemporary European writers Brecht and especially Kafka; and without really noticing it until later, our tale was taking on a very Kafkaesque tone. At first we worried that we'd be told to lighten it up. But happily we weren't; not that Leonard and Patrick weren't worried about it as being suitable children's-slot material – they were, but did nothing to actually discourage us.

As we wrote more, the more daring we became and *King of the Castle* turned out to be one of the most enjoyable pieces that Dave and I wrote together. We dared to put the boy Roland in a broken-home situation, having a stepmother as opposed to the conventional set-up. We made his father a mad-keen jazz musician who had little time for his son. The tower-block handyman becomes a sinister dark figure in the dream world our young hero creates to cope with the mysteries surrounding him. As a huge plus for the serial we had managed to get the really amazing, sharp, quirky and original director Peter Hammond, who showed his usual flair when directing episodes one and two, thus setting a cracking pace for the rest of the story.

Once finished, *King of the Castle* was a surreal, very offbeat piece and, as anticipated, Leonard White and Patrick had a good deal of talking to do to persuade the ITV network committee to take it. Thankfully they were successful and the show went out in April 1977. Apart from Peter Hammond's excellent direction, it was certainly helped by an equally excellent cast including Fulton Mackay, Talfryn Thomas, Milton Johns, Patrick Durkin, and newcomer Philip Da Costa who managed to do a superb job as the schoolboy mesmerised by life around him.

We dubbed it 'Kafka for kids' and, despite those qualms from the ITV network committee, *King of the Castle* was nominated for a BAFTA award as best children's series/serial. We went to the dinner where Princess Anne was presenting the awards. My heart was in my mouth when the winner was announced, but our hopes were dashed when we lost out to... *Ivor the Engine*! A children's cartoon show for very young kids. It seemed hardly to compare with our 'heavy' drama. We accepted it with steely grins. We couldn't complain about the category and *Ivor the Engine* was a very good show. But we'd got bloody near! 'Little HTV' was a force to reckon with in drama now.

After *King of the Castle* we were commissioned by Patrick Dromgoole to do another thriller set in Bristol. We understood that Leonard Rossiter was anxious to get involved again. So, our next opus was about a similar character to our safe-blower Eddie, but who'd gone in a slightly different direction.

Our new character was Cyril, who thinks of himself as a private eye, but in fact because of lack of detecting work he's ended up being a debt collector. We called it *Machinegunner* because of debt collectors' habit of rapping the door knocker long and loud. Rat-ta-ta-ta-ta-tat… like a machine gun.

Dave and I researched this one by meeting up with private-eye companies. They all said that work was very thin on the ground because, it would seem, divorce work was becoming rarer as divorce became easier to get – i.e. without needing photographic evidence of adultery – so the agency we spoke to told us they mainly did factory surveillance and debt collecting.

On the other side of the story, we'd got a bit involved in the politics of Bristol property dealers and found out that much of the power for making decisions on developments lay in the hands of the Merchant Venturers Society and that this 'club' had been exerting its influence over deals in the city since it was formed in John and Sebastian Cabot's days in 1500! It seemed that the Society was the real power in the city, from its formation, on down through the slave trade and up to the present day.

Our story involved Cyril, the male chauvinist 'private eye', who is asked to take on a divorce job. He discovers that not only is his client a woman, but she's black! Even worse, it is perfectly obvious that she earns much more money than he does. Cyril is on the back foot.

Nina Baden-Semper played the female lead, which I believe was the first time a black female actor had played a lead part in British TV drama. She carried it off beautifully, a solid, serene figure for the ferrety character of Cyril to play off. We of course had to go into the question of colour, since our lead character, Cyril, was a bit of a racist as well as a male chauvinist pig. I believe this may have caused the ITV watchdog some slight problems.

It seems strange now, but our character of Cyril, as a racist, came up with the following when he finds out that the work he's doing for his lady client is research for a TV documentary – and after he'd just been nearly killed doing it!

'What are you? Nothin' more than a jumped-up lah-di-dah black enamel bloody jungle bunny!'

It came back from the watchdog… with the word 'bloody' underlined in red…! We'd run out of our quota of 'bloodys'…

This time, Dave and I got to be two 'toughs' as small parts in the story, so we were practically at the shoot every day.

Machinegunner was another show that received some excellent reviews, one critic remarking that: '*Machinegunner* is an unashamed movie.' Such a nice compliment for a TV film. Dave and I couldn't have wished for more. However, it was stuck in the ITV network selection 'chain' for over a year so that it wasn't shown until 1978!

1977 was a year bulging with work. We managed to fit in yet another *Doctor Who* story, this time one titled *The Invisible Enemy*. It was in this story, based around the monster being a virus, that we introduced a new character called K9, a robot dog/computer owned by a Dr Marius who built him because he missed his real dog back on earth.

Dave and I have been asked so many times: 'How did K9 come about?'

As far as I remember, it was one afternoon after we'd returned from our lunch at the Anchor Inn to resume *Invisible Enemy* when we started to discuss putting something a bit striking in the show. After a few ideas flew around, Dave suggested a robotic dog that could be called… 'K9!' I interjected. That seemed to settle it. So we started to build up the character and discussed its capabilities and way of communicating etc. We ended up with what we know now as K9.

Dave's suggestion of a robot dog may perhaps have come about because he'd owned two dogs since moving to the country, both highly strung springer spaniels which were hell's own job to keep under control – in fact for my money they were both mad as hatters. Both of them died, one run over when it ran out of the gate onto the road and the other one in the exact same way. Following this, Dave entered a very dark period of mourning for the second dog; was it that, perhaps, that made him suggest an indestructible dog? Maybe… but it's pure speculation on my part.

It was Bob Holmes, the script editor, who rang us to say that they'd like to keep the dog on as a companion for the Doctor. We were delighted to have created a character which, like Terry Nation's Daleks, would be a regular on the show… and perhaps make us some money?

We were quickly disembowelled of that notion when we received a letter from the BBC asking if we'd like to contribute five hundred pounds toward the cost of building the K9 prop! We solemnly informed them that, sadly, we had no mechanism for returning money to the BBC…

And so K9, the Doctor's companion mutt, was born and stayed with the show for some time, mostly being loathed and detested by directors and producers for knocking sets over, with its erratic radio-control movements when K9 would either not move at all or career at high speed across the studio and smash into the set…

For diehard *Who* fans K9 was a love-or-hate figure; but the general public took to this rather lovable mutt, the only character who occasionally dared contradict the Doctor on scientific matters.

Tom Baker hated K9 and I can understand why: he always had to jig himself into a kneeling or lying down position to do a dialogue scene with K9. A continuing problem for us was that we felt that other *Who* writers were using him in their own stories as nothing more than 'artillery' or *Doctor Who*'s gun. (Shades of the current series where the sonic screwdriver seems to do everything but wipe the Doctor's bum!) Which is not, in my opinion, what *Doctor Who* is about.

It was in our original specification in *Invisible Enemy* that K9 would float just above the ground for movement, but this was of course beyond the powers of the BBC special effects department at that time.

Later on when John Nathan-Turner took over as producer of the show he determined to get rid of K9; and to further this aim he put the poor thing into really silly situations, thus losing all suspension of disbelief, including being constantly under repair and left under a bench somewhere, but worst of all having actors carrying his 'shell' around making it look as if it was made out of balsa wood.

Nathan-Turner called Dave and me in to see him at the BBC and told us of his intention to drop K9. We could do nothing about it so made our complaints as a matter of routine. In recompense, he held out the cherry that K9 might possibly get his own series. That made us feel slightly better. However, we were informed by letter about *K9 and Company* after it had been commissioned, written and filmed! We felt pretty upset that they didn't even ask us to submit a story idea for our own character. We were obviously rather disgruntled at this; but imagine how we felt when we saw the wretched *K9 and Company*? My first feelings were: well, if you want to destroy a character for good and all – this is exactly the way to do it.

Happily, K9 has survived that awful pilot episode and fans of the dog have remained faithful to this day. As I write I am planning the second series of twenty-six episodes of the new, improved, all-flying K9. Of which more later.

1977 seems to have been a bumper year for Baker and Martin. In addition to *Machinegunner* HTV told us of an 'experiment' with the Northcott Theatre in Exeter: a stage play that would be filmed *in situ* and then transmitted as a play on TV. It was a way of TV feeding back into theatre. Also the TV company could afford to splash out on the set, more than the theatre ever could.

Dave and I used our safe-blowing research for the very last time and did a stage play called *Rat Trap* (named thus in anticipation of a long run!) which combined pretty well all the research we'd done on the subject. Garfield Morgan of *The Sweeney* was to act in and direct it. With him were Dave King, Ram John Holder, Barry Stanton and George Sewell. It concerned a bunch of thieves who get themselves locked in a bank! It seemed to be going very well until, after we'd been to a pretty late rehearsal – two days before opening night – we mentioned to the director that Dave King was making his lines up as he went along. They were nearly accurate, but after we'd sweated to get the words right during the writing, we felt we had to insist that they were spoken as written. Dave King went ballistic and practically threatened to walk off the show. There was high tension for the whole day before opening night. Then to our utter surprise, relief and delight, by the time they did the dress rehearsal, Dave King was word perfect.

The play had a very auspicious opening night – seven P.M. on 7th July 1977… Indeed it ran for a week… with audiences figures rising from 40% to 85% on the closing night. The teleplay had been shot during rehearsals and on various nights during the performance. Patrick Dromgoole thought it might go out some time, but only in the Wales/West region; and left it at that. Left to happenstance, this is what occurred.

There came a time around a year later when several members of the network committee (those who choose what will be shown on the ITV network) were holding their meeting at HTV. They were left waiting in Patrick Dromgoole's office whilst he dealt with a situation that had arisen on the studio floor. To pass the time they decided to watch a video. They chose the tape that was already in the machine – which just happened to be *Rat Trap* – and were soon totally engrossed in it and apparently falling about laughing at the jokes (or perhaps that was Patrick's hospitality drinks cupboard?). When Patrick arrived, they insisted on watching it to the end. So, that's how *Rat Trap* got a showing on the network!

We also managed to squeeze in a play in the ATV series *Cottage to Let*, created by writer Richard Harris: a low-budget show with just the one set, a cottage. Our submission *The Last Day* was a black comedy with Richard Pearson, Pat Heywood and Megs Jenkins. It was during this time that we became good friends with Richard Harris, after our earlier somewhat shaky start when we were writing for *Hunter's Walk*.

Another piece we did for ATV was for a series called *Scorpion Tales*. ('Don't tell me – it's got a sting in the tail...') It was an hour-long play called *Killing* which starred Jack Shepherd and Angela Down. It was directed by Don Leaver and concerned a robbery. No safes involved! Honest! It was about a computer whizz-kid – what we now call a 'geek' – who worked at a bank and made electronic transfers of money at the end of the day's trading. He discovered he had around a minute to play the market in exchange rates and perhaps gain some cash before banking the bank's money; this way he'd built up a small amount of money which he put into a separate file. Then by gambling with his stolen money on currency changes he built up a small theoretical fortune... since it was all on one of the bank's files. When he gets sacked, he decides to get the money out of the bank, and run away with the lady who was brought in to surreptitiously investigate him and his fraud.

It was on this show that we met an actor called Michael O'Hagan, who played the enigmatic policeman. We noticed that he did his scenes with his ear stuck up with sellotape! He'd been involved in a fight the night before, trying to help a copper who'd been set upon by some youths, and came out the worse for wear. A warm but sometimes wild Irishman, Michael was to become a close friend later in my career, as we shall see.

Killing had good reviews, but, sadly *Scorpion Tales* were pretty well the last one-hour single plays that ATV ever did.

I find it hard to believe, but the statistics prove it. We also wrote for a brand-new cop series for BBC called *Target* starring Patrick Mower. It was produced by Philip Hinchcliffe who'd left *Doctor Who* that year. Philip very kindly gave us episode two to write; this is a favourite spot, since first episodes are usually weighed down by all the introductions that have to be made, but with the second episode all you need to do is concentrate on story.

We started researching drugs and addicts – not too closely this time! – but from newspaper articles and library material. The result was a story entitled *Big Elephant*, the 'street' name for heroin at that time, which concerned a merchant seaman who accidentally picks up a heroin consignment and tries to play the Mister Big between the police and the drug gang. Ken Hutchison was at his sinister best and dear Katy Manning, late of *Doctor Who*, played an absolute blinder as the pathetic young junkie.

We went on to do another two episodes of this hard-cop series. The second was *Hunting Parties*; and on the third story we met up again with the actor who starred in our very first TV play, Brian Cox. This one was called *Carve Up* where Brian starred as a cheeky villain alongside Pamela Stephenson. Brian was by this time a noted actor and had done several well received Shakespeare plays, including a highly praised *Henry II* for the BBC and *King Lear* at the National.

Again, I've still no idea how we did it, but we squeezed yet another *Doctor Who* into the year 1977: this time a story from the future based on the voyages of Jason and the Argonauts. This one (called *Underworld*) was memorable because director Norman Stewart chose to do most of it in CSO (Colour Separation Overlay). The series used it quite often for small sections; but this had the whole background set inserted via a blue screen, so that the actors had to work to floor marks instead of to the set. The problem was that this special effects technique was still in its infancy, but I believe the director did a very good job in the circumstances. The result was interesting to say the least and took another step forward in the use of CSO.

In my private life, I'd met the woman who was to be my second wife, Angela. She had a lovely young girl, Laura, from a previous relationship. We met while I was working on *Machinegunner*; she had some recordings for me to pick up of 'drum rimshots', made by the drummer in the band I was in, to serve as the door-knocking of the 'machinegunner'… Angela opened the door in a low-cut dress and I simply said 'knockers!' She saw the funny side of it and we chatted for a while… and as they say, 'that was the start of a beautiful friendship.'

Not long after, once the house was sold, I moved to Thornbury where I was fairly close to the barn where David and I worked. Fairly soon after, Angela and Laura moved in with me. We lived in a two-bedroom flat with a balcony and, as that summer was incredibly hot, we spent loads of time out there. As soon as my divorce came through I married Angela and we held the reception at the Anchor Inn at Oldbury-on-Severn.

That year we went for a holiday to Provence and stayed close to L'Isle-sur-la-Sorgue where Keith Floyd had bought a house which he was about to turn into a restaurant. We spent a fabulous time there eating like kings and taking trips to the beach at Saintes-Maries-de-la-Mer, where Van Gogh once painted fishing boats.

By this time Floyd had turned the wine-importing-to-the-UK business into a bric-à-brac-exporting-to-France business! The lorry was used to bring loads of car-boot type stuff from the UK to sell at the *brocante* markets around Avignon. He was now living with Paddy Stokes, our friend from Clifton. They had a pitch at the weekend market where they sold British junk to eager French buyers. They loved anything with a name on it; things like an ashtray inscribed 'A present from Weston-Super-Mare' sold like hot cakes!

When Dave and I went on frequent trips to London we always stayed with friends, Trevor Ray and Prunella Ransome. They were in *Oliver!* when they met and had been together ever since. We first met Trevor on that day in the BBC bar – he was with the *Doctor Who* producers as a reader and came along for the drinks. He offered us some accommodation if we ever needed to stay over. We accepted his gracious offer and felt obliged to take them out for a meal, and so that became the pattern of our London visits: we'd get the work done in the day, then go and have supper with Trevor and Prunella and sleep on camp beds in their lounge.

Prunella was beautiful and charming, with a terrific sense of humour. She'd played Fanny in *Far from the Madding Crowd* and she'd just finished playing the queen in *Alfred the Great* opposite David Hemmings. It was her first starring role and she was paid well for it, so she felt able to fulfil a secret wish: she bought herself a Mercedes convertible sports car. They had been filming in Ireland and the car was delivered there. She went out to find a road to really wind the car up on. There was at that time only one small stretch of dual carriageway in Ireland, just south of Dublin. It was there Prunella decided to see what this much-vaunted machine could do. She built it up to around a hundred before getting half way down the dual carriageway. Then, to her horror, she saw a tractor move into the central reservation. The driver stopped, looked, saw her coming – then calmly pulled out in front of her. She braked as hard as she could, the tyres screaming, and came to a halt just behind the tractor. The driver smiled at her and said, 'Now that's a handy little car...' That's Ireland.

Dave and I had gone through a hectic and exhausting year and I looked forward to having a relaxing Christmas holiday...

CHAPTER NINE
In Harm's Way, with Floyd

1977 HAD BEEN A mad, frantic year and I celebrated a very happy, tranquil Christmas with all the family. Everything was 'mellow' until the New Year…

New Year's Day dawned crisp and bright; I remember waking and feeling slightly fuzzy. The previous night's New Year's Eve party had been boisterous and I may well have had too much to drink. Never mind, a whole day to get over it.

Then the phone rang.

It was Keith Floyd, ringing from Peterhead in Scotland. He told me he'd been to Norway and bought a boat. Would I like to help him get it back to Bristol? I said yes of course, and didn't question him any further. I was to liaise with another friend of ours, Peter Gardiner, engineer and ex-racing-car driver. Another soul who happily cruised in orbit around Keith. Peter and I boarded the overnight train to Inverness having arranged to meet up with Keith at the station the next morning.

After the huge fluctuations in his business affairs, Keith had decided to take a sabbatical and think of some new way to make a fortune. He'd made a friend of an ex-naval officer, Willy Woodard, who'd been a submariner on conventional subs. He'd finished his stint in the Senior Service and told Keith he knew of some motor fishing-boats which were for sale in Norway at a very reasonable price. They immediately went off to check them out. Keith's idea was to get one back to Bristol and convert it into a luxury holiday cruiser in which he would get rich clients to sail lazily around the Mediterranean and dine on his fantastic food… for a shedload of money.

We arrived at Inverness and breakfasted at the Station Hotel: porridge with marvellous kippers to follow. We were served by a white-bearded Scot in a stiff white apron, who lamented the passing of the LMS (London Midland and Scottish Railway) to nationalisation as he served us.

Keith arrived in a hire car, introduced us to Willy Woodard who was to be our skipper, and drove us to Peterhead and the MFV *Solon*, waiting in the harbour. Firstly, Keith warned us, there were friends he had to bid farewell to. It was now 3rd January and the Hogmanay party we went to had been going on since midnight on New Year's Eve. We were plied with drink, which I didn't really want because we were going off in *Solon* at some unearthly hour in the morning. I crept into a bathroom with a glass and filled it with water; as I started to drink I was spotted by a reveller. 'Oh no!' he warned. 'A wee can or a wee dram is all ye'll have.' He proffered a can and a bottle of malt; I settled for the can.

The tide was right to set off at three-fifteen and we got ourselves aboard *Solon*. She was a sixty-foot fishing boat, built in Norway around 1939, and she'd been laid up in 1956. Willy, our skipper, told me *Solon* had been a 'Shetlands Bus' during the Second World War, running spies and refugees in and out of Norway and the Shetlands. An honourable craft then. I looked her over: a high wheelhouse and a single mast for'ard of the hold covers. I stepped aboard – and immediately slipped down on my bum. The deck was covered in fuel oil that had leaked from drums which were lashed onto the deck during the crossing from Norway, when, I gathered, the wind had abated to force nine! 'We sailed through the troughs,' said Willy in his jaunty manner. My thoughts were: I like it. I think I'll get on with this guy.

After slipping on deck, I was in for a few more surprises. I went into the fo'c'sle bunk room to find two teenage girls sleeping there. They were hitch-hikers – or perhaps fish-hikers? – on their way to Inverness, which was to be our next port of call.

Three in the morning on a frosty, cloudless winter night; the stars were painfully bright and the Milky Way magnificently clear as it swept across the sky above us. There was an eerie silence in the dock: no tinkling of stays on masts or motor boats chugging about, just an icy cold night without a breath of wind. Willy was about to start the engine and I heard him shout instructions down to Keith, who was in the engine room, to get the flywheel in the right position, then light the glow-plug, to heat the cylinder head, to ignite the spark… When all was ready Willy pulled a lever in the wheelhouse that released a blast of compressed air into the cylinder to get the engine going.

And fire it did! It was a brain-jangling explosion I can only describe as a *bop!* An agonising wait and then another *bop!* as the ancient single-cylinder Watts marine engine came to life. The whole boat shook to the *bop! bop! bop!* Then I noticed that even the mast, which weighed a ton at least, was dancing in time to the rhythm and any loose bits on deck were all dancing around in time to the thumping engine pulse.

I got into the wheelhouse and we discussed our duties and watches. Each of us would do a two-hour watch and oil the engine at least once during that time. There would always be two on watch: one steering, one keeping an eye on the course and a lookout for shipping. I hated going down into the engine room and so swapped it for an extra two-hour shift on the wheel. That was fine by me. I really enjoyed being at the helm.

As we rounded the harbour entrance we set out northward to hopefully reach Inverness by around afternoon the following day, and with any luck get into the Caledonian Canal by nightfall – around three-thirty P.M. at that latitude. On my first watch I began to feel a bit weird: the *bop-bopping* of the engine became a voice talking to me. It was telling me what a fool I was, going on this trip. I was able to put this down to sleeplessness and alcohol, but it was difficult to dispel the chanting voice. Then I saw what could only be a thin green trail of the *Aurora Borealis*, the Northern lights, in the sky on the far horizon; it was quite unexpected but very heartwarming. It also reminded me what I was on this trip for. Adventure! 'To boldly go…' etc… etc…

In the light of day *Solon* was a fine-looking wooden craft built along traditional lines; a little dilapidated from her long lay-up perhaps, but generally in good shape. However, as the journey progressed certain shortcomings came to light. One night when I was having a pee over the side I looked up at the lifeboat and realised to my surprise that I could see the stars… through it! Also, I noticed that the distress flares were no more than little piles of dust and paper. *Solon* had no ballast and floated on the water like cork. Plus, of course, there was no toilet. It was 'bucket and chuck it!' These shortcomings meant nothing as we chugged into the first lock on the Caledonian Canal.

The lock-keeper was waiting to take our lines, and pleasantries were exchanged. I was on the slippery deck ready to throw the line. The trouble was that the rope was around four inches thick and soaked with water – it weighed a ton… I was supposed to hurl it ten feet up to the keeper! After several attempts the keeper finally got hold of it, not without taking a bit of a risk himself by leaning over the lock. The rope had obviously been intended for a much larger vessel, but the keeper managed to tie us off. Then came an event of terrible embarrassment… As the water began filling the lock and the four-inch rope came under pressure, it snapped like a runner bean! I'll never forget the look of utter disbelief on the lock-keeper's face as he mumbled Highland curses at these Sassenach fools.

We had to make an unscheduled stop at the Inverness boatyard to replace the ropes. Having little or no cash, we had to find something in the dock scrapyard, and decided upon some nylon rope that had obviously been used on a trawl net. Unfortunately, these had seen much service and had developed a permanent serpent-like twist, so that after being neatly coiled, once thrown the rope reverted to the bent shape it had had before and flew off in any direction but the one I threw it!

We set off down the canal in the morning after a light snowfall. I was struck by the amazing beauty of the place. We passed alongside a wood, and a stag came through the trees and kept station with us for a while as we *bop! bop! bopped* our way to Loch Ness. We negotiated the deep waters of the loch, but saw no sign of its famous inhabitant; although when we studied the depth scanner, we did see a lumpy shape at the bottom… must have been a rock.

By the time we reached Fort Augustus it had got a lot colder. We ate at a pub with a welcoming roaring fire. It was nearly three o'clock so we were served 'high tea', something non-existent in England. Liver and bacon with sauté potatoes, with pots of tea or coffee followed by cakes; the whole meal cost less than the pub lunch. The warmth and food of the pub made us forget that we'd have to pull the stops out if we were to get to Fort William where the locks take you back down to the sea again. They closed from five P.M. Friday night until eight A.M. on Monday. We pushed *Solon* as hard as she would go through Loch Lochy, reaching a heady eight knots! Even this didn't save us from being 'weekended' in Fort William with just seven locks to go.

It was only a short walk down the towpath to Fort William, and there we found that the locals were still celebrating Hogmanay. It was somewhat disconcerting stepping over the bodies of drunken and collapsed revellers on our way to buy haggis 'n' chips. I decided that during our forced stoppage I would tackle the greasy-deck situation. I found some sand and sprinkled it over the deck, then swept it up; as I'd hoped, the sand absorbed the oil. The deck was now clean and unslippery at last.

It took us a while to get down the seven lock gates and we had to wait for the tide so didn't get moving until the afternoon. We chugged south and passed through the incredibly narrow Sound of Islay, and slipped through the 'neck' at two in the morning; even then people were busy on the dockside of Port Askaig. The weather was still crisp and clear: clear enough to see the city lights of Belfast over the horizon as we went into the Irish Sea, bound for Fishguard in South Wales which, if we kept up the steady six-to-eight knots we'd been doing, we should reach in about a day and a half.

I came on watch as the new day broke, and noticed that the wind was beginning to freshen from the south east. Not enough to worry us; ahead should be the Isle of Man. I heard Keith's voice shout from below. 'Where are we, Willy?'

Willy replied: 'How deep is it?' which was the submariner's way of navigating!

Soon up came the Isle of Man, right on the button, and we were pretty relaxed as we pottered down its north east coast. Keith always saw that we were well fed and regularly brought those on watch what he called 'a nosebag', or the human equivalent. It was full of little goodies, sandwiches, biscuits and sweets.

I was pretty happy until I saw something that quite put me off my food. Ahead of us, at the Calf of Man and between the mainland and a small islet called Chicken Rock, there seemed to be a line of white water crossing the gap, an edge like the Niagara Falls… I was reminded of lithographs I'd seen as a child of ships falling over the 'edge of the world'. I shouted for Willy: 'What's that, Willy?' He took a long look and told me to steer away and outside the islet. I got more and more nervous as we approached what was a race of tide, wind and current in the worst possible condition. We'd been happily sailing down Man's east coast; and unbeknownst to us we'd been sheltered and in the lee of a south-easterly gale.

All these elements clashed around Chicken Rock and turned the sea into a boiling maelstrom. We descended from the relative calm, over and down, down, down, into a swirling trough of sea and spray. As the unballasted boat hit the waves and was tossed all over the place, I lost control totally. The wheel slammed full over and stayed there as Willy frantically yelled at me to 'Steer for the gap!' But there was nothing I could do. Then the engine stopped... An eerie silence broken only by the moaning wind and the thump of the wheelhouse hitting the water as it rocked from side to side, the boat being tossed around like a rag doll. It was not so much if, but when I would die. I hung on to the wheel for grim death, my arms, hands and fingers in pain from the effort.

'Well I think it's a small suitcase when we hit the rocks!' was Willy's inimitable assessment of our situation.

The rocks were getting closer and closer. Peter Gardiner knew what had caused the engine to stop: 'A build-up of shit in the fuel filter.'

Keith said, 'Well let's clear it out and get the bloody engine started!' The two of them went down into the engine room to try and get the engine going. Willy stood by with the compressed-air lever. I could hear the shouts and curses from below where the valiant Pete and Keith fought to get the flywheel in position and then light the glow-plug in the gut-wrenching, sick-making, rolling belly of the boat. A shout from below told us the glow-plug was lit. The engine had to start first time, otherwise we would hit the rocks. In the few seconds before Willy released the compressed air, I saw in my mind's eye the broken lifeboat, the ruined distress flares and the lack of a radio or any lifesaving gear, just old-fashioned ring lifebelts...

All was ready down below and Willy released the lever for the compressed air. Nothing happened for what seemed a century... and then *MMMmmmmBop!*... a few stutters – and then she started her *bop! bop! bop!*

Our nearest port was Douglas, the Isle of Man capital. We all wanted to put in for a rest after our ordeal except Keith, who wanted to forge on. However, he changed his mind when he realised we were right out of an absolute essential: cigarettes. We all were pretty heavy smokers, but Keith was exceptional; he'd sometimes unwittingly have two on the go, one smouldering in an ashtray, the other in his fingers. After our near death experience we all needed to relax a bit... but mostly, we were all desperate for a fag!

We were not welcome in Douglas. The dockmaster screamed to us 'You can't stay here!' as we attempted to go into the harbour; then informed us that, if we did, we'd have to pay five pounds per head landing tax. A fiver to step ashore? That's no welcome for distressed mariners! He told us to tie up on the outer harbour wall, broadside on to the full force of the wind! We were slammed against the wall every few seconds. We raided a nearby Co-op delivery store and came away with some old lorry tyres that served as buffers to soften the blow of thumping against the dock wall. Peter had made himself ill with his heroic deed of cleaning the fuel filter and helping get the engine started down below, and couldn't stand the constant battering against the wall, so he booked into a hotel for the night.

That evening we all went to the Palace dance hall, an aircraft hangar of a place, and attended a very strange disco. The huge hall, meant for busy holiday-season dances, now held all of fourteen people. We danced in our wellington boots and polo necks with young girls who liked to make good use of the vast ballroom, so that you could at times be dancing as much as a hundred yards from your partner... weird!

We got under way next morning having heard a reasonable forecast for the sea area 'Irish Sea' on the shipping forecast: winds of around force five, moderate to good visibility. Within five hours the weather had deteriorated into another south-easterly gale. It got rougher and rougher and as we passed Anglesey, Willy was all for going in there until the gale had blown out; Keith, however, was insistent that we push on to Fishguard. 'It's bound to clear up soon'... but it didn't. It got worse – a lot worse. Soon, there we were butting head-on into a force nine gale on a craft with no ballast. It reduced our speed to around one knot, to the point where paddling seabirds easily overtook us! Consequently, a journey that should take around twenty-four hours was stretched into forty-eight hours, and still no sight of land. The Irish Sea is known for its short and steep waves, because it is comparatively shallow, and we were experiencing it at its worst.

I was glad to take the wheel in the dark hours, so that I couldn't actually see how bloody frightening it was. We just kept going up and down waves that seemed like grey cathedrals... I was so anxious to get ashore that I began to have delusions (it happens at sea!). I imagined I could see Fishguard, a town I knew from visits there; and even described how I could see street lights and buses going up and down the hill. I got some pretty funny looks from Willy, who was straining his eyes to see what I was 'seeing'. I then realised that in negotiating huge waves, there was no fixed horizon. I was hallucinating, joining the company of a good many sailors who were *in extremis*...

I finished my watch and went down to my bunk, praying that there would be a sighting of land on my next watch... There wasn't, but on the following watch at around eight in the evening Willy said, 'Did you see that light?' I thought: my god, is Willy hallucinating too? I didn't know whether to agree out of politeness or what, but then I did see the tiniest flick of light... In half an hour the light was clear, and sending out the code sequence for the Strumble Head lighthouse, just west of Fishguard Harbour. We were right on the button; Willy's navigation had brought us exactly where we wanted to be. At last we got into the lee of the storm and into calmer waters. Soon we were going over flat sea just outside the harbour. Landfall at last...

When we entered the harbour we heard the familiar cry: 'You can't stay here! This is a British Rail Ferry Dock.' We were instructed to tie up on a gigantic barrel-shaped buoy in the middle of the harbour. I begged the harbour master to let us tie up for long enough to buy a bottle of Scotch. He relented and gave us ten minutes on the dockside. I ran to the nearby Railway Hotel that was thankfully still open. I entered in my sea-boots and long hair sodden and streaked, all windblown and dripping wet, to find I was in the middle of a party, with everyone in evening dress. A 'yahoo' woman screeched with laughter at the sight of me and asked if it was raining outside. This caused loud guffaws from the 'Rodneys' around her. The situation was immediately summed up by the barman who understood completely. He swiftly brought me a bottle of Scotch. I paid and thanked him with a grin.

'Tying up to a buoy should be done in white shirt and plimsolls,' moaned Willy as he jumped onto the huge barrel-shaped buoy for yet another attempt to moor *Solon*. It took until one-thirty to get tied on. Then we sat round the cabin looking forward to a shot of whisky; but we were all fast asleep before a drop had passed our lips. We were moored but still tossed around by the gale… and there was no way for us to get ashore in the morning…

Next day the gale had abated to a fresh breeze. We stood on deck, frustrated that we couldn't get ashore to enjoy a gourmet lunch that had been promised us by Keith's ex-*maître d'* at the Bistro, who'd set up a restaurant nearby. Then we heard the sound of a Seagull: not the feathered kind, but the distinctive outboard motor that powered a rubber boat which was skipping across the harbour. We hailed the man and asked him if he would mind giving us a lift ashore. Unfortunately the boat was just a little too small for all of us and my luggage (since I had to return to Bristol, to maybe rejoin them later for the last leg up the Bristol Channel). As we approached the steps on the harbour wall the rubber boat began to fold in two! Something had to give and it was Willy who took the dip in the water to save the rest of us.

I took a train back to Bristol to finish a script that Dave Martin and I were writing, but I kept in touch with how things were going and I was prepared to go back and join Keith and Willy on the final leg of the journey. What was supposed to be a few days' delay turned into two weeks. Then communications stopped.

My house at that time, as explained earlier, was on an abutment sticking out into the Avon Gorge. The bedroom window looked out on the Avon Gorge and the Suspension Bridge about half a mile away. Some weeks after I'd left *Solon* at Fishguard, I awoke from a strange dream. In it a puffing boat was coming towards me and would at any moment run right over me…

When I became fully conscious, I could hear a familiar distant *bop, bop, bop*… I sat up in bed and looked down the river which was practically at dead low water; and there in the distance was *Solon*, only just managing to stay afloat in the shallow water. I quickly got dressed and ran down to the dilapidated dockside landing-stage for the defunct pleasure-steamers that once came and went along the Avon. I was well in time as *Solon* was hardly moving, but the tide was rising fast. And then I saw a most peculiar thing.

Alongside *Solon* on the Portway road alongside the river were three police cars and two large blue vans, creeping along the wrong side of the road to keep station with *Solon*. When she arrived I took her lines and was immediately pushed aside by several burly policemen and customs officers, who boarded *Solon* in military fashion. They started pulling the boat to pieces, examining every nook and cranny. I looked up at Keith in the wheelhouse and gestured, 'What's all this?'

I got a huge shrug in response. Keith shouted, 'For Christ's sake! Have you got any cigarettes? I'm desperate here!' I threw him a packet and he lit one gratefully.

After about an hour of rummaging searches, Willy was told to take the boat into the lock gate. I walked alongside until they tied up in the lock. Then I was allowed aboard. I went to the wheelhouse to join Keith and Willy and said, 'What the hell's going on?' They had no more idea than I had.

Then a police chief superintendent came in to join us. He looked at Keith. 'Who are you?'

Keith pulled on his cigarette and said, 'Keith Floyd.'

The officer asked sharply: 'Why have you come to Bristol?'

Keith almost smiled, and said: 'I live here…'

The 'super' was visibly deflated. 'Oh, you live here… Oh, I see.'

Keith explained the whole project and my part in it. The 'super' half-heartedly tried to explain the heavy-handedness of the police response. It was because when *Solon* was off Ilfracombe, the coastguard there sent several Morse code messages asking the boat to identify itself. On getting no reply, they immediately thought they were smugglers and alerted police and customs.

Willy confessed that he'd seen the Morse message but that his Morse was so rusty that he'd forgotten the code letters to reply… 'Sorry,' he said sheepishly.

Apologies were accepted and before long we were chatting amiably to the superintendent, who on departing asked Keith: 'If you ever do a project like this again… would you please keep me in mind as a crew member?'

What we didn't know until some time later was that on Christmas Eve, hardly a month before, a boat had arrived at Bristol Lock gates. The skipper and his three crew, all very jolly, wished the lock-keeper a happy Christmas, gave him a bottle of malt whisky, then went on their way into the city's floating harbour. Later that night, forty-two illegal immigrants left the boat and disappeared into the UK.

With Keith and *Solon*, the police and customs were shutting the stable door very firmly after the horse had gone.

Solon never was converted into a gourmet floating dream-palace. Keith had other dreams and sold her to a man from Falmouth. *Solon* somehow got mysteriously sunk… some said for the insurance money. If true, what a sad ignominious end for a boat that had served us so well in the Second World War…

It was not long after this that Mum told me that Dad was unwell. I took him to hospital for tests and, sadly, it turned out to be stomach cancer and poor old Dad wasted away and within six months he died. He'd left an unfinished painting of a sailing ship and as a kind of homage to his talent I finished it and gave it to my brother Roger. Mum then came to live in a flat at our house.

CHAPTER TEN
A Parting Partnership

1978 TURNED OUT TO be another busy year. We did what now seemed to be the obligatory annual *Doctor Who*, this time with a new producer and script editor – Graham Williams and Anthony Read – who decided to do a linked series of stories called *The Key to Time*. The premise was that the Doctor has been requested by the White Guardian to find the Key to Time and stop it falling into the hands of the Black Guardian... the usual God vs. the Devil sort of thing. Each story concluded with the Doctor finding a segment of the Key; Dave and I were to do the sixth and final story, a six-parter in which the Doctor eventually finds the carefully concealed last piece. Again we did some research on the subject we'd chosen to frame the story: two worlds who have been at war for aeons, not even knowing much about the reasons for the conflict, but with each side out to flatten the other. We chose an underground shelter as our main set.

For our research we wondered what the – highly secret – Regional Seats of Government looked like inside. RSGs, as they were coded, were hydrogen-bomb-proof shelters for the government to safely retire into should there be a nuclear war with Russia. There was a huge fuss when their existence was discovered and made great satirical fun of on BBC's *That Was The Week That Was*. That had been a decade before; we decided it would have quietened down by now, so we contacted a friend who'd been in the Territorial Army and he told us that there was an RSG just outside Bath, near the racecourse.

We decided to investigate. We passed a sign saying 'W.D. Property – Keep Out!' and went to look at it from the outside; but there was nothing much there, just a heavy locked door in a kind of grass-covered bunker. We decided the best thing to do was to tackle things head on. After all, it had worked with the nuclear power station. So we decided to get in touch with Bath Territorial Army and see what happened. When we phoned them, the person on the other end of the line was highly suspicious – even more so when we explained that we were writing *Doctor Who* and were researching bunkers for a story. He took our phone number and said somebody would be in touch…

A week later a man rang us. He sounded very amused and said in a high-pitched voice, '*Doctor Who* here!' then roared with laughter. This was a major in the TA who was an avid *Who* fan. He gladly showed us over the bunker, which was a bit of a disappointment as a possible set. It was, as expected, grey concrete walls and banks of telephones. Anyway, it just goes to show what you can get away with if you're genuinely working on *Who*.

The Armageddon Factor was the last *Doctor Who* that Dave and I worked on together. He'd been warning me for some time that he had to write novels and that TV was a terrible distraction for him. I was not only sad but a little frightened even when Dave said, quite bluntly, that this would be our last writing collaboration. He was moving house to Dorset which would absolutely finalise things. I knew how much he wanted to write novels and wished him well.

We took a while getting the story exactly right and pushed for the final piece of the Key to Time to be a 'being' – in this case, the Princess – and finally got our way. The character was played beautifully by Lalla Ward. *The Armageddon Factor* was a great story to write; I feel we managed to get a real sense of 'total war', and John Woodvine as the Marshal was a marvellous piece of casting. Dave and I created a character we hoped might become an occasional regular: Drax, the recalcitrant Time Lord, an enjoyably quirky character; but he didn't feature again.

On reflection, I feel that *The Armageddon Factor* turned out to be a fitting way for our writing partnership on *Who* to end, although I must admit to feeling a wee bit apprehensive when we wrote the last scene… wondering what lay in store for me.

However, it turned out not to be the last thing we worked on. When Patrick Dromgoole at HTV found out what was happening he offered us one more TV film with HTV. We managed to build it into four one-hour episodes.

We called it *Murder at the Wedding* and we put our all into it. The story touched on many of the people we knew, including my previous mother- and father-in-law and a Floyd-like figure who is a restless, unfulfilled 'star of his own life'. Peter Sasdy was the director and the cast we got together were marvellous: Bryan Marshall, James Hazeldine, Diane Fletcher, Liza Goddard, Caroline Mortimer, Angela Pleasence, Christopher Biggins, Janine Duvitski, Trevor Thomas and, as the bride's parents, Cyril Luckham and Eleanor Summerfield. The film was all shot on location in Somerset.

It was our swansong and we waited with bated breath to see what the critics thought of it.

I simply could not believe my eyes when I read the critics. Every paper, without exception – sorry, one exception, Philip Purser of the *Mail* – totally slammed the show with a kind of vicious fervour. I felt ill for days… weeks! I hid away from everyone. It was my dark night of the soul. It was like being beaten for some misdemeanour you hadn't committed. Dave was really hurt when his mentor and favourite person in the whole world, Clive James, also panned it.

Well, you have to learn to take the rough with the smooth and it had seemed all plain sailing for us before then. We'd received praise mostly, and even more than that here and there. One redeeming thing about *Murder at the Wedding* was that it launched Dave's book-writing career when he was commissioned to write the book of the TV serial. I was touched when he dedicated the book to me. Dave then moved yet again, to West Bay in Dorset, and set out on his new career writing novels.

The best and happiest thing to happen for Angela and me around that time was the birth of our son Andrew.

My writing partnership with Dave had lasted for ten years… ten fantastic years, going from speculative writing and filling in our time as 'extras' and working on comedy snippets, then into writing films and TV shows in ever increasing number. We were always looking to come up with something a bit different. Our greatest successes were perhaps *Thick as Thieves* and *King of the Castle*. Dave once described our working life together as 'like being in a marriage without sex'. I'm sure that's a pretty apt description, because we were two minds in tandem, always up to speed on what the other was thinking and for the most part thoroughly enjoying work and play together.

CHAPTER ELEVEN
The Sound of Silence... Working Alone

FOR SOME TIME AFTERWARD, I was very aware of the silence in the room as I typed. Things were different in another way too. I was with a new wife, Angela, and family, Laura and Andy. All I had to do was wait for commissions to come my way. So I waited... and waited... but commissions came there none.

I took an office in the Thornbury High Street as there was no room to write in the flat where we lived. After about six months without a commission, I began to wonder why. I didn't want to start ringing round to people I knew in the business – that would perhaps prove that I was scared...

As the work drought went on, I began to feel pretty lonely, although I did go on writing. I did a TV film idea about the characters that I'd met in the Anchor pub. During this time I received a commission from the pub's landlord, Mike Dowdeswell, a dashing gent who has the most amazing memory for names and faces, which is a distinct plus when attracting custom. To wit:

Some years before, I went to the Anchor for the first time with the boat-builder who built *Strongbow*. I was welcomed by Mike and made to feel very much at home. I didn't go there again for at least a year, but when I went in Mike gave his usual greeting: 'Well hello there Bob!' I was amazed he'd remembered my name.

So it was Mike, when I was in my 'doldrums', who asked me to write a pamphlet that he could give out to customers who enquired about the history of the pub and village, as they quite often did.

I went into it with gusto, since I was keen to know more about the village anyway. I read loads and loads of books and visited the Gloucester museum and records office for older information in dusty tomes. Oldbury-on-Severn, I found out, contained a Neolithic ditch settlement, now called – as many of these are – 'the toot'; this was in turn occupied by the Romans around 100 B.C. to 100 A.D. A rather unofficial archeological dig had taken place in the twenties and uncovered several Roman coins.

The village is mostly known for its salmon fishing in the river of its name. For hundreds of years these fish had been caught by the 'putcher' (an old word for basket or bag, as in the saying, 'Never buy a pig in a pouch') method: that is, conical withy baskets tied to a wooden fence that stretched from the shore for about a hundred metres out into the river, three rows high and facing downstream. Salmon, since they swim against the tide, would swim into the 'cone' on the falling tide and get stuck fast. As one of the fishermen once explained: 'They can't swim back'ards can 'um?' The fish were taken out when the tide receded.

I once watched the biannual rite of putting the putchers out at the start of the season. The Severn mud is sticky and smelly, and a bit like quicksand, which made working extremely difficult; walking up to the waist in mud is the most tiring thing imaginable. The work was done by the then license-holder of 'the fishing' as it was called: a young woman called Christobel who, along with her husband John Tymko plus a few willing helpers, slogged back and forth pulling a mud sledge which carried the putchers out into the river, then tied them securely to the fence. They had to work fast between the tides.

The other local fishing method is by lave net, a triangular net on a Y-shaped pole about eight feet long, which is used to net the salmon as it swims by. This is done from a rocky rise in the middle of the river where the Severn is nearly a mile across. The Severn tide has the second highest rise and fall in the world, up to fifty feet high. On a spring tide, around full moon, the tide comes in at an alarming rate, as I was to witness one time when I was taken out lave netting by Doughnut, one of the licensed fishermen.

We spent a fruitless three hours without seeing a fish, then just as the sun was going down he spotted the tell-tale 'V' wake from a salmon's dorsal fin. He was determined to stay until the last moment, but as the tide had begun to turn Doughnut told me to go back to the shore, then added, 'Whatever you do, don't run...' I started back through the murky waters; and when I looked down-channel at the oncoming tide, it was frightening: from sea level I could see a mass of water swirling over the mud coming towards me from the shore. Suddenly the water started to rise around me. I began to move faster, but my waders acted like a buoyancy aid, threatening to topple me head first into the water. I began to run... but found it exhausting and several times I felt myself falling over. After what seemed an eternity I reached the end of the putcher line and was able to grab hold of it and drag myself foot by foot toward the shore. I finally made it and lay down exhausted. At that moment I heard sloshing water and Doughnut appeared out of the water and guided me back to safety. It was certainly one of the most hair-raising moments in my life.

On 'putcher nights', the evening after assembling or dismantling the putchers at each end of the season in May or September, there was always a sing-song at the pub. The Anchor would be packed out and a squeezebox player would accompany the songs. One obligatory ditty was by Tony Day, the regular folk singer at these do's, who would sing a lament called *Dead Dog Cider*, which of course concerned a dog that got drowned in the vat! The singing went on well into the night.

The village of Oldbury had several what might be called festive occasions. One special time was the Bath Race. The sea outlet for the rheen, or stream that runs through the village, was closed and the fresh water allowed to fill the rheen to a depth of about ten feet. Boats were constructed from baths or oil drums, or anything that could be made to float! The races were watched by thousands who came from miles around.

The boys in particular made it into a gladiatorial struggle and ended up trying to sink opposing craft. There was great rivalry between the Anchor teams and the Ship, the other pub in the village. They took to ramming, beating off with oars and general skullduggery. All in all, it was an hilarious day enjoyed by everyone; and, apart from a few cuts and bruises, no casualties. However, the Oldbury Bath Race was closed down for reasons of 'health and safety'. A sad loss to some wild exuberant fun!

Another event was Bonfire Night, which, to be frank, I didn't quite fully understand. Some days before Bonfire Night, the lads from the village would first steal, then hide an authentic old wooden Gloucestershire farm cart; then on the night they would fill it with faggots of fence wood, set it alight and roll it down the steep hill from the church. It was quite a spectacle to see this antique cart – which many a museum would cherish – going up in flames. It appears they'd been doing this for ages, at least as long as old people remembered. It was also a night for revenge. One year I was there they placed the cart against a gate that had been put up in a place the villagers felt was wrong, so they 'accidentally' burned it down on Bonfire Night. Both young and old joined in the rite, and some people would go a bit mad. One cidermaker went through the throng dressed as a woman and brandished a knife, telling people drunkenly that he was going to get even with a real or imagined enemy. The whole thing was mad from start to finish; it was a village-wide act of disobedience and the police stayed well out of the way, until Bonfire Night went the way of the Bath Race – banned on grounds of health and safety... Also, they'd burned the last cart. Extinction...

I guess there was a touch of *The Wicker Man* about it all, but it was for me something unique and special to experience; but it's all gone now. The salmon run has declined to a trickle so it's not viable to put the putchers out; and the lave netting couldn't compete against the farmed salmon from Scotland, so that has stopped too. I feel privileged to have been able to witness these events and I mourn the loss of Putcher Night, the Bath Race and Bonfire Night.

There are, though, some sort of replacements. The Anchor has a strong *pétanque* team and has won all the major British championships. Then there is the Oldbury Fun Run – a charity run for CLIC, the Lifeboats and a few other good causes. Happily, the day attracts the same kind of numbers that the Bath Race used to.

Oldbury also has its own saint, Saint Arilda, an early Saxon martyr who preferred to throw herself down a well than be defiled by a man called Muncius. The church, perched high on a pointed hill, is named after her.

Meanwhile, back at the coalface, a year had gone by and still no work came in. I had been driving a Mercedes, but I had to tighten the financial belt. I got rid of it and bought an old Ford Anglia, the kind with a sweep-back rear window. It had been modified by the previous owner and ran as smoothly as a sewing machine. It was perfectly acceptable. However, one thing dogged this machine and that was that, just as you needed power and gunned the engine, it would cut out! I tried and tried to get to the bottom of it and took really bad advice. One friend told me it was definitely plugs and points. I renewed them. The car still stalled! Another motorhead friend swore it must be the carburettor; I fitted a new one and still it stalled…! Another told me it was definitely, but absolutely definitely the diaphragm. I didn't know what that was! But I had one fitted anyway – and at great expense. Still it stopped. I paid out more and more money on examinations that came to nothing. I went to my local garage man, Mike Cumber, in despair. He asked me if he could have a go at solving the problem. 'Be my guest,' I said. He kept it for a day or two and discovered that when the previous owner had been 'souping it up' he put a new fuel line in, but the metal pipe didn't quite reach, so he'd put on about two inches of plastic piping to bridge the gap; unfortunately the plastic pipe had a kink in it and when more fuel was suddenly required, as on accelerating, the fuel couldn't get through the 'kink' and caused the engine to stall for lack of fuel… Total repair bill: labour £100, parts 2p!

Cars and me somehow just don't go together.

It had been about a year since I last had any work and my residuals from overseas sales were beginning to wane. I phoned all my contacts, but not one seemed to have any work. I began to think that this was definitely the end of my career as a writer and started to try and think of alternatives. But I could see nothing but what I'd been doing. I was kept pretty busy with our new arrival too. We put a bed for him in the broom cupboard, and at first he slept in a drawer of the chest. I know Angela, who'd previously had a very successful career in an architectural practice, would love to have got some work, were it not for the children. I was facing a very uncertain future.

Chapter Twelve
Regeneration

It was at the end of my *annus horribilis*, 1978, just before Christmas, that I got a call from the writer Richard Harris. He and another acquaintance of mine, Robert Banks Stewart, had come up with a new private-eye series for the BBC and they'd decided to set it in Bristol. They wondered if I might help them find some interesting locations. I of course said I would be delighted.

As I waited for the day they were to come down, an idea started eating into my brain. They won't want to commission me to do a script because they obviously think that without Dave I wouldn't be up to it. I found I was still suffering from that kind of agonising self-doubt now that I was on my own.

I met Robert and Richard at the station and we had a really great time reminiscing on the things we'd done and the people we'd met. After showing them around the city, the time came for them to go back to London. Thanks were given and goodbyes were said, but nothing else.

I returned home in a dark depression, convinced that I was useless. Then later that night, the phone rang: it was Robert Banks Stewart calling to thank me for giving up my day to help them. And as a parting shot he said, 'By the way, would you like to have a go at a script for us? We'd like you to do episode two.' A warm glow came over me as I accepted the offer to do the important second episode of the new series, which I now knew was to be called *Shoestring*…

Robert Banks Stewart was to produce it and Richard Harris had written the first script. During a script session with Robert about my *Shoestring* episode *Knock for Knock*, I mentioned my work drought of the previous year. Robert explained why he thought it might have come about. He said all the producers he'd spoken to about Dave and I going our different ways felt that, if they commissioned a script from me, they'd have to offer one to Dave as well. I explained that, at least for the while, Dave wanted to concentrate on novels and not do any TV at all. Perhaps I should have sent a round robin to all the producers I knew?

Since *Shoestring* was set in Bristol it meant regular visits to the city from Robert to oversee the filming. One time, when they were filming in Clifton, I met up with him. We went for a coffee and discussed scripts; then, out of the blue, he asked me if I'd like to be his script editor on *Shoestring*. I was delighted that he'd asked me and took the job like a shot.

Script editing meant working in London three or four days a week. Richard Harris kindly offered me a room at his Ealing house to stay in while I was in town. I found working with Robert both tough and exhilarating; he was a stickler for getting the story just right, and would keep on nagging at it until he felt it was ready to be shown to a director; then there was more refining and more detailing, this time with the director in with us as well. We'd sometimes change whole facets of the story to make it stronger, which I then rewrote for the rehearsal script. It was often gruelling, but I loved it, all of it, seeing a script come together stronger than it'd been before.

Working in London meant being in the place most writers felt they should be – 'where it's happening'. However, I found that unless you frequented certain Soho pubs, living in Ealing is much the same as living in Truro or Edinburgh... or, of course, Bristol. One got used to the local places and a trip to the West End hardly entered your mind. What was fantastic about being script editor on *Shoestring* was not only getting deeply involved in the scripts, but going to the studios with Robert to see rushes or rough assemblies of scripts we'd – as it were – performed surgery on!

Courtesy of Richard's and Robert's concept, *Shoestring* had deeper layers of back story for writers to work with. Eddie Shoestring was a complicated character who'd previously worked in computing; but there is a hint that he'd had some kind of breakdown, a very human failing for our hero. So now and then he seeks solace on a boat he owns but will never sail in. Eddie also had some really oddball ideas about life which enhanced his character. Here was detection through observation and understanding; he was never one to instigate violence or bullying tactics, which came as a change and a breath of fresh air from the then current cop series.

Working on the series I was introduced to the worrying situation of not having a script ready for production after the crew and director had joined. Rarely, but sometimes, it came about that a script which had been commissioned, written, and rewritten after Robert and I had given its author notes, still wasn't right. This meant a total reconstruction. This always came about on a Friday afternoon and circumstances were that a script had to be ready by the following Tuesday at the very latest. (This was because the production ball had begun to roll; all the crew needed to know what the new story entailed and to know what to get ready – locations, props etc. needed for filming which was on a strict schedule.)

Consequently, there would be a very charged meeting where Robert and I would take the story to pieces in order to rebuild it into something that hopefully worked better. These exercises are a bit like unravelling knitting. You always end up with the wool all over the floor! We would work well into the evening and hopefully have the outline of a story that worked. I would take notes and at around nine I'd leave to get the last train back to Bristol. I then had the pleasure of working the entire weekend producing a script from the notes I'd taken, so I could go back to London on Monday with a finished – albeit a first draft – script. Robert would give it what he called a 'brush-up' and produce a second draft, which was then passed out to the cast and crew. However, there were the occasional nailbiting times when we couldn't get the finished draft until Wednesday or Thursday. This would result in the office being stalked by the production manager, a rather nervous director and others, all waiting for the script.

Not knowing what to expect in the job, I found the whole process incredibly enjoyable. After my year of no work, I positively threw myself into it, and in so doing lost all the nagging fear I had about not being able to write solo. I felt I could take anything on. The hard work on *Shoestring* received some recognition when it was nominated for a BAFTA award as best series. It didn't win, but *Shoestring* was transmitted during the ITV strike and secured top viewing figures for a couple of months. Sadly, it only ran for two seasons, but for those who saw and enjoyed *Shoestring* they've never forgotten it.

The *Shoestring* office was in Threshold House on Shepherd's Bush Green, the same building as the *Doctor Who* team. As I was coming to the end of my stint there, I'd heard through the proverbial grapevine that they were looking to save some money on a cheaper script. I came up with an idea which I passed on to Graham Williams, who then introduced me to the new script editor on *Who* – none other than Douglas Adams, author of what must be one of the greatest science fiction ideas of the time, *The Hitchhiker's Guide to the Galaxy*, which had gone from radio to book, book to television. I discussed my ideas with Douglas and we refined it into a four-parter. My ruse for saving money was to use a device in the plot, the 'Continuous Event Transmuter', a machine which grabs a piece of a planet and keeps it in suspension so that it can be projected and studied at leisure – explained by the Doctor as: 'So you've left bald patches on planets all over the galaxy!' The savings came from the fact that the 'other planet' was no more than a tiny set. I must confess that when I saw the finished show it looked as if they'd spent more on it than any other !

This, my last *Doctor Who*, was particularly memorable for meeting Douglas Adams. We had some great times, especially as his idea of a good script session was lunch at one of the excellent restaurants around 'The Bush'. He was brilliant at inventing obscure jokes, which I confess is not my bag; but I do remember once trumping him with one that I made up when I was in France with Floyd. It went: if I was in the back of an open-top Rolls Royce drinking Pernod, would it be a Corniche Pastis?

Nightmare of Eden, my only solo *Doctor Who*, had some highs and some very low lows. The spaceship collision and all the space work was commendable, but the monsters were terrible – not in a horrific way, just plain bad, made worse by the fact that they were always seen in broad daylight. You could see the feet of the actors playing them which made them totally lose all suspension of disbelief when they were on screen. A pity, since I'd tackled a pretty revolutionary theme for *Who*, that of drug addiction. Finally, I was amazed by the music-hall German accent that the villain decided to (or was encouraged to) use.

On finishing *Nightmare of Eden* and my contract on *Shoestring* ending, I looked around for more work. Then I had a call from Patrick Dromgoole at HTV. He wanted to talk to me about a possible position with the company. It turned out that since my absence, HTV had become a major player in the realm of international co-productions, and because of Patrick's fluent French and German he found it easier to set up European deals. The deal he was doing at that moment was a co-production with Télécip of Paris; it was a series called *Hi Champ* which needed some work in the script area, since it was a raw translation from the French. It was the story of a French sports journalist who was friendly with all the champions of various sports, and who would get involved with some problem they had, such as a false accusation, an injury or just depression at not being in the limelight. Patrick said that if I accepted this job, I could also take charge of all scripts coming into the station, both solicited and unsolicited, and deal with them.

I thought long and hard about accepting, since I would no longer be my own man; I'd be on a salary, which somehow had a warm and comforting feel – but that's the danger of course.

I accepted, and on my first day of the job found myself taking an Air France flight to Paris, the first of many. I met my French co-producer, Jacques Dercourt, a really wonderful man who was so patient with me over my very limited knowledge of French. He determined to give me a good time when I was working there and in the evenings took me for meals at La Coupole, where famous artists from the past including Modigliani and Soutine had painted wall murals to pay for their meals, an Alsace restaurant and an exclusive bistro next to Hotel George V. I was enjoying the whole experience until I met the man who'd written the original idea for *Hi Champ*. He was, of course, a sports writer. I was as pleasant as I could be with him, but he was a sullen sort of guy with very little sense of humour – or perhaps it got lost in translation? I soon began to realise that the French don't have such things as script editors; there, for better or for worse, the writer's word is law. In other words, if that's how I've written it – that's it! No one can question what's there.

He suddenly realised that that was exactly my mission: to make some changes. He then became quite unpleasant and called me 'the script doctor' with a kind of snarl. I really began to think he was going to thump me. In the end I just smiled at him and assured him I would only make changes that affected the English version. That at last placated him.

There were problems with the deal and *Hi Champ* got made in France but there never was an English version. It was not the only co-production that fell through because of money and contracts. The second co-production was an hilarious comedy, again with my friend Jacques Dercourt and RTE, the Irish TV channel. I thoroughly enjoyed working on the production; all was ready to go ahead. I knew it would be a huge success. Then, only weeks before filming, it all fell through. I felt as if I'd lost a child. Sounds melodramatic, but I was really hurt that after so much work and effort on the scripts it was to come to nothing. Apparently the reason was that the British film union, the ACTT (which was really powerful at that time), had insisted on huge pay and overtime perks for work on co-productions. The French and Irish, seeing the stratospheric budget figures, pulled out.

Following this, Patrick Dromgoole sent a memo around to the film personnel to the effect that asking for unrealistic wages on these projects seemed to be becoming the norm, but that all it did was price us out of the market. After that disappointment, I approached the work perhaps a little more circumspectly, always wondering if it would get pulled.

However, I had plenty of other work to do. HTV received several scripts or ideas every day from hopeful authors and more official ones from agencies. All these submissions had been neglected for some time and it became my priority, when not script editing, to clear the backlog. That meant I had to read everything, make written comments on it and return it. If I felt any particular piece showed extraordinary merit, then I would refer it to Patrick for his comments. I was given help with this enormous task, having three writers who agreed to take a number of scripts each month. One of these was Tony Robinson, who always had amusing comments to make on some of the scripts. At that time he was an aspiring actor living in Clifton and was involved with the Avon Touring Company of actors. I was delighted to see him later in the series *Who Dares Wins*, which was his stepping stone to his most well known and brilliant character of Baldrick in *Blackadder*. I believe it was a good year and a half before we got the script pile down to a manageable level.

A third arm to my employment at HTV was to encourage, as much as possible, writing and theatre in the region. One of the in-house directors and I encouraged a new 'lunchtime theatre' at Bristol and Bath, the bait being that HTV would film the best one at the end of the year. It was at the

Bristol lunchtime theatre, held in the Bristol Old Vic basement, that I met John Collee, an aspiring young playwright who was studying medicine at Bristol University. His play, about Bristol estate agents, was witty and highly entertaining, but pressure of his studies made meetings with him pretty scarce. However, I did manage to catch up with him for my series *Function Room* – of which more later.

The next European co-production was a series of plays by various authors to have French directors and a British cast and film crew. They were sort of in the horror genre, and were part of a series of ten stories with the umbrella title of *Night Voices*. One of the directors was Juan Buñuel, son of the great Luis. He was to direct a fairly straightforward film, a 'body behind the wall' story. I suddenly noticed in his budget a bill for 'butcher's products'!

'What's this for?' I asked.

'Ah, that is for the dream sequence.'

'What dream sequence?' I enquired.

It seems he was about to distort the whole story to do a dream sequence of blood and gore, just like what his daddy did!

There was one story short of the ten and I suggested that Dave Martin and I had written a script that would fit in perfectly with the series. It was called *Succubus*. It is worth mentioning how this came about. Dave and I were in our local pub, the Nova Scotia, when we decided to try and get a film off the ground. Another bloody epic! Based around the Siege of Malta in the sixteenth century, when the Knights of Malta held out against a huge attacking force of Turks. We were looking something up in a dictionary when Peter Gardiner, our engineering friend, spotted an interesting word. 'Look,' he said, 'succubus', and then read out the definition: 'an evil female spirit; one who lies beneath…' A way of explaining away masturbation and nocturnal emissions in a monastery.

As expected the 'epic' came to nothing, but Dave and I decided to write a script entitled *Succubus* anyway, basing it yet again on one of Keith Floyd's fantasies, of buying the aforementioned empty monastery at St Didier and turning it into a fun palace. To quote Keith, he could see 'girls in flowing white dresses serving drinks whilst the Rolling Stones play on the lawn…'

Our premise was that, yes, you can buy the monastery, but you have to take what comes with it. In this case we schemed that our hero has bought the incumbent succubus who had maybe plagued the monks in previous centuries and sent them mad. When the script was finished, we sent it to our agent, who told us that she'd heard that a producer who'd made *The Greek Tycoon* starring Anthony Quinn on the island of Paxos wanted to follow it up using the same facilities.

The producer read the *Succubus* script and asked to meet us. He was keen to do the film but wondered if we could translate the story from Provence to Greece. We of course said we would and started work on doing it. We thought it would be fairly easy, but in truth it meant a total rewrite. The real problem was that there was something creepy about the Catholic idea of celibacy connecting to succubi, which gave the script an edge. This became lost in the Greek connotation. The Greeks didn't, as far as we could see, have huge hang-ups about sex. In the end it didn't matter. It happened again. The production manager rang us up and said, 'Hey, we're gonna make a movie!' From then on we never heard another word. And the producer's phone had been cut off…

So here was a chance to revert to the French version of *Succubus*. Patrick loved it and wanted to direct it; it was right up his street. So although it was against the European co-production deal to use a British director, we got over it by making up an anagram of Patrick's name, a weird sort of Jewish/Irish amalgam… Mordecai Klogport! Since it had originally been a feature film script there was a good deal of cutting to do and it was fun working with Dave again; we hadn't lost any of our former rapport and quickly got the script into shape. We were invited to go to France on the recce. It was a marvellous few days. The French production manager had managed to get the empty Abbaye de Montmajour, the one often seen in the background of Van Gogh paintings. Barry Foster was cast as the lead, the entrepreneur who arrives at the place along with his girlfriend and his son from a previous marriage; this combination and the succubus create a pretty toxic situation. Others in the cast were Lynsey Baxter, Pamela Salem, Jacques Feriere and – as the young son – the very talented Jeremy Gilley.

The series *Night Voices* was not really a success and was shown at a very early hour of the morning…

Now that I was on a salary, Angela and I decided it was time we bought a house and took a sixties semi-detached near the main street in Thornbury. It had a large roof conversion that I used as an office, though that didn't last long. My first wife Vicki had been having very bad bouts of her illness; she sometimes stayed in bed for up to six months. Catherine, my oldest daughter, had left home by now and Paul, the middle boy, seemed not to mind things as they were; but the youngest, Martin, was getting a bit depressed by it all. When Vicki asked me to take him, I was more than glad to, and Angela was happy with it too. So, at sixteen, Martin came to live with us. He was brilliant with the kids. I'm sure Andy, the youngest, looked upon him like a god when he played football with him on the lawn.

As soon as Martin was seventeen we gave him driving lessons and happily he passed first time. We then bought him a Mini so that he could go into Bristol (a drive of around thirty minutes) and enjoy himself, since night life in Thornbury was a bit restricted. I hoped that he would soon figure out what he wanted to do in life. But I didn't want to push anything.

We took a holiday in the Scilly Isles with Dave and Celia, and Keith with his son Patrick, but the travel arrangements were a bit diverse. Dave and I, Martin, Keith and Patrick were to sail down on Hywel's fifty-foot, multiple-chine boat, *Lydney Maid*, one of the new designs he hoped to sell. Celia, Angela, Laura and Andy were to come by air from Plymouth.

Our trip down on the yacht was fairly uneventful until we rounded Land's End, heading for a lunchtime stop at Newlyn. Hywel put *Lydney Maid* on a broad reach and she was heeled right over; suddenly there was an almighty crack! The sail started flapping wildly with its sheets writhing around the deck like demented rattlesnakes. One of them got tangled around Martin's ankle. My heart was in my mouth as I couldn't get to him to help. Luckily he was wearing a pair of Hywel's wellington boots and he allowed the rope to whip the boot off his foot and throw it overboard.

Finally she was righted and we found that the stays were fastened to the deck, but should have then been connected to the anchor-chain housing. Hywel was mad with himself for not seeing to this and got to work tying off the stay down below in the bilges. The boat sailed on with only a handkerchief-sized staysail. There was relief all round when we moored in Newlyn. We went straight to the pub which was just about to close and ordered pasties and two pints each. Amazingly, we all fell asleep in the pub before finishing our first glass…

Hywel had noticed the cool way Martin had reacted when he was in danger. He took a shine to him, as they say, and asked him if he'd like to become his apprentice on a youth employment scheme. Martin accepted and started a life in boat-building, with oak, plywood, and finally fibreglass, working on the Nigel Irens boat *Apricot*, winner of the Round Britain Race. His experience found him work abroad, and culminated in building ocean-racing multihulls in France, including the eighty-five-foot catamaran *Fleury Michon* which won the Guadeloupe race. Also, to his credit, he learned to speak perfect French. The little bugger also sailed as crew across the Atlantic in eleven days on the eighty-foot Nigel Irens-designed *Formula Tag*'s shakedown cruise! His comment afterwards was: 'It was bloody fast!'

Back at HTV, another co-production. A fascinating one for me. It was to be an Italian/French/British tripartite production. Yet again the French company was Télécip and Jacques Dercourt was the producer. This time it was about the French Foreign Legion, a subject I was fascinated by and delighted in learning more about. It was about the Legion at its outset: that is, in 1831 when it was first formed... Twenty years after the French Revolution there were thousands of mercenaries roaming around France, from disbanded private armies; they were jobless, hungry and armed! They were becoming a danger. A quick fix was to form a *légion étrangère*, or foreign legion.

A decree was issued for anyone wishing to join the new legion to be in Marseilles by a certain date to sign on – no questions asked. Around three thousand signed on and were immediately shipped to Algeria, where France was waging a colonial war against the Arabs... but not to fight: to build roads! Whilst building a road, the legion were called in to help the French army who were making heavy weather of trying to take a town, because of the withering fire coming from the city walls. The legionnaires lined up and walked into the town and took it, totally regardless of casualties... and a legend was born.

The series was to be filmed in Morocco and the Italian company had made some deals with the Moroccan film industry to make props and provide extras. The producer for the Italian company was an effete young fellow called Stefano.

We were in for thirteen one-hour adventure stories: a fantastic challenge. The scripts that were already written were pretty rough, suffering in translation from the Italian. Before getting down to scripts, Jacques, Stefano and I went to Morocco to be shown around by the

Moroccan equivalent of Richard Attenborough: Suiel Ben Bakka, a charming and very cultured man, who was the one setting things up at that end.

When I arrived in Casablanca it was winter and it was still around seventeen to nineteen degrees. I looked around for Rick's Bar, to no avail… We set off on our search for locations one evening to stay the night at a hotel in the hills. I woke next morning thinking I was in Switzerland! The landscape around was under ten centimetres of snow. We were in the foothills of the Atlas Mountains. I was to discover that more legionnaires died from frostbite than ever died of sunstroke, or amazingly even in battle!

We travelled the length and breadth of Morocco to see old forts (built by the lesser-known Spanish Foreign Legion), found souks that Westerners never venture into and huge swathes of desert near the Mauritanian border. It was all perfect. On our journey, Suiel gave us a special treat: it was his nephew's name day (birthday) celebrations, when the family held a feast and we were invited. They'd cooked a whole goat for several days in a pit oven, then added the succulent herb-infused meat to a gigantic cous-cous which we ate with our hands; tea was served by the women in a ceremonial way. It was there that Suiel told us the fantastic story about how his mother and father got married.

Suiel's grandfather was from Timbuktu and ran a camel train trading salt from Algeria to the Lebanon. He became immensely rich and when Suiel's father accompanied the caravan as a young man, he would stop off to stay in the best hotels. Came the time in the thirties when he started taking trips from Beirut to Paris, where he enjoyed the western lifestyle. There he fell in love with a Parisian girl, swept her off her feet and they got married. He then took her back home to the mud town of Timbuktu! She was in shock and demanded she go home immediately. Her husband said she could go any time she liked, but there was no way she could have made the journey. Her next ploy was to say she was a Catholic and had to say mass or face hell. The husband arranged to fly a priest in every week for her to take communion… They had seven children of which Suiel was the youngest.

I returned to HTV and reported to Patrick. Everything was go! I had to get thirteen scripts rewritten, and I suggested bringing Dave in to help me. Dave was now living with his family in West Bay, Dorset, in a fantastic cottage that looked out over the beach to the sea. (The pebble beach was the one used in the opening title sequence of *The Fall and Rise of Reginald Perrin* which shows Len Rossiter scrambling down the beach taking off his clothes.)

For his writing work, Dave rented a small office in the neighbouring town of Bridport. He was at that time in the middle of his first novel, but gladly took the work on *Legion*, since he hadn't been published yet and was in need of some cash. By the time we'd written six episodes and after a lot of research, I heard that the Italian producer, Stefano, had sold his interests to another Italian TV company who worked out of Milan. I went to Rome with Patrick to renegotiate the deal. It was hard going and they had an American writer who wanted to do some script editing on the series. He'd married an Italian girl and settled in Rome. I found we got on better after we'd gone on a pasta crawl! We could use his help anyway.

I had a great time in Rome, including a frightening tour of the city riding pillion on Stefano's huge 1000cc motorbike!

In a lighter moment, Patrick was asked up into the Frascati hills outside Rome to see a contingent of the Sadler's Wells ballet performing at a village fete. We were promised dinner after the performance, which ended around seven-thirty. We were beginning to get a bit hungry by nine... Then we were told that the dinner was to be at a certain restaurant, but nobody knew where it was! By the time we found it, tucked away up a narrow street, we were ravenous, and finally got around to eating at midnight! I was seated next to the ballerina, a fragile Hepburnesque woman who totally amazed me by how frank she was about everything. And I mean everything! She spoke in a very refined voice and used the most foul descriptive language I've ever heard about her sexual exploits with men... and women... and both together! I thought I couldn't be shocked... but I was! I was convinced that – with certain modifications – she was a character I had to use in a future script... And I did: she cropped up in a *Call Me Mister* story and gave it quite a lift, plus the part was played by an ex-ballerina.

I flew home from Rome full of ideas about the *Legion* series and got down to more scripts with Dave; but then, you'd never guess what happened... Yes, it all fell through.

I still had plenty of work to take my mind off *Legion*, which included script reading. I had a call from Robert Banks Stewart, who asked me if I'd like to write episode two in a new series he'd just started at the BBC called *Bergerac*, about a Jersey cop. I was just a shade concerned as my contract with HTV forbade me to work for other companies. I told him I'd have to do it in my summer holiday. I went to see Robert and we thrashed out a story. I based it on an old Richard Widmark movie called *Pickup on South Street* which had a pickpocket pick up more than he'd bargained for: in the stolen wallet is microfilm, possibly worth more than any money. I did a similar set-up, only the pickpocket – or 'dip' as these villains are called here – finds himself with a fair load of heroin. So, the police are after him, the drug dealers are after him too – who will find him first? It was called *Unlucky Dip*. I just managed to write it during my summer holiday in Dartmouth. I sent Angela and the kids off to the beach whilst I typed. A real busman's bloody holiday! I was very pleased with the result when it was transmitted; it had a superb performance from Prunella Scales as a dipsomaniac one-time pools winner. I saw it recently repeated and I feel it still stands up well.

Since I had nothing but compliments on my *Bergerac* break from HTV, I felt I might try doing a surreptitious second episode. I did, and wrote a story that was getting a bit near the edge for a popular genre cop series: *Moonlight Girls*, about prostitution at 'the top'. I seemed to manage this whilst still working full out at HTV.

Peter Graham Scott was now part of the production team at HTV for overseas co-productions, so during a lull in new deals he suggested I come up with a very low-budget series to keep the production team ticking over. We got Patrick Dromgoole's approval, but with the proviso that it was not just low budget... or incredibly low budget... but infinitesimally low budget!

So I set to work on doing an outline. It had to be a seven-part action adventure series in one set only! Quite a brief.

I began to put the thing together; and as inspiration I came across an old Christmas present, a set of eighteenth-century parlour games. One of them, a card game, featured a devilish character called Rothgo. I decided he would be my time traveller. I then set about putting the story into a pitch to show the bosses.

I've never enjoyed doing the one-page outlines, but here, things began to flow. I looked into women goddesses and came up with 'Belor'; then I needed the 'MacGuffin' and came across the word 'nidus' in *The Explosion of Science*, as the centre of the nucleus. I worked the three together into a scenario where the baddy goddess Belor was after something from Rothgo: his life force – the Nidus. The outline took several days to refine; and when I read it through I honestly believed it to be one of, if not *the* best I'd ever done! Well, it was about time I learned.

Peter Graham Scott took me to lunch, one I shall never forget for two reasons. First, that he chose Black Tower sweet wine to go with the meal! Second, that after reading the outline and saying he was highly impressed, he took it to Patrick Dromgoole separately... and for the price of a crap lunch, I suddenly found that Peter Graham Scott was now co-creator of what was to be called *Into the Labyrinth*. P.G. Tipps (as we called him) didn't even mention sharing the credits with me. It was simply fait accompli as far as he was concerned, a power thing... I could only smile through gritted teeth and get on with the show.

It was with some pleasure that I learned that Ron Moody had accepted the part of Rothgo, and I was pleased that Peter's suggestion for Belor was accepted. She was played by Pamela Salem who was to become a very dear friend.

The set was a cave system modelled on the caves at Cheddar near Bristol and the title sequence used film shot inside them. All the rest was polystyrene tunnels moulded and painted with a couple of larger areas built into them. In each episode we reset the caves to try and look different from the previous one. I chose my writers carefully and they included two former *Doctor Who* script editors, Bob Holmes and Tony Read; one or two new ones, including Andrew Payne who went on to greater things including devising and writing the cook-cop series *Pie in the Sky* (he now is a regular writer on *Midsomer Murders*); and some local talent, Ivan Benbrook and Gary Hopkins. One real surprise was when we had an unsolicited script in from a writer called Jane McCloskey; we thought it would be a good idea to feature a totally new writer and proceeded to commission her. We invited her to the studio for the recording of her episode, *London's Burning*, and found out that that very day was her birthday... her seventeenth! She'd written her episode while she was still at school. We were pleased to welcome her to the world of television and it gave us some newspaper publicity for the show. Thereafter, Jane went onward and upward and after finishing university she became Head of Programmes for the Plymouth-based ITV company, Westward; then went on after the amalgamation of the regions to become Head of Programmes for the whole South West area, including HTV West.

Labyrinth was a pleasant series to work on in that it was – apart from the leads – almost entirely cast from local actors, both famous and less so, plus actors from the Bristol Old Vic. They were given some pretty meaty stories to work with, including the French Revolution, the Alamo, the English Civil War, but all underground – the history was being made up above. We even managed a Robin Hood story set indoors! On that occasion Marian was played by Patricia Driscoll, who'd played Maid Marian in the fifties series *The Adventures of Robin Hood*.

The making of the series went well, except when Ron Moody would… well, do a moody. He'd suddenly set off on a tirade, telling us what a load of amateur shits we were and that without him the series would be nothing. On this we would all wholeheartedly agree which sort of took the wind out of his sails. He would spend the next few hours apologising for what he'd said, and then go on as if nothing had happened. I must say that he and Pam Salem really gave *Labyrinth* a lift and took it to a level I hardly expected it would reach. This I believe was down to the excellent writing, which allowed us to completely suspend disbelief at witnessing an important historical event taking place entirely underground!

Having been introduced to Pamela Salem, we got on like a house on fire. After the first week of filming she told me her partner Michael was coming down to Bristol. Amazingly it turned out to be Michael O' Hagan who I'd met and become friendly with on the ATV play *Killing*. From then on, whenever I was in London there was always a place to stay overnight with Mike and Pam at their flat; in fact I stayed there for the duration of my script editing on the BBC private-eye series *Call Me Mister*. Mike and Pam were away working on separate projects, Pam in Rome doing *Salome* and Mike making a film in the US. So they just gave me a key. It was amazing: their flat was like a theatrical hotel. They are such generous people.

It was during the filming of *Into the Labyrinth* that I first met the Aardman Animations team, Dave Sproxton and Peter Lord. They showed me their showreel and I was quite frankly knocked sideways by the ingenuity and sheer inventiveness. On their piece called *Animated Conversations* they used sound recordings of actual events – like one incredibly good example of an impoverished old gent trying to get a room for the night at the Salvation Army. It is unbelievably moving, and as I said at the time I saw it – 'It's more real than real!' I decided that although financially we couldn't commission them to do a half-hour animated piece, I could at least get them in to do some special film for *Into the Labyrinth*. I think they would be the first to admit that it didn't work that well. The good thing was that I kept in touch with Dave and Peter thereafter.

After the first series of *Labyrinth*, HTV partnered a company called Gatetarn (who had previously done the successful *Dick Turpin* series) and a German company in a spirited series called *Smuggler*; Oliver Tobias played the swashbuckling lead Jack Vincent.

My job was to oversee the scripts on behalf of HTV. This meant doing some interesting and enjoyable research into eighteenth- and nineteenth-century smuggling and the force formed to combat it, HM Customs and Excise. Most of the scripts were pretty good; however, I began to get a little concerned about the rather crucial second episode, which all involved agreed was a bit of a problem since there was simply no mystery involved in it at all. It was much too straightforward; so much so that anyone would know who the villain was from the beginning. So Patrick, with agreement from Paul Knight, Gatetarn's producer, asked me to rewrite it. Happily, it turned out to be a really strong episode. As thanks for the work I'd done on episode two, Paul Knight asked me to write a further episode for the series. I was only too willing and set about using all the research I'd done.

I was a little worried that although the title of the piece was *Smuggler*, with all the excitement that it conjures up, not one of the first seven scripts had any smuggling in it! I pointed this out and came up with a story that actually entailed smuggling and a sea chase with cannon fire. In the story, titled *Forced Run*, Jack is on a routine trip to France for brandy when he's intercepted by the Revenue cutter. The series needed a boat, and a skilled sailor; so who did we get? My good friend – the old man of the sea... Hywel Price.

Smuggler was proof that with the right stories you could make an expensive-looking series on a fairly low budget. I remember at the preview in BAFTA there was a huge indraught of breath from the critics when, in the first episode, there is a violent swordfight between two rival gangs of smugglers, which was shot during the fast-rising tide at Clovelly and in pouring rain.

Further co-productions came and went. As for my second brief of encouraging new writers from our region, I felt I'd hit a brick wall. I remembered how Dave and I had started with the half-hour play all those years ago. That was the thing that set us alight; seeing your name on screen as writer of a TV play made you feel like a real, proper writer. I suggested to HTV that we do a similar thing for new authors in the region, but this time we would advertise it in the local papers and see what the response was. For me, the only way to encourage writers was for them to see their work produced on TV.

HTV were broadly in favour of my suggestion but the problem was fixing it with a budget; there was so much else going on at the time. However, Patrick Dromgoole asked me to come up with an idea and a budget. I recalled doing an episode of the ITV series *Cottage to Let* – nice and simple, the same set with different tenants each week; only mine would have fewer sets… just one in fact. Having rented loads and loads of pub function rooms for band rehearsals, I immediately thought that 'the Function Room' might make a nice simple set for writers to set a story in. Our designer was asked to build a model – and make it cheap! It was a bit like a giant shoebox, but perfect for our use.

I got the go-ahead and put the notice in the papers. I asked for outlines of one or two pages in length. From around a hundred and twenty entries, once we'd discounted the ones who'd totally misunderstood, or decided to ignore, the 'one room' brief and had put battle scenes in (and even spaceships landing!) we were left with seventy entries. From these I chose to commission seven – hopefully as the start of a regular yearly showcase of local talent.

As usual, things never go quite as expected. For some reason HTV didn't think I was capable of producing the series and brought in Peter Miller to produce the first play. (Peter was the producer Dave and I had a run-in with when he was producer of *Arthur of the Britons*.) He chose the one I thought was absolutely brilliant. It was written by Matthew Bardsley and entitled *Cary Grant's Nose*, a wry comedy about a punk kid auditioning for work as a Cary Grant lookalike. It at once had worldwide appeal and obviously had local interest as well since Archibald Leach aka Cary Grant was a Bristol lad; plus it was sharp, very modern and funny. However, Peter Miller thought not; and disregarding the intention that *Function Room* was a showcase for new writers and their work, had Matthew Bardsley do a total rewrite exactly to his instructions!

I might have understood if this was a running cop series or something where I myself had writers totally reconstruct an episode, but this was mutilation of a sensitive first play. It ended up being called *Wingers*; a bizarre and crass piece which I don't care to go into. I was so angry about this, since *Function Room* was intended to showcase new writers and not old producers!

Finally I regained control of the series and went on to produce the other stories. Since *Wingers* was so unlike *Cary Grant's Nose* I felt honour bound to do that one too, only properly this time. It went very well and starred Rula Lenska as a jaded lookalike agent who suddenly sees something in the punk who says he's 'got Cary Grant's nose', implying that his grandmother knew Cary Grant before he left Bristol and that he could possibly be his illegitimate heir… Happily, its author Matthew Bardsley has gone on to a career of writing for television. Another one that stands out for me was a comedy by John Collee. He used the Function Room for a pork-pie-eating contest in a story starring Ewan Hooper as the pie-eating champ. John Collee of course has progressed through novels like *Paper Mask* and screenplays such as *Master and Commander* to be an internationally acclaimed writer. Another of the writers whose name I don't remember went to live in New York and wrote off-Broadway plays with some success. All in all, I feel that *Function Room* did what it said on the tin: encouraged those with real passion to go on writing.

After *Function Room*, I was offered an episode of the ITV children's drama series *Dramarama* to produce. I chose Matthew Bardsley to write it and he came up with a real gem. It was titled *Purple Passion Video*, since the overall theme of the *Dramarama* compilation was 'fame and music'. We had Bobby Gee playing the lead, from the then hit group Bucks Fizz not long after their Eurovision success with the skirt-stripping performance of *Making Your Mind Up*!

Matthew Bardsley's piece was an intriguing one to be part of and I was thoroughly enjoying my position as producer. All seemed to be going well… then it happened.

A day's location shooting was planned: we were filming in an office in Queen Square for the morning. We then took lunch and Terry Miller, the director, wanted to set up the next location which was on the Bristol Docks only a few hundred yards away. We needed to be set up for around about four that afternoon. Timing was important since we'd hired a steam train, which was pretty expensive, and we only had it from six P.M. till ten P.M.

I suddenly became aware that things were going wrong when I sat in the control box at four o'clock waiting for the first shot to be done. Time was moving on; it was nearly seven o'clock and still nothing was happening. I was then told that the train had run over the cables and we were waiting for replacements to be delivered from HTV base – a five-minute drive away! I wasn't sure if I believed that or not. So, we waited and waited. Still nothing happened. The director did a few pick-up shots to keep things ticking over, and finally at nine o'clock we were able to get the first shots of the train. There still seemed to be troubles and I was informed, by a loyal mate, that the crew were out to 'break in a new producer' and get some extra pay, by taking the shoot into overtime… and that started at ten o'clock.

By ten o'clock, we hadn't done half the shots needed for the train sequence; we also had a dozen or so extras to think about – they had only been called until ten… Things were getting pretty tense and I negotiated with the train people to carry on for an hour or so. Things got slower and slower; every little thing seemed to take much longer than usual and we were already into double time for the crew. I further heard that the crew were going to try and take the shoot into what is known as the 'golden hours', that is after midnight when it goes to triple and then even later into quadruple time!

And so we went on shooting until one-thirty A.M. I had an unpleasant feeling in my stomach. My first network production and I'd blown the budget sky-high. One day had cost nearly half the whole shooting budget… What really saddened me was that this crew were the same people who'd worked with me back in times when there was a family feel to the proceedings. Don't get me wrong, I know that sounds pretty dewy-eyed and nostalgic; but it was a shock, since I know there once had been a genuine desire to get the job done as well as possible and have pride in doing it.

All that had gone now. I guessed that this must be the result of working on co-productions with a lot more money sloshing about, and them feeling it was about time it got sloshed their way. To be sure, HTV was now a major co-producer and many of the projects were very good, but others just had to be finished and got to market. What was lost was the pride in the efforts of a small TV company always up against the 'big boys' like Thames, ATV and Granada and making a real winner; all that was no more…

My immediate problem was that I had to explain the huge overtime bill to the executive producer at HTV, Patrick Dromgoole. He was in a really good mood when I met him in his office. I went through the woes of the night before and saw that he was smiling. He offered me a drink and said, 'Forget it.' He then told me he'd put the whole costs onto the *Robin Hood* budget…! That was a new one on me: of course, if you've got plenty of money in one account, as it were, you can use it to help out on another… simple. I was relieved, but still a little sore that I didn't handle the crew with more determination. I'd learned my lesson.

More co-productions where I was only involved in the script followed. Next was a French/Canadian/HTV co-production: an historical piece called *Frontier* set in Canada during the 1740s. Again I dived into the research of a subject I knew little of and found it really fascinating, since it was a French view of the American Colonial war. The whole thing was to be filmed in Canada and much of it in the museum town of Fredericksburg (where, I was told, actors not only dress up in period costume, but assume the identity of a 'character' of the period like a blacksmith, a soldier a milkmaid or whatever, and apparently have a huge database of facts about 'themselves' so they can answer any question that might be put to them by tourists). That was all very well, but I was having real trouble with the script. It was written by a very highly valued French writer – of novels it must be said – Didier Decoin, who seemed to have real trouble writing a film script. I read his episodes over and over but I couldn't get what it was all about. I tried cleaning up the dialogue, which yet again was a straight translation from the French, but everything seemed complete gobbledegook and sounded stupid… There was no alternative but to start again.

I was doing reasonably well with a new script when I was told to expect a visit from the French director, who wanted to work on the script with me. He arrived with his beautiful wife Li: she was much younger than him, but you could tell they were very much in love with each other; very French, very sweet. His name was Victor Vicas, in his sixties and something of a celebrity in the French film world. I was a little wary of him, until he told me of his adventures in Hollywood in the fifties.

After making an acclaimed French film he was invited by Paramount Pictures to go to Hollywood and direct a movie. When he got there he was full of himself: 'I'll show these Yanks how to make a film.' He was handed a script called *The Wayward Bus* from the novel by John Steinbeck. Quite a gem to be offered! On reading it, he decided on the perfect casting: he wanted Anthony Quinn and Shelley Winters. Victor was offered Dan Dailey, a well known song-and-dance man and terrible actor; and then for the leading lady… Joan Collins. He was stunned. He smiled and said in Victor's inimitable way (imagine a thick French accent), 'But this is wrong! I insist on my choice of cast!' Things got a bit heated; then again as only Victor could say it, 'If I don't get my cast I resign!' Next morning an airline ticket for Paris arrived on his breakfast table. Needless to say, Victor made an 'artistic decision' to make the movie with Dan Dailey and Joan Collins. The result, given the source material, is in my opinion quite forgettable.

Victor and I started work on the scripts; there were eight episodes, and he insisted on being with me as I wrote. This led to the most marvellous situation of commuting to Paris every week. I'd catch a plane from Bristol to Paris on a Monday and back again on Friday.

I must confess I found Victor rather heavy going: he was a bit of a manic depressive if allowed to be. Just to emphasise this, I was at a party to celebrate Patrick Dromgoole's son getting his degree at Cambridge when Victor edged up to Patrick and asked what the party was about. A very proud Patrick said, 'My son's just got his degree at university.'

Victor twisted his lips down on one side and said in a very flat voice: 'My son has cancer…' That was Victor.

When I was in Paris we worked in his apartment on the south side of Paris and I travelled there each day by the Metro from my hotel. It was fantastic to feel a part of Paris and see all the non-tourist places. Li, Victor's wife, was a fantastic cook and prepared some delightful meals for me. At other times we'd go out to eat in a restaurant, always in Li's Mini, which she explained was perfect for parking athwart a zebra crossing!

Victor invited me to his country house in Île-de-France for a change of scenery but I found him too much for twenty-four hours a day. He never stopped working or being depressed – and depressing! His ideas for the script I found amazing. Having got to a point in a scene where we had a spy and the leading lady playing mind games with each other and I was wondering what might happen next, Victor said, 'Then he slaps her face.'

I frowned and asked: 'Why?'

'Because he wants to,' said Victor.

This was fairly typical of the whole French approach: sod subtlety, a pox on the plot, let's do melodrama. These co-produced series were so full of these weird sudden out-of-character acts that I found it hard to keep my sanity at times. Then to my horror I found out after Victor and I had done months of work that the whole thing was to be re-edited by Didier Decoin. Peter Graham Scott, who was to be the producer for HTV, told me that he and Victor were made to hang on every word that Didier, the great French writer, uttered; and when he came out with a line, Victor would say: 'Oh brilliant, Didier!' It was at that point that I decided to pull out of *Frontier* since I knew that we'd be back where we started once Didier rewrote it.

The resulting series was a bit of a disaster, one that bears telling. (Not because of the script which wasn't too markedly changed; I think Didier got fed up with rewriting and decided to leave it as it was.) On lots of the interior shots, there seemed to be a fire-glow flickering in the background. Strangely, this flickering fire effect was on everything. Even the exteriors! It took them a while to realise that they'd failed to change their electrics from European AC to American DC. So all interiors, whatever the background, had this flickering fire effect... The much-vaunted Fredericksburg 'actor' extras, given free by the Canadian Tourist Board, simply could not act! Also, Victor obviously wasn't used to handling large numbers of extras, since when appearing as background fillers they all walked awkwardly and at exactly the same speed and all of them constantly looked at the camera. One particular oddity was a man pushing a cart, who seemed to pass by in the background of every shot in a slow lumbering fashion! Another amazing thing which managed to get into the broadcast tape was a scene between our heroine, played beautifully by Mel Martin, and the French male lead who had been made up in a full moustache and beard. As he is beginning a particularly passionate speech in a close two-shot, his false moustache begins to unravel and a strand of it drifts off for about two feet out to the side of his face! It stays there, waving in the breeze throughout the shot.

I wasn't a great fan of Victor Vicas. He was a deeply serious man and still retained the early sixties' fear of nuclear war and would join in Paris Peace Marches; despite all his foibles, he was a man of humanity. Sad to say, during the filming of *Frontier* Victor had a heart attack and died…

During the late eighties, HTV were doing more and more quite big and important co-productions. Sheer favourable economics brought some pretty hefty productions to HTV's door. I was not involved in many of these since they were all ready to shoot with screenplays already written. It also brought some pretty incredible casts to our little regional station.

One morning I came in to my office as usual around about nine-thirty to find a bed on the floor and, lying on it, Sir Laurence Olivier! Quite a shock. He was full of apology and said he'd been given the room to rest in between takes. I told him that it was fine and that I had another room I could use. I was to find out later that in fact he was quite ill and had a lingering cough after a bout of 'flu. He was appearing in a TV film for HBO (Home Box Office) called *Mr Halpern and Mr Johnson*. Olivier was playing Mr Halpern, a Jewish man who has just buried his wife after a long marriage. Jackie Gleason played Mr Johnson, a mysterious stranger who turns up at the funeral… The director was Alvin Rakoff.

I felt I ought to try and see these great people work, so I found a monitor well out of the way of the action and settled down to watch. Jackie Gleason seemed to be a bit aloof and only called from time to time for his factotum, a strange streak of a man, to 'light me!' At this, the man would rush onto the set and put a cigarette into Gleason's mouth and light it. Jackie Gleason was a chain smoker. He smoked throughout the scene; his smoking sent Olivier into paroxysms of coughing, which he had to control for his speeches. He would hold up his hand to say he was ready to go, then do his piece to camera with Gleason puffing smoke at him. He did it perfectly and as soon as he heard the word 'cut' he would start coughing again. What a pro, I thought.

BOB BAKER

I was lucky enough to meet John Schlesinger when he came to HTV. I was a great admirer of his work and I particularly liked his rendering of *Far from the Madding Crowd*, which of course included my friend Prunella Ransome as the hapless Fanny. He'd come to direct *Separate Tables* which starred Alan Bates and Julie Christie. Schlesinger had never worked in a TV studio and although he had three cameras available to him, he only used one, more or less like a 35mm movie camera. Again, I felt honoured to be able to watch them work.

Richard Burton and Elizabeth Taylor came to HTV to film *Divorce His – Divorce Hers*. There was a huge security guard in place at the time, to protect Liz's diamond ring I was told. Lots of stories surfaced during this shoot of Richard Burton's drunkenness. He apparently travelled with two Rolls Royces: one for him and his bodyguards, the other for his booze and its bodyguards. It was said that he needed to finish off a bottle of vodka before he could do a first take and then have one of his bodyguards hold on to his legs, out of shot, to stop him trembling…

Sometimes there were some very unexpected pleasant surprises. I walked in through the front door and recognised Van Johnson, an American star of the forties and fifties. I couldn't believe it. He was there to star in a children's series. He was a charming man and, considering his movie career, extremely modest and easy to get on with. A lovely guy, not unlike many of the fifties characters he played.

Meanwhile another two series of *Into the Labyrinth* came along. It was unfortunate that Ron Moody was unavailable for the third series. Peter Graham Scott suggested we try a local actor, Chris Harris, who was very active in the Bristol Old Vic. I knew Chris and had enjoyed his productions at the Old Vic, especially a clever piece called *The Bristol Twins* where he played the part of both twins. I felt Chris would be great for the new 'Rothgo', but realising that there was such a sharp contrast I felt a completely new character was in order. I did the first script of series three and introduced the new character 'Lazlo' in a story based on Long John Silver and *Treasure Island*. Chris brought a completely new dimension to the show, that of physical in-your-face comedy, whereas Ron Moody was all looks and sharp dialogue. It was of course different but I wouldn't say it was inferior in any way.

176

I began to feel, after *Function Room* and having now got the 'pile' of scripts which were sent to the station down to manageable limits, that my job with HTV was completed. There was one more programme I was attached to which I feel broke new ground. It was another HTV co-production, this time with Chatsworth Television. I was shown a Thames TV series on teenagers that had gone out at around eleven-thirty P.M. and it tackled all the usual problems which beset teenagers and their parents, teachers and the law. It was a very good hard-hitting drama series, but apparently after sifting through the viewing figures ITV realised it had hardly been watched at all. By anybody! So the same idea was pitched to me. Patrick Dromgoole asked me to 'put a series together for teenagers; don't hold back and make it work.'

I must digress now. During a long stint going through submissions of plays and ideas, one of my colleagues drew my attention to a piece by a writer named Jack Allen; it was a full novel sent in the hope of making it into a series. The size of it was a bit off-putting as I had so many things to read. It was called *When the Whistle Blows Stand Still*, an hilarious, yet harrowing satire about the state of education and teaching in the eighties. As I read it, I remembered meeting a guy called Jack Allen in the fifties. He was a professional rugby player and played for a Rugby League club up north somewhere. He was a strapping lad, six-foot plus, and had a beautiful girlfriend who was a jazz singer. I was playing in a band with Ron Caines at the time, called Soul Brothers, at a pub in Bristol.

Jack and his girl came up to chat with us in the interval. We were amused to see that Jack's leg was in plaster and Jill's arm was plastered in the comedy raised-and-bent-forward position. (We learned that Jack had pranged his brand new Mini a couple of weeks before thus causing the injuries.) Jack introduced himself and asked if we'd mind Jill sitting in on a number in the second half. It's always an awkward moment when an unknown person asks to sit in – you never know if it's going to work – so we asked her what her repertoire was and it seemed fine. She was to sing on *Georgia*. All turned out well; she was a terrific singer and came along to sing with us for quite a while. We got friendly with Jack, and even after he and Jill split up he still kept coming to the club when he was around. That was in 1956 and I'd never seen him since then.

So, after reading the book by 'author' Jack Allen, I contacted him and asked him to come and meet me. I recognised him immediately as the rugby player who I'd met all those years ago. I soon got up to speed with the years in between. He had to give up rugby because of a knee injury, and had then become a teacher: first in a junior school and now in a rough, tough comprehensive on the borders of St Paul's, a district of Bristol largely occupied by black, poor white and Indo-Pakistani people. Jack told me of the trials and tribulations of trying to teach in the remedial class to kids who didn't want to learn anything, and who were willing to confront any teacher who was even a teeny-weeny bit scared of them. Jack's huge presence helped him a lot; and out of what frankly sounded like misery came a fantastic book, wild, zany and right on the mark.

When I was constructing the 'teenage show' I thought, who better than Jack to come up with some real stories wrought on the anvil of truth? So, we got busy. Some of Jack's stories were too horrendous to use, but we managed to cover the basic brief. There was a further element to the storyline, and that was music. The Chatsworth co-producer was very much into the recording side of music and he insisted on using some of the top groups and performers of the day. Certainly music to my ears!

Ever since I'd been a 'musician' in a production of *Marat/Sade* I'd wanted to break up conventions in television in a similar way. Here was a chance to be innovative and subversive at the same time. We decided it should be called *Jangles*. Jangles was a nightclub where our teenage characters met and this was where it was literally 'at'! The shows were directed by the two youngest and best in-house directors at HTV, Kenneth Price and Alex Kirby. I devised the Herald character, superbly played by David Delve, who was the resident DJ. Dressed as a ringmaster, he narrated the series and, by suggestion, never left the place. The lead was taken on by Hazel O'Connor, hot from her success in *Breaking Glass*. She was ably supported by Jesse Birdsall, who has gone on to be in some pretty awesome series.

The other contrived convention was that in contrast to the richly coloured interior of Jangles, everything that happened outside the club was in black and white, desaturated and dull. We covered the areas of education, bullying, drinking, drugs and relations with parents and the law, then even ventured on to teenage sex and living together. In addition to this we featured a new band, sometimes two, each week at the Jangles venue, including heavy metal band Tank, Bananarama and several other top-line bands; and of course Hazel O'Connor giving terrific renditions of her own and classic songs, like *School's Out for Summer*.

I believe it is fair to say that everyone concerned with *Jangles* thought it was fast-moving, very relevant and highly watchable with that extra something added into it. It was a success as made, and was immediately chosen as the ITV entry for the Prix Jeunesse at Monte Carlo. However, all depended very much on how it went down with teenagers in the UK.

It was disaster… This highly charged series concerning teen-to-adult subject matter was screened on the network at four-thirty P.M.! Just in time for the junior-school kiddies coming home! What idiot(s) thought this was a good time to show the series? They must've needed their heads examined. We had calls from irate mothers and fathers from all across Britain asking what the hell was going on. The series was, of course, taken off the network and never seen again. A tragic ending to a piece of really innovative television.

Glad to say, Jack Allen finally got his book *When the Whistle Blows Stand Still* published and there are rumours of a series…

There were a few more international co-productions and more disasters of a similar kind, including *She Wolf*, a co-production with Universal Pictures, which was a stark and sexy piece about a female werewolf; again well-scripted, acted and directed, but it went out on the UK network at five-thirty P.M. Again, howls of objections from parents, but not least from Universal who'd been promised a late slot. This became the source of a law suit, which of course Universal won.

My final co-production was on something called *Jenny's War*. This was taken from a book, a true story of how a mother travelled to Germany in 1945 to find her son, who as an RAF bomber pilot was shot down over Germany and captured after he parachuted out of his doomed plane. An American director got hold of the rights and wrote a script from the story idea, but changed the mother to an American and set it in 1941.

Now that might sound alright, until you realise that he knew absolutely nothing about history. I read the script with mounting incredulity. Tony Robinson had also read it and we had a conversation on how to report back to Patrick Dromgoole – in how many ways can you say 'it's a load of crap'? Even with the best will in the world, nothing stacked up. I was given the task of trying to get the writer/director to allow me to make little alterations to his script; and to point out that changing it to 1941, before the Americans entered the war, made a radical change to the story. The director also assumed that Americans could come and go as they pleased. When I enquired how Jenny was going to get to Germany in war-torn Europe, he assumed she'd take a plane. 'Where? On what airline?' I enquired. He didn't know. I had to point out to him that as a neutral American, her only way to get into occupied Europe was a dangerous flight to Lisbon, then a train to Madrid and then another on to Switzerland and into Germany from there.

A more important historical oversight was when he had a Russian POW camp next to the British Stalag. Since Hitler had only invaded Russia in June of '41, he'd hardly have POW camps in the Reich! And anyway Russian prisoners weren't brought to Germany until 1944/5 as the Germans retreated. I could see he was getting a bit angry at all these unfortunate facts coming out. The final straw was a scene where Jenny has found her son and they are escaping when, just about to be caught, they are helped to avoid capture by some kindly German farmers. All I said was: 'By the end of 1941, Hitler's Germany was at the zenith of its power; the Nazis controlled all of Europe and were deep into Russia, barely thirty miles from Moscow; in North Africa the British were in retreat from Rommel and it looked as if Egypt would fall; the battle of the Atlantic was going well for Germany and Britain was facing starvation. Why would German farmers want to help an American and especially a British bomber pilot escape?'

He made a snarl and said: 'Fuck history!'

And at that point I said bye bye salary, bye bye HTV...

Looking back on my four years of employment at HTV I feel pleased at achieving one or two things. Firstly, my readers and I, in three years, reduced a pile of unanswered requests for an appraisal of work submitted in the hope of getting it to the screen. These varied enormously from the clever and witty, to the dour and serious drama with 'meaning'; and included several comedies, one of which I begged HTV to do, since it was really hilariously funny – very off-beat and set in Shropshire.

It was written by actor Tim Preece who had been in the cast of *Machinegunner*, the TV film with Len Rossiter. Patrick agreed Tim's script was a superb comedy but he just couldn't fit it into the schedules. Anyway, I'm pleased to relate, it was made by the BBC some years later and I was lucky enough to see it. Likewise, the Tom Sharpe book *Blott on the Landscape* was offered, but not taken up because the cost of production couldn't be borne by HTV alone. Again, it was later done by the BBC and launched David Suchet's career.

I hope and believe that the would-be authors of the HTV area felt they'd been fairly treated. I'd also had a hand in starting up the lunchtime theatres in Bristol and Bath where new plays and actors could be showcased, and one was chosen from each venue to be televised. This gave me the idea of pushing for *Function Room* which I believe in terms of its brief – to encourage new authors – getting three new authors turning into professional writers out of seven productions was a success. It is something I'm quite proud about. I know how difficult it is being on the 'outside' wondering how the hell do you get your work produced? The other thing is keeping contact with hopefuls: authors you know have something, but who would wither on the vine if left totally to themselves. I regularly held what would nowadays be called 'surgeries' with writers to discuss their work and – hopefully – push them in the right direction.

Then there was *Into the Labyrinth*, an object lesson in low-budget action adventure. Twenty-one episodes filmed on one set! Now that's economy. Again, apart from guest stars, all the smaller parts were played by actors from in and around the area. I also managed to slip in some very new writers among the big name pros: Gary Hopkins, a writer I'd met at a *Doctor Who* convention who'd asked me to read some of his scripts, but missed out on *Function Room*; an Indian writer, Yogesh Asthana; and the already mentioned 'schoolgirl' Jane McCloskey.

Jangles was yet another achievement. Whatever the end result, transmission wise, it was a real shake-up of the children's genre. It was like *King of the Castle*, challenging the norm, breaking new ground: an almost Brechtian surrealist situation used in tackling important issues, and the whole thing awash with lights and music; a perfect example of what three or four like-minded writers and directors can do, given the chance.

Quite apart from the pain of some co-productions (which could at times resemble toothache!) it did of course broaden my travel opportunities and I can remember wonderful times I had in Morocco, Rome and particularly Paris where I was always given a fantastic welcome by Jacques Dercourt of Télécip.

Chapter Thirteen
Days of Wine and Roses

NOW I WAS BACK in the world of freelance writing; and, on the home front, Angela and I decided to move house. We tried in vain to find a cottage in Oldbury that we could afford, but the prices there were a good bit higher than anywhere else around. In the end we decided to tear ourselves away from Oldbury and the good friends we'd made there, and looked elsewhere around Bristol.

We came across a house in Portishead further down the Severn where it meets the Bristol Channel. It was a beautiful thirties cottage-style house, one of six with huge sweeping tiled roofs, overlooking the Bristol channel with views across at Newport on the Welsh coast. In front of that was the Portishead boating lake and a cricket field with white wooden pavilion, from where, sitting in the garden on a quiet Sunday afternoon, you could just hear the sound of 'leather on willow', the shouts of 'Run!', 'No!' and 'Howzat!' Immediately opposite, across the road, was a manicured bowling green. It was a beautiful house in a fantastic location. Furthermore you could watch ships, from tugs and coasters up to hundred-thousand-ton container ships, gliding by on their way to the Portbury Docks just around Nore Point and its lighthouse. One unexpected extra that came with the place was a 1940s Anderson shelter with the original wood and steel-strip bedsteads.

I worked in the small bedroom at the back of the house; and I knew the time of day by the unmistakable passing of a Concorde which crossed the sky, a sound like no other aircraft, at exactly eleven-oh-three every day on its way to New York.

I must recount an amusing thing that happened whilst living there. I became aware from the local newspaper that a Radio Portishead had started up and they did daily broadcasts, for two hours from four till six. I'd never actually listened to it; but one day a very young man came to the door. He was accompanied by one of my neighbour's children who introduced him. He asked me if I had indeed written *Doctor Who*. 'Yes,' I replied; and he asked me if I would be interviewed on the fledgling Radio Portishead? I agreed, and a time and date was set. I arrived at the 'station' – a back room in a high-street shop – to find that the whole operation was run by schoolkids. Well done, I thought: good to see the kids getting involved.

When my time came I was put in front of the microphone and the very young DJ/interviewer told his audience that he had a very special guest and went on about *Doctor Who* for a while – a really big build-up. Then he introduced me: 'Ladies and gentlemen with me this afternoon – Tom Baker!'

I had no choice but to tell him that I wasn't Tom Baker, but Bob Baker… There was an agonising silence as the DJ went into a state of shock. I started telling him that I'd written *Doctor Who* for Tom Baker, that I'd created K9 and was involved with writing for television, but this was to no avail: the poor DJ was totally bewildered; so I ended up interviewing myself as the DJ sat staring at me in total silence.

I had a call from an old acquaintance, a director who'd worked on *Doctor Who*. He wanted to introduce me to some Dutch people who were looking for somebody to rewrite a police TV film from Dutch into English. I was given a meal at a London hotel and introduced to the producer, a lady called Wilma, who questioned me very closely on my past work. The man with her seemed happy with my CV and they invited me to go to the Netherlands and help do an English version of a police series with the author of the story; he was a journalist on the Amsterdam daily newspaper, *De Telegraaf*.

I worked in Holland off and on for about six months, and the series was made in Dutch and in English the following year at the fine old studios at Hilversum. I travelled around Holland looking at locations and found it fascinating; everything is about water and keeping it at bay. Canals, sea walls, banks and windmill pumps keep the Dutch from drowning. I also spent a day with the Amsterdam equivalent of 'the Sweeney' and I accompanied them to watch – at a discreet distance – a raid on a house thought to contain money-counterfeiting machinery. I noted how rough the uniformed branch were when handling alleged villains – plenty of punches and kicks – and again in the streets of Amsterdam, the uniformed cops came down physically hard on people like vagrants sleeping in doorways. In my innocence I thought, well our policemen don't do things like that... now, after seeing some recent TV reports, I'm not so sure.

I had a message to ring Robert Banks Stewart. He asked me to be his script editor on a new series he was planning, a private-eye series (shades of *Shoestring*?) called *Call Me Mister*. I of course accepted and met Robert in London. He was back in Threshold House on Shepherd's Bush Green; it was just after he'd got back from filming the first episode in Australia. (Oh shit! It was yet another co-production.) The series concerned a Sydney cop, played by Steve Bisley, who I'd seen and liked in *Mad Max*. Steve was a big star in Oz and we hoped he'd get an audience here in the UK too.

Steve played the estranged son of a British lord, who'd grown up in Australia from an early age. The father had recently died and the lowly Sydney cop was now a lord! This brought him to London where he meets up with his rather snooty brother and sister who are contesting the will. There is no money to inherit as yet, not until all the claims are settled, so our man is in London and broke. He finds himself a job as a private detective. What better job for an ex-Sydney cop? Dulice Liecier was the female lead. Her character was a nightclub singer who was struggling to get by and had a young daughter to look after.

I was back on the treadmill with Robert Banks Stewart and really enjoying it. Still going through the agony of the weekend writing, producing the draft script by the following Monday. This time, during the week, I stayed with Michael O'Hagan and Pamela Salem; again they left me to fend for myself as they both went off on film work. They lived in a flat in Earl's Court and I got to know the area quite well during the time I lived there.

I could see that *Call Me Mister* was building into a strong series, script wise. Robert and I worked long and hard in producing, in my opinion, some of the best stories I'd ever worked on. Furthermore, on watching the rough cuts, the episodes themselves were coming on well too. Steve Bisley was an out-and-out movie actor and seemed to give the series that special extra little oomph. He had a great supporting cast including Haydn Gwynne, Dermot Crowley and Rupert Frazer. David Bamber played the wheelchair-bound head of a private detective agency which was set in the Spitalfields area.

Robert ran into trouble over David Bamber's character. There was strong lobbying to cast a real disabled actor in the part. Robert had auditioned several, but came across the same problem that at one time plagued black and Asian actors: that they didn't get much work, so they didn't get the experience. So do you cast someone simply because they are disabled, or do you go for the best actor for the part? I was glad that was a decision I didn't have to make. Happily things are different now.

The other fun thing about the series was that directors were encouraged to use locations around St Paul's Cathedral and the City of London. It was amazing how we came across unfamiliar locations in an area we thought we knew, like a Victorian shopping arcade, a beautiful little park hemmed in by skyscrapers where City workers munched their sandwiches to the music of a brass band. There was of course the occasional howler. The top-floor conference suite of what was then the tallest building in London had been selected and hired as a location for one of the scenes. The huge windows looked out on a marvellous view of central London. Yet the scene was shot in close-up on the actors without even a glimpse of the fantastic view!

After nine months of work on the series, we waited in anticipation for the reaction from viewers. Unfortunately, *Call Me Mister* did not take off. The public seemed not to have any like or dislike for Steve Bisley. There was absolutely nothing wrong with his performance, and nothing wrong with the scripts, or the direction; there was just something about the lead actor that didn't click. The series became the proverbial damp squib.

I left the BBC and went back home to Portishead, where I was asked by HTV if I would be interested in writing on a project they were working up. It was a subject matter close to my heart: wine. Although it was another bloody co-production. Again I would be working with Jacques Dercourt, so at least that was a plus. It was to be a series called in French *Les Grand Années* ('The Great Years'). Apart from the obvious connection with wine, there was to be a story of families: one in Bordeaux and the other in Bristol. Harvey's wine and sherry company was one of the oldest in the country, so there was that extra attraction of historical Bristol. I came across some interesting facts in a book I read called *Bristol Cream* about the history of Harvey's and I decided to base the English family on elements of it.

As I began assembling some ideas for the French series, now called *Vintage*, I noticed something rather strange. On checking my bank account, I found I was still receiving my monthly *Call Me Mister* script editing salary from the BBC. I didn't worry too much at first; it seemed rather amusing. Then the ugly thought of having to pay the money back came over me. I asked a few friends what was the best thing to do. Most said, 'Take it, it's their mistake.' I then asked Robert Banks Stewart and he was amazed. The series had been finished six months previously, but he said he'd quietly ask around. To my utter surprise he found out that the BBC do carry on paying script editor/writers for an extra nine months in the expectation that they would come up with a new programme idea during that period.

Jesus! Why didn't anybody tell me? I had recently written a children's series idea based on a private helicopter rescue service. I'd been asked by a friendly neighbourhood millionaire to help his wife, who'd come up with the idea, to write the series. He himself ran a helicopter and, as a special perk for the series, offered the helicopter for the filming, free, *gratis* and for nothing, thus saving a huge chunk of the budget. I first offered it to HTV, who after doing a budget found that since the whole thing was on film and on location, the helicopter costs were infinitesimal compared to, say, overtime, lab costs and hotels. I offered the series to Graeme MacDonald, the BBC's Head of Series and Serials, as the work I'd been doing over the paid period. The series was rejected. My greatest regret was: why wasn't I told about the pay thing? I could have come up with something of my own if only I'd been told. Bugger! Such is life.

I became deeply involved with the French series *Vintage*. I was to work with an English-speaking French writer, Jean Paul. I don't remember his surname. I went to Paris to meet him and was invited to dine with him and his family. He was a good bit older than me and was serious and meticulous with everything, and especially over wine: beginning with fussing over the temperature of the champagne we drank as an aperitif.

Then to see him opening and serving the red wine was something out of this world! He would painstakingly ease the cork out, then sniff it for a good minute, then pour a little drop into a balloon red-wine glass, swill it around and look through it up to the light. Then sniff the aroma deeply... After about five minutes of this rigmarole, he eventually took a sip, replaced the glass on the table, then held both hands flat against each side of his nose and made sucking and sloshing noises with the wine in his mouth as if he were cleaning his teeth. Finally he pronounced the wine drinkable and poured it.

I noticed (having done my research) that the wine was a Bordeaux, chateau-bottled, and was vintage 1976 and was of the *deuxième* Grand Cru; it would have cost in the region of thirty pounds (sixty to eighty today)... It better be bloody good! I must say it was what I call drinkable, not unpleasant; but it set me off on trying to expose the myth of French wine... Not that I disagree that the very fine and very expensive Bordeaux wines are fantastic, but you have a ten-year-wait before it becomes mature. I just wanted to use the series to clear the air around the mystical 'quality' of French wine without the French realising... some hopes. But the *Vintage* series seemed an excellent place to start from.

The next day Jean Paul drove me down to Bordeaux. On the long journey I asked him who his writing influences were; I was ready to answer with mine: Osborne, Pinter, Brecht, Arthur Miller... His sole answer was *La Comédie-Française*. An eighteenth-century form and genre. I was shocked and I couldn't think how he might apply it to the serious, hard-hitting drama that I had in mind... I was soon to find out.

Meanwhile we were to be staying in the grandest hotel in Saint-Émilion: the white building in the square that is on all the guide books. It was a superb hotel and everything was being paid for by Télécip, the French co-producer. Jean Paul ordered more and more expensive wines, up to a hundred pounds at one time (a white Chateau Talbot). The problem for me, as one who loves food, was that France and indeed the UK was going through the *nouvelle cuisine* fad; and although we had fantastic wine each night, the food, while very prettily presented, was minuscule. I was hungry after the evening meal. At one outrageously expensive place he took me to, the first course was the plates! Very artistically decorated plates were put before us with great aplomb... We waited for about ten minutes, and then they were taken away again with another great flourish. When the starter came it was a baby lobster tail very daintily placed on the plate with a few snail trails of a sauce in a pattern around it. The lobster tail was just for decoration… it was empty! After a few days of this I just needed to eat something solid. I begged Jean Paul to take me to one of those simple French restaurants with bentwood chairs and good homely cuisine.

He took me to just the place. It was in the centre of Bordeaux. As we tried the door, my mouth was already watering at the sight of the place: the Ricard signs, the *pression* beer pumps and a waiter in an oversize white apron. Just what I wanted. I could already imagine the stale Gauloises smell… The door, however, was locked. We knocked on the glass and the waiter came over to us and tapped his watch and shouted through the glass: '*Sept heures et demie!*' It was only seven o'clock. I was starving. Jean Paul told me he knew another restaurant just down the road. What he didn't know was that the restaurant had changed hands. It was in a basement and had become the chicest of chic, specialising in… guess what? *Nouvelle* fucking *cuisine*! I went to bed hungry yet again.

We visited many vineyards in Saint-Émilion. Jean Paul had a good friend who had a chateau, but he could only make wine that was Saint-Émilion *appellation contrôlée*, a long way down the scale from the vaunted Grand Cru classes. He asked us to lunch and brought several examples of his wine for us to try. The first he described the taste of as 'blaring like a trumpet!' For this, read sharp and vinegary, as were all his other wines. I was beginning to realise that the whole thing about the 'greatness' of French wine was perhaps derived totally from semantics, the flowery descriptions rather than the actual taste being what mattered. I enquired discreetly of our French producer, Jacques Dercourt, if I could bring up themes about the French wine industry that might be thought of as sacrilege? Happily he was all for it.

Next, Jean Paul showed me around the famous Médoc chateaux which were all of the first Grand Cru class – in other words, rare and very expensive wines such as those produced at the Chateau Mouton Rothschild, which had a gigantic underground cellar like a rabbit warren with little side tunnels, each with the year written above the arch. It went back to 1912!

Jean Paul bombarded me with details about the composition of the soil around the river Gironde and how perfect it is for viniculture. I then found out that it was only perfect as long as the weather was right for maximum growth, i.e. no frosts in late April or May; so in reality it's at the mercy of the weather. The other thing he kept banging on about was the 'great Grand Cru scandal' going on at the time. It seems a wine can only be called Grand Cru if it uses grapes from certain prescribed vineyards, the old vines that have been around for many years. Of late, some Bordeaux growers had been redefining their vineyards so that new vines crossed into old. Since the harvest from that field would contain a certain amount of the Grand Cru grapes, they were claiming a higher status for all the wine from the vineyard. Gee whizz! Or as the Aussies say – well hooray fuck!

I certainly didn't want such idiosyncratic details to weigh down the drama, otherwise we'd be making a bloody documentary. We visited Chateau Latour, which just happened to be owned by Harvey's of Bristol at that time. For me that was the perfect place to build a story from, since Bristol and Bordeaux are twin cities, mainly because of the trading that went on between them for six hundred years. Trade in claret, the English name for Bordeaux red wine, was even getting into Bristol during the Napoleonic wars! Trade being more important to both than war.

When I got home, I began to put a story together and I got another writer, Michael Aitkens who I'd met on *Call Me Mister* (he was later to devise the series *Waiting for God*), to help me with it. I received a draft script from Jean Paul for the first episode. I was amazed. He'd opened this new exciting series with a twelve-page scene of eight people in a room being nice to each other! In my mind this would have viewers turning over channels in droves. I rewrote the first episode with plenty of oomph in it. Everyone seemed to agree the rewritten first episode was what they were looking for.

It centred around two families, one in Bordeaux, one in Bristol. The French family was ruled over by a sort of matriarch who kept an ailing Grand Cru class vineyard going after her husband died. It had strands from World War II, politics, rugby; New World winemakers buying up established vineyards, and of course passion and anguish for families and lovers. It even touched on alcoholism.

When Jean Paul saw the rewrite, he resigned, with a grand flourish. With him went the French government co-production money and down crashed the series. *C'est la vie!*

As a coda to this I spoke with Jacques Dercourt, who went on and made the series in French only. He thanked me profusely for doing what he thought was a superb script and told me he'd used it and Michael Aitkens' scripts – translated of course – in the French series. Some time later, I was in Paris once again on some other business when I saw the first episode on my hotel TV. I felt a warm glow of pride as I saw the series unfolding just as I'd hoped it would.

Back at HTV things were changing; the whole TV world was changing. The unions were a broken force and could do nothing about the redundancies that were being handed out by every TV company across the UK. In order to be profitable by the time the next franchise round came up, HTV had to shed some seven hundred jobs. BBC West were being even more rigorous in shedding jobs. Consequently, a load of ex-HTV/BBC West employees became freelance companies, supplying their previous employer along with editors and film producers. Several of these companies lasted less than a year, others struggled on; but in the end, very few lasted more than five years.

It was at this time that I ran into an old friend from my rock 'n' roll years: Roger Crago, who was in partnership with my musical agent John Miles. He'd gone into property as a diversification from the agency. They were looking for a property portfolio and one of the houses I'd done up suited their budget.

I met him at Bristol airport as I was on my way to Amsterdam. He was waiting for his partner to arrive from Spain. Her plane was late and as it happened my plane was delayed too, so we had a damn good chinwag about the intervening thirty years since we'd last met. I gave him a rundown on my career as a writer; then Roger told a fantastic story of how, when he was building villas in Spain, he got unwittingly involved with the Mafia. He'd met an American guy in similar circumstances – at an airport, both with time on their hands. The American was a wheeler-dealer, interested in anything he and his associates could make money in, and bullshitted about the million-dollar deals he'd done. Roger then told him about a holiday-villa project he was about to get involved with in Fuerteventura, but at that point he was only just discussing obtaining the land. The American said he'd love to get involved with him, gave him his card and vowed he'd be in touch. Roger thought that it was just a chance meeting and that nothing would come of it.

He did get in touch and it led to an amazing series of events whereby Roger was sucked into a huge con. He went to America to meet with his new friend's 'associates'; this was in a hotel penthouse with around a hundred Runyonesque characters all doing deals on telephones. Roger's new-found friend introduced him to the dealers; and then the frightening figure of the 'Mr Big', the boss of the syndicate, entered the scene, wearing only a dressing gown and trailing a pretty blonde girl. He looked at Roger and his welcome was: 'Who the fuck are you?' He was quickly introduced and made aware of Roger's plan for Fuerteventura. 'How much d'ya need?' enquired Mr Big. The price for the land and infrastructure would be around a hundred thousand dollars. He was given a cheque for that amount. A company was then formed and floated on the New York stock exchange. Amazingly, Roger's project was attracting investors at an incredible rate. It got up to an amazing one million dollars... Then came the sting. He looked at the figures one morning to find that it had all evaporated. All the equity had been drawn down... by his new-found partners. They then tried to get him into money-laundering to get himself 'straight'. He refused.

I thought it a tremendous subject matter for a feature film. Roger didn't quite believe me, and took a bit of persuading to tell me more details so that I could write a screenplay. Eventually he was convinced and we formed a company to produce the film called R&B Productions Ltd. I wrote the screenplay and called it *The Killing*.

With a first draft finished I used all my connections to try and get the film made. Dave Martin helped me out by introducing me to feature producer Steve Lanning, who read the script and liked it. He was at that time making a film with the very actor we felt was just right for the lead in ours – Timothy Dalton, who'd just finished his stint as '007' – so we hoped we might kill two birds with one stone. It was not to be, however, and the Dalton film went straight to video. Roger and I were invited to the preview. It had a great cast: Timothy Dalton was partnered by Anthony Edwards (just out of *E.R.* and well known for his portrayal of 'Goose' in *Top Gun*) and the fantastic Janet McTeer, so it wasn't the cast; for me, the whole thing came over as being totally daft. Roger met one of the investors in the loo during the preview. He was hiding away, petrified about the reaction to the film. It was Barry Gibb of the Bee Gees.

191

The Killing was still not made and a friend of mine told me he knew a guy in Amsterdam who did feature films on low budgets: why didn't we try him? So, Roger and I took a trip to Amsterdam to meet one Sidney Ling. He was incredibly young, hardly twenty, but he had the spiel and knew all the right words to use. Sadly, dear Sidney was another con-man on the make; but in finding this out, we met with another film-maker, a Spaniard, José ('Pepe') Maesso, who was going through with one of Sidney's 'deals'. Basically you paid Sidney a lump sum of money, say a hundred thousand dollars, and he would lay the whole thing on for you in Amsterdam: studios, locations and equipment, actors and extras. One evening José, in desperation, told us that all the locations Sidney had set up were bogus. José would turn up at a house and say, we're the film crew to shoot here today – only to be met with frowns, hard stares and bewilderment. The householder knew nothing about it!

We kept in touch with José (who had worked with Sergio Leone on several of the 'spaghetti westerns'). He came to see us in our office in Bristol and said he'd like to do a 'western', as the sets used by Leone in the mountains above Alicante were still there and he could get them cheaply. He needed a foreign co-producer to qualify for the Spanish government grants. Would we like to be that partner?

It looked an exciting prospect, but things were happening closer to home.

At HTV, Patrick Dromgoole, who'd been such an important element in my writing life, was to retire after the franchise was won or lost. As part of a presentation package for HTV's franchise bid I was asked to write a two-hour film for television. The new Head of Drama for Wales and the West was Alan Clayton who'd worked in the Cardiff section of HTV. He'd read an outline I'd written called *Jazz Detective*. It was a thriller, a murder story, again set entirely in Bristol. I was commissioned to write it as a two-hour drama.

It sort of combined at least two of my strong interests, thriller writing and my love of jazz; bring in the Bristol element and I was as happy as the proverbial pig in shit!

However, as I was writing *Jazz Detective*, I found out that Angela, my second wife, after several – as it's put – 'irreconcilable differences', wanted out of our relationship. She explained that as a couple she felt we'd 'decoupled'. I was unsure what to think; maybe she was right? I didn't know, but I was really shocked. However, I quickly realised that there was another man involved. Then one day she left, taking the two children. I was rattling around in our house on my own. She hadn't moved far: only into Portishead village itself, less than a mile away, so I could keep in touch with the kids and they came to see me a lot of the time. I was deeply unhappy, but the work kept me sane – or so I thought.

My personal life hit me with yet another blow. Not long after Angela left, my mother had a stroke and was in hospital, virtually paralysed. At the same time I knew my brother Roger was not well, but I hadn't seen him in a while; when we were together visiting Mum he told me he had cancer. He'd just had a son with his second wife Ann and he insisted that he was putting up a fight and was determined to get through it. He'd been having chemotherapy and looked pretty rough, but full of spirit. Mum died in the September and, sad to relate, Roger followed her within six weeks! I couldn't believe how quickly it had happened.

Feeling a bit lonely, and at the suggestion of some friends, I joined Dateline, where you are supposed to be put into some computerised matching system. Quite honestly I don't believe it, since every one of the ladies I met was a schoolteacher, and at least fifty per cent of them talked of nothing but their exes! However, it kept me from getting too depressed and I may even have found a few ideas for a story…

Jazz Detective was filmed in the summer of 1990. I went to as much of the filming as I could and was very impressed by Danny Webb, who played the lead. I wasn't quite so happy with the music. I had asked and hoped that the innovative Bristol saxophone player Andy Sheppard would have been used, but Alan Clayton chose a friend of his from the Welsh side of the company. When I asked what his music was like, Alan Clayton said, 'Oh he's great, and he does the jazz as well.' At this, my heart sank. It was the tell-tale 'jazz as well' that worried me. In the event it was okay, but not unique: not different and not inspiring. The end result was, I feel, patchy; there were some great bits in it but it lacked real pace. In hindsight I can see that it was too long: ninety minutes would have been more suitable for the story. I was to find out that Alan Clayton was always trying to stretch drama out as long as he could.

HTV regained the franchise, Patrick duly retired and HTV West was under new leadership. There had been vicious restructuring and shedding of more jobs. TV companies were now in the business not of making drama, but commissioning outside production companies to do it for them. This saved keeping on salaried employees and all the expenses that came with it such as pensions.

I had a meeting with Alan Clayton and gave him the latest thing that Roger and I were working on, again based on a true story. It was a fantastic love story of how, through unexpected circumstances, a young Sikh boy falls in love with an English woman twice his age; of how the boy is made to go through an arranged marriage to a beautiful Sikh girl and what happens as a result. It was called *Loving Son* and was written as three one-hour episodes. Alan Clayton felt it would be a good drama for the refranchised HTV to kick off with.

Clayton was to produce; and, in line with the then present system of television, I was encouraged to form a company to do the work and a deal would be put in place that meant, roughly, they paid for the scripts and any rewriting, after which they owned the copyright and our production company would make the film at an agreed fee. Roger and I were happy about this and felt able to move from our rather shabby premises in Gloucester Road on and up to Clifton, where we took offices in a strange turreted gatehouse that suited us perfectly. I got into scripting *Loving Son* and all went reasonably well until Alan Clayton suggested making it into a four-hour piece. I wasn't too keen, but I did, and immediately regretted it. Another episode stretched the story too far and it went limp in the middle, as they say.

Even though *Loving Son* was going along nicely, we had to keep other projects moving as well. Our Spanish producer friend, Pepe Maesso, came to see us with a proposition. He reiterated that he could get a government film grant if he could secure a European co-producer, and asked us to consider coming in as that partner with him. We assumed he meant the 'western' idea. We were interested but decided to keep that in abeyance for the moment and get on with *Loving Son*. We'd asked director Alex Kirby, who I'd worked with at HTV, to direct; he'd since gone on to do episodes of *Lovejoy* and *Boon*. (*Boon*, incidentally, was devised by Bill Stair from our film group in my early days, who had now returned from Hollywood.) Alex was extremely excited and got moving immediately to get a production team together. Everything was under way for filming in around six months. This left us some time; so to fill it, we took up Pepe

Maesso's offer, and decided to try out his method of financing film by using the Spanish government grant.

It seemed to work pretty well, if pretty illegal! Pepe was able to cut his own (Spanish) budget enough to allow us to put up a still sizeable amount of cash on our side as mandatory equal co-production partner. We were to make a feature film in Madrid; it was not the western, but a film called *Cthulhu Mansion*, which was to be written and directed by a horror-genre adherent, Juan P. Simón, director of a truly unbelievable film (and I mean that sincerely folks!) called *Slugs* – which featured action adventure at the speed of a slug!

J.P. Simón was an H.P. Lovecraft fanatic (maybe that's why he put his name like that?). He'd written the film we were to shoot as a sort of homage to the master. I felt rather nervous at first, but soon got into the swing of things. The British side of the co-production was to provide the actors, their flights to the location and hotel. We managed to get Frank Finlay to play the lead. He was fantastic as usual, but of the rest of the film I can only quote one science fiction film magazine: 'This is possibly the worst film I have ever seen!' However, it proved that Pepe's budget-juggling worked and we looked forward to doing another one. Perhaps the western this time?

We'd finished the film in Madrid, and on our return Roger and I were going to the office when we saw a headline in the local newspaper: SHOCK FOR LOCAL FILM COMPANY. We read the article only to find that it was us! It seems that HTV had decided to drop *Loving Son* from their books to concentrate on a new series based in the West Country.

We had a rather nervous meeting with HTV bosses who were adamant they could not proceed. We argued that we had been promised certain sums of money which we had accepted in good faith; but they had put nothing of our financial plans in writing and even denied ever saying it. They offered us a lump sum: 'Take it or leave it.' We took it, of course; but now it was all hands to the pumps, to fill the gaping hole made by *Loving Son*.

The worst thing about the HTV affair is that they wouldn't tell us why they'd built us up and then dropped us. Later, from some questions I was able to put to the few people that I knew at HTV, it would seem that the unspoken division and enmity between the Wales and West sections of HTV had, in the absence of strong leadership, begun to flare up again.

Alan Clayton was from HTV Wales and he'd done all of the dealings on *Loving Son* which was to be filmed and paid for by HTV West in Bristol, but to be counted as an HTV Wales production. A petty squabble over money and territory left R&B Productions in a parlous state. The lump-sum payoff would only keep us going for a few months, and of course we'd just moved to more expensive offices. In hindsight we should have gone back to cheaper premises and tried to weather the storm, but that's hindsight... It's hard when you've moved upward to move back down again...

We had another project to get on with: still not the western, but a new co-production Pepe had come up with in Prague. Again the script was by Juan P. Simón; called *Nexus*, it was a lavish sci-fi piece set on a distant planet. I read the script and again my heart sank. It was childishly, ridiculously awful... Pepe said he'd like me to rewrite it and I was only too willing.

When Pepe had visited us to discuss *Cthulhu Mansion* he also brought a script for another movie, a Russian one. A Russian producer had sent it to him and he asked us to read it. It was superb! Titled *Shalom Vavara*, it was a tragic love story that had lots and lots of wry, very Russian humour.

We made contact with the Russian writer, Oleg Ramarov, and thought it worth a visit to Moscow to meet him and his producer to see if a deal was possible. We were treated royally in Moscow and were put into an amazing hotel which, apparently, was specially built to be used by higher members of the Stalinist Politburo to stay with their mistresses or whatever. Everything was decorated in heavy dark wood, with gigantic carvings and paintings of 'heroic tractor drivers on a collective farm', 'heroic factory workers sweating for the common good', and portraits of the Russian communist government leaders. Our suite was also gigantic and had two separate bedrooms with en suite bathrooms divided by a lounge which sported the biggest radiogram I've ever seen, with piles of 78rpm records to play on it!

We had arrived in 1990, just after the virtual collapse of the Soviet Union. The currency, the rouble, was in freefall with hyperinflation; when we went out to a restaurant they had to take a money carrier with a satchel full of banknotes to pay the bill!

The Russians laughed at us because we didn't drink vodka with our meals. We were derided as 'water drinkers'. However, our negotiations went well and it looked as if *Shalom Vavara*, suitably rewritten, could be made in Moscow for a fraction of doing it in the UK. So, we returned to England with high hopes that there was a possible deal on the table.

That summer, I went on holiday with some good friends from the HTV days; it was just the usual package deal to Corfu. I guess I must have seemed pretty quiet and lonely, because apart from a few short-lived flings with Dateline partners, I'd been completely on my own. One of my friends, Julie, claimed she knew just the girl I'd like. Julie was in advertising sales for the West section of HTV and the lady in question was her counterpart on the Cardiff side. She gave me her telephone number and I said I'd call her.

I eventually got around to ringing the lady and spoke to Marie; she lived in Pencoed near her work in Cardiff. After a pleasant conversation, I suggested we meet up and have a drink. Then my mind went daft, as it occasionally does. 'How about half way, in Chepstow,' I said, 'at the Salmon pub?' We agreed on times. I then realised what a prat I'd been. Chepstow was a mere ten miles for me, but nearly fifty for Marie... Duh!

I arrived at the pub at the appointed hour and waited where we said we'd meet, in the car park. The time was set for seven, but at around a quarter to eight I decided that Marie wasn't coming. I eased the car out of the car park and passed a car going the other way, driven by a lone female. I stopped and we rolled windows down.

'Marie?' I asked.

'Bob?' she said.

Neither of us had realised that there were two car parks!

We had a good evening together, and our relationship has gone on from then to now. Marie and I have been married for twenty-one years! Gor blimey! Soon after, she moved into the house in Portishead with me, bringing her four children, Jo, Clare, Rachael and Sarah Jane with her. Including these new stepchildren, that meant I now had nine children!

There were hard times ahead. I returned from filming in Prague on the Spanish/Czech/British co-production *Nexus*, of which more later, to find that Bill Stair had leukaemia and was in a hospice in Bristol and not expected to live much longer. I went to meet him and he looked pretty scared. He asked me to hold his hand as we went over some of the crazy things we'd done in earlier years. Three days after that meeting Bill passed away. I was pleased to see John Boorman had made it to the funeral, and that he'd kept up with the things I'd done during my career.

A few days later, I woke up with Marie and kept forgetting what time and what day it was. She's a very perceptive lady and called the doctor; he came and immediately called an ambulance, suspecting a heart attack. Whilst in the ambulance, still believing I had had a heart attack, the ambulanceman gave me warfarin to thin my blood (which, when they finally found out what was wrong with me, was the total opposite of what I should have been given!). I was taken to Southmead Hospital in Bristol and kept under observation. I was quite unused to hospitals and the protocols of being in one. I was dying for a pee; so, being me – 'Oh I'm fine, don't worry' – I got out of bed to go to the toilet, but immediately collapsed… I couldn't feel my legs! I panicked and screamed out for help; then another patient pressed the red button to summon a nurse. I went into a kind of dreamy sleep and woke to find myself being pushed on a gurney down to surgery; my son Martin had signed the release forms for an operation to be performed on me. I really had no idea what was going on. Poor Marie was frightened to death, especially since, as she wasn't a family member (as yet) and even though we lived together, she couldn't make any decisions about what would happen to me. After twenty-four hours they still didn't know what was wrong with me. So, they put me in an ambulance and transported me to Bristol Royal Infirmary, where they had recently acquired a scanner. They found out that I'd had an aortic aneurysm which had ruptured…

Someone who looked to me like a boy in schoolcap and short trousers was introduced as the heart surgeon who was going to operate on me! I must have been delusional by that time… but he *was* young.

I underwent a six-hour open-heart operation. Marie was gently warned that people with ruptured aortas don't usually make it…

I came to in the recovery room, my ears bombarded by the *peep-peep-peep* of automatic blood pressure machines; and so began a slow painful recovery. 'So, you have kissed Death,' Pepe Maesso aptly remarked when we next met…

Marie and I got married just before Christmas that year. She pushed me up the aisle in a wheelchair. There was no escape!

I began to recover slowly, but was back at my desk within a month, now walking with a stick and a very uncomfortable leg-strap fixed on with

Velcro. My first task was to rewrite the sci-fi movie *Nexus*, but things had moved on there since my illness. Writer/director Juan Simón pulled out of the film because of illness and was replaced by José María Forqué, a bit of a Spanish aristocrat and doyen of the Spanish film industry. He decided to rewrite the script for himself to direct. I guessed he was of about the same standing in Spain that Michael Winner was in the UK.

He chose to reconstruct the already flimsy script to suit a very young actress he'd obviously fallen for. (She was nineteen and he seventy!) I was under the impression that the female lead was a huntress-type character, full of energy and daring. I had already cast the part with a very talented young actress, Oona Kirsch, who'd been in my HTV *Dramarama* film.

When I read Forqué's rewrite, I was astounded: the part of the kidnapped princess, originally a very tiny role in the film, was taken by Forqué's young lady friend. She was now the female lead! Not that that was too big a deal, but the script was now full of totally static chat scenes between her and the arch baddy, Tarn, played by Oliver Tobias. These scenes only served to slow the action down, simply because there was no point to them other than to provide exposure for the young actress. At this point I decided to step back from the script side of *Nexus*.

It was to be filmed in Czechoslovakia, with the special effects done in the Barrandov Studios in Prague, who had a peerless reputation for animation and special effects.

We were in Prague following its recent release from Russian occupation, and a kind of misty-eyed euphoria abounded in the place. And who could blame them? At the same time the people seemed rudderless and just jogged along in the vague glow of 'freedom and democracy' – the era of the Russian tank in Wenceslas Square painted pink. This atmosphere also pervaded the Barrandov animation studios who were doing our special effects; and to my horror I found that, virtually to a man, the animators were pissed out of their heads most of the time! When you visited them, they would always offer vodka or wine from their office fridge; wanting you to join them. I began to smell vodka and disaster approaching... and when, after the first day of filming, director Forqué through interpreters told the whole Czech film unit: 'You are all cretins!' I knew all was not right.

The film lurched on with dispute after dispute. The director became very sullen when his 'protégée', as he called his teenage lead, started sleeping with one of the British contingent.

One day the Czech producer called a meeting to inform us that they had gone a million dollars over budget. This was seen as no big deal, since our agreement only dealt with tasks and not costs – i.e. we asked 'Can you cover this or that part of the filming?' and, when agreed, your share of profits amounted to the percentage of the budget you'd undertaken to cover. Actual money costs were irrelevant in this type of agreement.

From beginning to end *Nexus* was a total disaster. The budget dispute ended in a lawsuit between the Czechs and the Spanish and included us. It was to be settled in the European Court. Somehow, it doesn't seem to matter how, the Czechs won their case and stripped Maesso and us of our sales territories. The final film would be virtually totally owned by the Czechs. Things got worse. With no money coming in, it was like riding a runaway train toward the buffers. Should we jump or hang on? Roger and I decided to leave our office, and I moved house with Marie and the children to a rented cottage in Oldbury-on-Severn.

The previous year had been quite hard to believe. They say that, separately, a break-up of a relationship, or a death in the family or particularly moving house can all cause terrible anxiety. Not one to do things by halves, I did all three at once and things were looking more than a little bleak.

Chapter Fourteen
One Man and His Dog

BACK FROM PRAGUE, THERE was still more bad news. The Czechs had taken the whole thing over... but at last it was finished with...

I had a call from Aardman Animations; they wanted me to meet their new partner, Nick Park, and talk about possibly doing a script. Nick had recently joined them and was the one who'd done the brilliant Heat Electric ads with the animals talking in human voices, thus combining the best of *Animated Conversations* that I'd found so marvellous with really funny animal characters that had crazy things going on behind them. It looked like, in Nick Park, Aardman had found the perfect man to enhance their style of animation.

We met at their studios in Clifton where they showed me Nick's first Wallace and Gromit film, *A Grand Day Out*, and said they'd like to do another half-hour story. Nick told me that *Grand Day Out* was in fact made at his film school as his final graduation piece. I was intrigued by his humour and we were left alone in a room to discuss possible ideas. I had the distinct feeling we were left alone to see how we got on and that somewhere there must be a two-way mirror and that we were being watched.

The man who was commissioning the new programme was someone I'd met in 1968, Colin Rose; he was one of the directors of the late night comedy shows I'd written for and acted in for BBC West. He was now Head of Animation at BBC2. It was he who had suggested me as a possible writing partner with Nick.

Nick and I soon got on to talking about films: British film comedies – which ones we liked, and didn't like; cartoon characters like *Top Cat*, *Roadrunner* and especially *Tom and Jerry*; then about paper comics. We are both keen *Beano* fans and before long we were laughing at some of the old *Beano* stories together.

We were commissioned to write a thirty-minute Wallace and Gromit adventure. The Aardman guys sent me a load of ideas they'd been working on: a huge sheaf of drawings, all possible as fantastic story ideas, but there were scores of them! They included giant robots, spacemen, zoo stories starring a penguin, underground creatures… I have likened getting the final story of *The Wrong Trousers* out of it as resembling making up a story 'train' out of a virtual marshalling yard full of ideas. We started to select specific items: one was the Techno Trousers (ex-NASA!) – a beautifully mad *Beano*-type idea. Nick and I started building the story around them.

We felt the Penguin had promise too, so he was taken on board along with something to do with a train set. We thought Wallace would be the sort of man who would not only own a model train but set it up for some ingenious purpose, like serving at the table… Again, Wallace is unashamedly a bit of a geek but it just makes you admire him more: for being so English, the man that never grows up, the cheese-loving Peter Pan of Preston and his faithful dog Gromit. Wallace and Gromit enjoy a cosy spouse-like relationship. Gromit though is more intelligent than his master, or perhaps more 'streetwise' would be the modern equivalent. As for plot, we were happy with the domestic set-up, a nice simple one: the day of Gromit's birthday, and the Techno-Trouser present from Wallace that wasn't for Gromit at all – it was to save Wallace taking him for walkies! It then builds to show how Wallace gets caught up in events, not having the nerve to stop them; Wallace is crass enough, and daft enough, to allow the sinister Penguin to take over Gromit's room instead of the 'room to let'… I've always enjoyed thrillers, especially fifties *film noir*, and the film edges that way for the robbery sequence. Then the finale – the amazing train chase: Nick's *pièce de résistance* perhaps?

After I'd finished my work on the script, I remember being asked if I'd like to see rushes of the previous day's work on *Trousers*. I was eager to see how things were going, so I drove the twelve miles into Bristol full of expectation. At the studio I waited for the (16mm) film to be looped into the projector and then watched the fantastic shots of Gromit track-laying ahead of himself in the chase.

The rushes lasted for fifteen seconds!

Working with Nick was quite different from working with Dave Martin. Although we had a similar attitude toward working on the scripts, Nick was always on call to the studio for meetings, or perhaps work on a commercial, so that there wasn't the same nine-to-five-every-day continuity I'd known with Dave. Nick would give me a list of days when he was available and I would fit in with him. When we did get a day's work it wasn't hard going by any means, since we spent most of the time laughing at ideas that might be put into the script.

On seeing the final cut, there was a kind of suppressed euphoria; after all, we didn't yet know if we'd hit the right note. Then Nick told me of the various European animation awards the film had won. Aardman were also submitting it to the American Academy for consideration for an Oscar. I just smiled; and thought to myself: 'Oscar? That's the Hollywood I saw in the cinema with my mother when I was a kid – clips of the glittering ceremony shown during the *Movietone News*, watching people like Gregory Peck and Katherine Hepburn grasping their golden man... nothing to do with me and little old England... no way...'

I saw Nick accepting the Oscar on morning TV. I couldn't quite believe my eyes. I was walking on air for days. There were some deserved celebrations on Nick's return from La-la-land. To hold an Oscar is a special feeling and I took it home for a day so that my family could share the feeling, before it joined the growing case of awards won by that very special Bristol enterprise. It was at another award ceremony for another Wallace and Gromit success that satirist Willie Rushton remarked that the world's animation centre of gravity used to be Prague, but that now it had shifted to Bristol.

I was asked to join Nick again for a second thirty-minute Wallace and Gromit. I sat down and began to think, 'How the hell do you follow that?' So Nick and I got down to what is now called some 'blue sky' thinking. We watched a lot of films to inspire us. One of the things we wanted was for Wallace to fall in love. We watched loads of films but finally decided on *Brief Encounter* as a model for the love scenes with its very British reserve.

If anything, Wallace is the epitome of that particular British attitude toward emotion where burning desire is restrained to the point of agony.

The other thing Nick wanted to do was have sheep in it, since in the Wallace and Gromit household there is a painting of a sheep on the wall. I recalled some of the research Dave and I had done in the eighties for an episode of the countrified police series *Hunters Walk* which was about sheep rustling. I'd always imagined rustling as being confined to Texas ranches in 'B' movie westerns, but we discovered that it was rife in rural England at that time. The creation of the lovable escaped lamb, Shaun, came about as he progressed in the story from naughty lamb to hero. At one point we were worried that Shaun might take up too much of Gromit's role, but I feel it came out pretty well in the end; they seemed to be about equal, with Gromit having incredibly funny scenes like the one where he's cleaning Wendolene's window on a bungee rope, the sad scene when he's in jail and not forgetting the exhilarating aeroplane sidecar sequence – done perhaps, I like to think, in honour of my love for aircraft?

Again the Aardman fun factory came up trumps with the finished film. Called *A Close Shave*, it was entered for various awards, and again it won the American Academy Oscar, the BAFTA award and the British Animation award for best script. That was a nice one to receive since it specifically honoured the script.

It was a time for celebration. Nick had now won three Oscars, a very rare and amazing achievement. At the BAFTA party after the award ceremony I was talking with Peter Sallis who, in honour of Nick and his animation, said: 'I've met two geniuses in my life – one was Orson Welles, the other is Nick Park.' I'm sure most people wouldn't disagree with that sentiment.

After this, Nick and Aardman went on to make the film *Chicken Run* which I wasn't involved in. It was their first feature film and their first outing with DreamWorks in the deal they'd made to make several animated feature films.

Around this time I was contacted by a man called Paul Tams. He'd worked on *Doctor Who* as an illustrator and prop designer. He asked me if I might be interested in resurrecting the Doctor's doggy companion, K9? But doing him in a completely revamped way. In a word, the mutt was to be – like his erstwhile master – regenerated... The thing is, as previously mentioned, when Dave Martin and I first suggested the character in *The*

Invisible Enemy, it was our intention that K9 would hover and float just above the ground; but unfortunately, being long before the days of CGI, it was not achievable by the BBC at that time. I wondered if I should get involved, it having been twelve years since K9 was on screen; but then I decided – why not?

I did a series idea and based it all in space, so that the CGI would be easier to do. I also wrote a first episode. Paul and I then formed a company to market our new series idea. We had some interest from the BBC initially but also from Buena Vista – the Disney arm in the UK. Things progressed with them on *K9*, but had to be put on hold as I was asked to work on an animated feature film in the USA.

A highly successful series of children's books called *Miss Spider*, written and lavishly illustrated by David Kirk, were published in America in the eighties. They quickly became extremely popular and were even read aloud on a US children's TV channel by the then First Lady, Hillary Clinton; later, I met Alec Baldwin and Kim Basinger when they did a reading from the *Miss Spider* books at a New York book fair. The books were bestsellers and came to the notice of Universal Pictures, who asked David and his publishers to put together a film idea based on them.

However, David Kirk had an idea he desperately wanted to work on in advance of a *Miss Spider* movie. He was passionately into robots (apparently he went to loads of fancy-dress parties as a kid and always went as a robot!) so he'd come up with an idea called *Nova's Ark* – Nova being the main character, a young robot, in the story. I was contacted by David's publisher, Nicholas Callaway of Callaway Editions, who told me that both he and David Kirk were avid Wallace and Gromit fans and that they'd contacted Aardman to see if Nick Park would be interested in doing the work. Nick of course declined since, having started his own feature film, he was too busy working on *Chicken Run*; so he recommended yours truly. Nicholas Callaway invited me to go to New York and meet with David to see if I'd like to work on the project.

New York had always been on my list of 'must see' places, so to maybe go there to work would be especially exciting. We met in the Callaway Editions office in Greenwich Village. David Kirk was a studious type whom I felt would take a while to get to know, but I judged that it was worth going along with for a trial period. David lived in upstate New York with his daughter Violet, from his first marriage, in a tiny village. No more than a crossroads with a garage and a shop, King Ferry is on one of the Finger Lakes – five long narrow lakes stretching down from Lake Ontario to around the university town of Ithaca.

I flew up to Ithaca from New York's La Guardia regional air terminal on a tiny commuter plane, to be met by David. We spent several days talking over his ideas. I saw how he worked on his illustrations; it was amazing – he was absolutely meticulous, painting every last tiny detail on the creatures and plants in his books. As a bit of a painter myself I really appreciated the work that went into his pictures. We talked of all sorts and found we were in general agreement about most things; and, even in that short first visit, I got to like and admire David, a committed conservationist and animal lover – too much for me sometimes, like when the pet mouse was allowed on the dinner table! The clincher of course was that *Nova's Ark* was firmly in the science fiction genre and I was a sucker for that!

Returning to New York, I met with Nicholas Callaway again and said I'd love to work on *Nova's Ark*. So, a deal was done with my agent. I was to spend my time in King Ferry with David, putting together a treatment of around thirty pages outlining the story of the proposed movie, and then submit it to Universal. The idea was that I stayed in upstate New York with David until we'd finished it. I began to realise that this could take a lot longer that I'd imagined, since David's painting work was so much in demand that we rarely had time to get stuck into the story and I reckoned I could be there for up to six months.

From time to time we'd go into Ithaca, which for me was a godsend: I needed coffee bars and shops. Even though I lived in the country at home, the feeling of isolation in King Ferry was pretty powerful. I hired a car and felt free at last to wander around the countryside, which as it happens is a lot like England – or perhaps Scotland.

Along came Christmas, and Marie came over to stay for a couple of weeks and we spent time in New York doing all the touristy things; the only trouble was that it was twelve degrees below zero! We went on an open-top bus tour of the city and sat in the front seats, freezing to death. The driver called up to us: 'Hey, you gotta be British sittin' up there!' We stood it for around ten minutes, then scuttled down into the relative warmth of the bus interior – warmer, but you couldn't see much above street level. Then we went to the Empire State Building. Marie was really keen, but I'm not too good on heights (once having had vertigo on the Pont du Gard in France). Anyway, we got to the observation platform; I took a quick look around and then waited for Marie to take her time. I noticed that the building was moving slightly, rocking from side to side in the high wind; Marie suddenly turned to me and said, 'Right, let's get down.' Next, Staten Island; the Statue of Liberty followed.

We spent the Christmas with David and his girlfriend Kathy. As if on cue, snow fell on Christmas Day. I cooked a goose for lunch, but David felt it looked too much like the real, live bird to eat. Marie popped it into a picnic basket for Boxing Day, when we took a trip to visit Niagara Falls, which was only about a hundred and twenty miles from King Ferry. The snow got worse as we reached Buffalo, but we managed to get to the Falls without mishap. I don't think I've ever felt so cold in my life as I did on that Boxing Day. The Niagara Falls were magnificent, but as we watched in awe, the spray froze on us! It's not until you see something as powerful as Niagara Falls that you get a real shock at the power and energy of nature. I hate the word 'awesome' as currently used, or overused, but that's what the Falls are. Totally, utterly awesome. Marie spent a few more days in New York before going home to the girls and another family gathering.

Not long after, Universal Pictures asked to meet with David and me to discuss the direction of the movie. So, along with Nicholas Callaway we went to Los Angeles to meet them at the studios. A new editor had been put on to our project and was very helpful, except she kept reminding us she'd worked on the *Tarzan* cartoon which I personally hated. It was the victory of crazy frenetic movement over action and content – it went at top speed from beginning to end, lacking any moment of reflection on what Tarzan's goals, aims or feelings were; it just rattled on without pausing for breath. The producers at Universal told us that they felt what we were doing story wise was pretty much as they'd hoped, but they had to know what the lead character's 'issue' was; without that, they couldn't proceed to a script.

It seems to me that if you'd asked what Wallace's 'issue' was in *The Wrong Trousers* I wouldn't be able to tell you. The story works, and that's it; you could try imposing 'issues' on him or Gromit, but I'm sure they wouldn't sound true. The Penguin had an 'issue' though: he wanted to be rich!

We came back to New York determined to find an 'issue' for Nova, the young robot that the film centred around. Then came a shock. David had been commissioned to paint a calendar and it had a contractual delivery date on it. David with his slow meticulous way of working was way off the deadline. There was only one thing to do: to remove any distraction so that he could finish the commission. I suddenly found myself living in a New York hotel on Times Square with a clear view out the window of the moving newsflashes on the sign across the street.

I soon began to feel my way around the Big Apple and decided that the best way to get around was to walk. So I walked all over the place: to the Hudson River to see the USS *Independence,* an aircraft carrier moored in the dock and converted into a museum; to the Rockefeller Centre, the Guggenheim and the New York Metropolitan Museum on Central Park. One evening I accompanied some of the Callaway people to Radio City, an amazingly beautiful Art Deco building, to see the British group Radiohead. To cover themselves on health and safety grounds, the Radio City management handed out earplugs on entry!

I discovered an amazing little lunch bar, frequented by the comedian Jerry Lewis, invitingly called Caviarteria! Soon, however, all thought of leisurely lunches dispersed when I became one of the workers at the publishing office of Callaway Editions. I walked the two miles to Greenwich Village every morning, eyes agog at the streets which resemble deep canyons of concrete and glass. Once there I would spend my day at the office, which was full of interesting and friendly people. There, there was no lunch break: all employees were expected to eat their lunch at their desks. And certainly no cigarette breaks! I got on really well with most of them and especially with the assistant editor, Antoinette White, a highly intelligent, dedicated and talented lady. She was doing a 'coffee table' photo-memorial book to Princess Diana whilst I was there and worked long hours to make sure everything was exactly right. Her partner was a Mormon from Salt Lake City and had been mayor there for a while. He was always up for a spirited political discussion. I think he had ambitions to run for President, and I remember thinking: 'President? A Mormon?' How wrong I was.

I was in the Big Apple, the bustling metropolis in total contrast to the remote country upstate, and I got to love it more each day I was there. David's publisher, Nicholas, was now working with me on the Nova story and we reported back to David each time we got a section finished. During our script sessions I found out that Nicholas was rather a good golfer. In fact, I should have realised, but there is a complete set of golfing paraphernalia – clubs, balls, gloves – with the trade name Callaway, and Nicholas' father was founder and head of that company which is perhaps most famous for the gargantuan driver club nicknamed 'Big Bertha'. So Nicholas had golfing in his blood! I was a keen golfer myself at the time so Nicholas invited me to his Long Island 'cottage' – a five-bedroom mansion with a swimming pool and huge garden – so that we could play a round of golf at his club: the Golf Club of America, their equivalent of St Andrews and in fact, I was told, designed by a Scot and based on that course. Nicholas played off four, which is in the big league; I was off a lowly eighteen, but the handicap system of the game is more than fair for players of differing abilities. We played a foursome, but unbeknownst to me they were playing their regular betting game which, although it sounded like small amounts of money per hole, began to accumulate over eighteen holes. I guessed I'd better be prepared to part with some cash when I noticed that the members did practice shots with brand new balls, hitting them into the sea which skirted the course! I held my own and didn't disgrace Nicholas, but I found my tally for their arcane betting game was a hundred and twenty dollars. Though at least the golf round was free!

After eighteen holes I was starving as usual and we went into the clubhouse for lunch. I wasn't allowed in without a blazer, so an ill-fitting one was found in the locker room for me. This caused me to be late for lunch and they were all sitting around the table waiting. They said they'd ordered me something light as a starter. To my surprise, and delight as it happened, along came a huge lobster which was delicious; then fabulous crab cakes as a main, all washed down with an excellent Oregon Pinot Noir. I thought: this is going to set me back a few quid! But the other two, our opponents who'd won the game, insisted on paying for everything. Nicholas told me later that one of them was Diana Ross's manager and the other was a banker. I accepted their generosity without a qualm.

Nicholas and I were getting on well with the Nova story; there seemed to be a spark between us. He suggested that I move into the new house he'd bought in Brooklyn Heights, a typical 'brownstone' Brooklyn house. It was four storeys high, and from the hallway a wide central spiral staircase connected each floor. Every curve of the staircase wall was adorned with nineteenth-century murals, from the bottom to the top of the house: scenes of the British surrendering New York to Washington, and another of Indian peace-talk meetings. The whole thing was lavish and magnificent.

The house was on Willow Street, one of the more salubrious streets of the Heights. I was to stay in the basement. I occupied a large room next to the old servant's kitchen range which had been completely refurbished, so I could do my own cooking instead of going to restaurants every day. Through the back window I could just see the garden and the roots of a giant wisteria tree that covered the balconies at the back of the house.

Nicholas lived there with his Japanese wife Ukiney and his two lovely kids whom I rarely saw unless I went to Long Island with them at the weekend. It seemed that number 70 Willow Street had strong literary connections; there were stories that a previous owner, a philanthropic businessman who had a great admiration for writing, would let rooms to struggling authors such as Norman Mailer and Truman Capote before they made it on the literary scene. I came across an autobiography of Truman Capote, and on reading it came to a chapter where he recalls living at none other than number 70 Willow Street, Brooklyn Heights. It was eerie reading his description of the room he occupied in his day – in fact, exactly the room in which I was reading it! It was in that very room that Capote penned *Breakfast at Tiffany's*. That can't be bad, I thought to myself.

My walk into Greenwich Village now took me over the central footpath on the magnificent Brooklyn Bridge, through the Wall Street area and then on up toward midtown. I must say, before I lived there I always thought of New York as a bit of a violent place (maybe because of the movies I'd seen?). However, I was surprised to find that I've never felt so safe anywhere as I did in New York. It wasn't long before I was driven to the office by Nicholas when he took his delightful kids to school, way uptown: a forty-minute journey up the East River and across Central Park to the West Side and then back down Broadway and Third Avenue to Greenwich Village – a huge 'U' shape drive during the morning rush hour. Again I lapped it all up.

Nicholas and I were getting to a point where we thought we had the *Nova's Ark* story in good shape, so we got David to come down to New York and go over it before we went to present it to Universal again. We felt we'd got the 'issue' thing cracked and had conceived what we felt was a fantastic OTT baddy robot we named Kaali. David was a little bit resentful not to have been in on all the story, and who can blame him? However, that's what comes with being very talented. People want to buy your work and if you're commissioned to do a picture or, as in this case, a calendar, then you have to fulfil that contract.

We departed for Los Angeles in good spirits. Nicholas had booked us into the highly posh Beverly Hills Hotel where, in the famous garden restaurant, film deals are talked over, scripts commissioned and stars are cast. I was agreeably surprised and delighted to meet and briefly pass the time of day with Jamie Lee Curtis, who was occupying a room next to mine. (Show-off!)

We went to Universal and were shown into the boardroom; and then something very odd happened. Three people completely unknown to us were welcomed by those present, and we were told that these were the new heads of Universal Pictures. They had us pitch our story in its burnished condition, then in a quite brusque manner told us that they'd seen the project when it was offered to Columbia Tristar, they didn't like it then and still didn't like it... We were out... The entire Universal board had been replaced by the heads of Columbia Tristar in a kind of top-executive musical chairs! We just happened to be unlucky in getting the ones who'd seen the project before and had for whatever reason rejected it.

I went back to England, sad about the project, but feeling personally enriched by the whole experience. So I was back in Bristol with a bump.

After all the trouble with the Portishead house and three years of renting a place in Oldbury-on-Severn, Marie and I found ourselves in a position where all four girls had finally left home. The oldest, Sarah Jane, had married a colleague of Marie's at her college. Rachael took herself off to university, and we got the two Down's syndrome girls into a residential home not far away. There was a sudden feeling of freedom and we decided to buy ourselves a house.

The best place we came across was a neat little townhouse in Bristol, a three-storey place with the ground floor as a garage and workshop; first floor, lounge and kitchen; and on the top floor, a bathroom, two double bedrooms and a single. The first thing we did was convert the garage into my office. And so we'd fetched up in a pleasant leafy road in Westbury-on-Trym, near Marie's work at Filton College, where she was now Head of Drama. Perfect. Things were nice, for a while… Then, for one good reason or another, the girls all came back! We now found ourselves squeezed into a tiny house with every space filled. Even my office had to be sacrificed as a bedroom (moan, groan!). So, things were a little rough at home when I was asked to go down to see Aardman, though not to see Nick Park.

The producer of the first two stories I'd worked on was keen to keep Wallace and Gromit in the public eye and he asked me to come up with some ideas for five-minute stories, as some slots of that length could well become available. I was to work with Steve Box, a brilliant animator who'd done some fantastic work on *Wrong Trousers* and *Close Shave* as Nick's second-in-command as it were. We began to get some ideas together and agreed to then separate to work on them alone. It was during this period that he then came up with a new idea of his own and approached the producer with it; since Steve was 'in house', I didn't know much about it until we met again and I realised the producer had received a completely new story, one which I knew nothing about. It was a wee bit off-putting; and, through working with Steve, I realised that perhaps he believed that scripts weren't necessary for animation, and that the animator could do them by storyboarding ideas, that is, do drawings in the story sequence. I began to realise that it was also his opinion that writers were totally unnecessary. I was pleased when that particular relationship came to an end. He is of course entitled to his opinions, though I don't think many people in the business would necessarily share them.

Aardman were in a partnership deal with DreamWorks and had several visits from their Head of Animation, Jeffrey Katzenberg. There were rumours that after the success of *Chicken Run*, it was time there was a Wallace and Gromit movie.

Nick and I spent a good few days setting out a situation and possible storyline, starting from story threads we'd done after *Close Shave* of Wendolene maybe returning and merging her in with a typical British country fruit and vegetable competition. We decided upon the vegetable competition idea, and that Wallace and Gromit would be pest controllers ('Antipesto!'); then, after watching a few Lon Chaney werewolf movies, decided to try and combine the two and create… a Vegetarian Horror Movie!

On the home front we had no alternative but to move into a bigger house and, rather hastily, bought a five-bedroom house not far up the road. This house had the space, but it was on a busy main road right next to traffic lights. As cat lovers, we obviously brought our moggies to the new place, but it was so close to the previous address that one of them – a great big grey fluffy ball called, rather unaptly, Willow – kept going the five hundred metres or so back to the old house. He was a tactile gentle giant of a cat and was loved by all the little kids nearby, the only problem being that when he lovingly brushed himself against their legs he would knock them over! Another person who absolutely adored him – she used to send him Christmas cards! – was Gladys, a widow who lived three doors away from our old house. She fed him on his daily return to our old address. After several trips to get him back, we gave in and asked Gladys if she'd like to keep him, since we didn't want to risk him getting run over on the busy road outside our new address. She was, of course, delighted to take him. We often dropped by to see how he was getting on; one time, Gladys informed us that she'd opened a Post Office account for him… I looked at Willow and I swear he grinned at me!

I'd started painting again and so I was very pleased to receive a birthday present from Marie of a wooden garden shed, more of a small summerhouse really; this was my studio and sanctuary where I could go to draw or paint or just contemplate… I might even think up story ideas.

There was a big meeting at Aardman to discuss the ideas Nick and I had come up with for the movie. DreamWorks was represented as usual by Jeffrey Katzenberg. Nick and I pitched 'Antipesto' and the vegetable competition where a mysterious Were-Rabbit is destroying all the entries. Jeffrey warmed to the idea, but was a bit concerned about the Britishness of the basic story and how it would 'translate' to American audiences; but we agreed to disagree about how much that really could influence the film. What was needed was a film that should be fast and funny and rely on solid storytelling and strong characters to provide a unique platform for – we hoped– hilariously funny jokes.

I also remember Jeffrey wondering what Wallace would learn from this adventure. 'He must learn something.'

The answer was, 'No. Wallace never learns anything. He is an utter and complete lovable moron.'

After a moment of thought, Jeffrey smiled in agreement.

In the coming days I was to learn that Steve Box was to co-direct the film with Nick. On hearing this I began to worry that he would want to be involved in writing the script; given my previous dealings with him, it was something I would be concerned about, but I was given assurances that he would only come in at stages of the script for discussion. This, of course didn't happen and from day one, the script was written by a troika: myself, Nick and Steve Box. It was not something I was looking forward to. Soon disagreements began to erupt and I always seemed to be in a minority of one. However, I stuck with it. I could not believe that after a year and a half of writing we still hadn't got the thing cracked. Or even half cracked!

Inevitably, the rift between myself and Steve began to affect the way we were working, so I was hardly surprised when I was asked to become a 'consultant'. I left with a sour taste in my mouth. All I will say is that Steve Box is a brilliant animator, as testified on the Wallace and Gromit shorts and other things he's done; but I wouldn't have the brazen cheek to tell him how to animate – yet somehow, sadly, everybody thinks they can write as well as, or better than, a dedicated professional writer.

The writing went on for another two years and I got more and more worried by how the film was going and sent impassioned 'devil's advocate' criticisms. In the end, the final shooting script reverted to – with modifications – pretty much the script as it had been when I left.

Wallace and Gromit in The Curse of the Were-Rabbit turned out to be a terrific success, winning an Oscar for Best Animated Film and the Alexander Korda Award for the most outstanding British film. To be the best British film was a wonderful accolade. We couldn't have wished for better. Another thing: to my surprise and delight, I was nominated for a BAFTA award. Standing there on the stage, grasping the award, I couldn't help wishing my Mum, Dad and Roger were still around to share my joy. The rest of the evening, the dinner, the mingling with guests all seemed like a dream – or maybe the whole mad wonder of it all fuelled with champagne caused me to float around like a butterfly with a daft fixed grin on me boat!

The BAFTA award mask is a really heavy piece of kit, as they say; and after the ceremony, when I was getting back to my hotel, I found that there was no pocket I could put it in. So I had to carry the bloody thing – and me in my penguin suit as well! I finally decided I had to find a bag to carry it in, so there I was with a BAFTA award left sitting on the pavement whilst I looked through a rubbish bin to find a bag! I found a suitable one, a Tesco bag, and finally got a cab. The cabby, noting my attire, enquired if it was really necessary to dress these days for shopping at Tesco? I smiled. The perfect end to a fantastic night.

After the euphoria had died down, there was another character begging for attention: K9, the metal mutt from *Doctor Who* in his regenerated form. Firstly I had to clear things with Dave Martin, and asked him if he'd like to be involved. He was well into his third novel by then and was happy for me to exploit our character and to get paid for its use. With that, Paul Tams and I started sending the series idea around. We had a positive response from a producer I'd met and got on well with at London Films, the lovely Rosie Bunting. She was at the BBC as Head of Children's Programming.

However, just as we started talking seriously about making the K9 series, Rosie moved to Buena Vista, Disney's arm in London who, as previously mentioned, had seen the project. Rosie was to occupy a similar post as at the BBC, so all was not lost. Rosie felt that K9 would be a suitable piece to fill a Disney children's slot in the *Power Rangers* area. It appeared that all the British employees thought a K9 series would be fantastic, but all the American ones thought not. I must commend Rosie for working so hard to get the K9 series away, but first she asked if I could make it a fifteen-minute show. Paul Tams and I went over it again and worked out that, yes we could do it, but that several episodes would have to be two-parters that joined up into half-hours… We waited some time for a response to this, but then Rosie asked if we could make *K9* into a three-minute interstitial… whatever that was! It was time to say no. It was impossible.

We had, of course, pursued several other possibilities; and, after Disney, the best one was with distributors Park Entertainment, headed up by Jim Howell who had a reputation for putting deals together, usually with South African, Australian or Canadian partners. Park had taken an option on *K9* and, over a period of three years, come up with several possible deals. They too approached Disney; and with a new man in charge there, we were back with them again in a mooted Canadian/UK co-production.

The doing of deals was a new and frankly unnerving experience. I'd previously been used to people wanting me to write something and paying for it. 'Simples,' as the meerkat says. I thought I'd just get on writing it and bring in other writers to do other episodes. However, in this situation, in the world of co-productions, despite the fact that Paul and I came up with the series idea and K9 was, of course, my character, I found out that the first thing to happen in any such deal is that the creator is downgraded, pushed aside and kept out of all decision-making. In my naivety, I thought my reputation on *Doctor Who* and Wallace and Gromit and other things would be enough: but no. Our new man at Disney, after a rather heavy conversation, told me that he knew two Canadian writers who would love to do episodes one and two. Park Entertainment's Simon Barnes hinted that it was a question of standing my ground and not doing the series, or allowing it and see the series go ahead. Which did I want…?

Of course I wanted the series to go ahead. The two writers did the first two episodes of the new K9 series. I edited them pretty thoroughly and felt that things would be okay if I had that amount of control over the final scripts. My integrity seemed intact again. Paul, Simon and I went to drink our success in doing at least a partial deal with Disney; all the rest should fall into place in no time…That was 6th July 2005, remembered because it was the day before the London bombings.

The setting up of the K9 series was to rumble on over the next few years. I went to see Dave down in Dorset where we were interviewed for a *Doctor Who* video. When I told him about the K9 situation, he recounted how he'd undergone a similar situation when he'd come up with an idea for a series called *Harbour Lights*. His opening episode was rejected and the whole series written by someone else; and, despite the fact that it was filmed in West Bay, where he lived, Dave wasn't welcome anywhere near the set of any filming! 'Be warned,' said Dave.

A call from Nick Park. He asked me to come and talk about a new Wallace and Gromit 'short' since the BBC were interested in doing another. We met up and began to talk over ideas. There was still a sort of hankering to bring Wendolene back, but then we thought it would be better if it was a new character altogether. Then we thought it might be nice if Gromit found himself a 'bitch'! We found ourselves harking back to

216

the early thoughts on *Were-Rabbit*, when Lady Tottington was a far less posh character. We had ideas about this lady inheriting a bakery and having to keep it going; then the *Psycho* influence came into being, and as we worked the story it became clear that our heroes should be the bakers and the woman be a bread-hating, baker-hating psychopath! A gentle woman turned into a monstrous multiple murderer by cruel circumstances and… the bitterness of rejection. Gromit's bit of fluff would be the brave lovely Fluffles who finally rebels against her cruel mistress to protect Gromit and is welcomed into his and Wallace's world.

Yeah, that's a good theme… why not.

Our research took us to working windmills, watermills and powered bakery mills, but we needed something creepy as well as sweet old working windmills. We got a copy of Hitchcock's spy film *Foreign Correspondent* and studied the creepy windmill chase scene – that was more like it.

Working on *A Matter of Loaf and Death* was sheer pleasure. Nick and I found ourselves laughing about the characters more than ever before. It seemed a lot easier to write, maybe because we were more relaxed; and once we'd found the character (and the 'issue') of Piella, the overweight ex-Bake-O-Lite girl, the script took flight, so to speak. We went to the BBC in London and pitched the story and had a very positive response, and so the film was on! I was very flattered to have a claymation model character of myself as Baker Bob… even though he does get killed in the first minute! I got to sing *If I Knew You Were Coming I'd've Baked a Cake*! Of course I was hoping for a spin-off series, but it hasn't happened yet…

On *Loaf and Death* I got much more involved in the making of the film and worked at Aardman during the animatic stage, the black and white storyboard filmed and then cut to length, changing Peter Sallis and Sally Lindsay's pre-recorded dialogue to fit and cutting it where necessary. I got on famously with the producer Steve Pegram and under his supervision it all went like clockwork… or should I say animation? The completed film was finished in exactly the predicted time – almost to the minute at six o'clock on the last day.

In parallel with *Loaf and Death* the K9 series was beginning to come together. New co-producers had been found willing to come on board with us in Australia, and amazingly even after our Disney contact in the Canadian deal had moved on, his replacement was still interested in coming in as a third co-production partner to take up the European satellite rights; but there were several knotty problems to get over before we could go ahead. It was our intention to use the original K9 in our opening episode and see him 'regenerate' as the new improved version. We realised that because of existing rights to the character and design of K9, if we did an independent story, nothing to do with the BBC, it would not be possible to relate the new series to *Doctor Who* in any way – even though Paul's and my idea was that K9's regeneration powers had been bestowed upon him by the Time Lords.

It is worth mentioning that we offered the series to the BBC twice: once when it looked as if *Doctor Who* would never come back in 2003, then again when Russell T. Davies created his very welcome and amazing reinstatement of the Doctor in totally new glossy feature-film style. A spokesman for the BBC said: 'A K9 spin-off would be a spin-off too far.' So Paul and I, having expended so much effort on the series, had no alternative but to look elsewhere to get the show up and running. It was at this time that Russell T. Davies contacted us and asked if it would be possible to use the original K9 in an episode of the new series, Christopher Eccleston having passed the role of the Doctor on to David Tennant. It is just the utter contrariness of things that this situation conspired to arise just when we'd made a deal with a co-producer. I was disinclined at first, after the BBC's outright rejection of the new K9; however, we felt that a re-emergence of K9 would be good bit of 'reminder' publicity of the dog for our own series. I thought *School Reunion* which brought back K9 and the late, very sadly lamented, Lis Sladen as Sarah Jane was the perfect mix of old and new *Who*. Everything seemed to blend in exceptionally well. There was also talk of a series for Sarah Jane for which K9 might be needed…

Once we'd established a deal with our Australian partners and the Disney part was put in place, there was a meeting with Disney, our London distributors Park Entertainment, Paul and me. It was good to hear the new Disney executive talking about the show in a very positive way. The surprise was that, in his opinion, the show should be earthbound and set in 2050s London – which, of course, would be shot in Brisbane! He moved quickly on and announced that he knew a couple of writers in Australia who would be perfect to work with us to create the new earthbound series.

Over the following month Paul and I started to address the Disney requests, and found that the series worked perfectly well in the 'future Earth' scenario; and it didn't matter a jot that we would be filming in Brisbane, since with the marvels of computer graphics we could 'drop in' such iconic features as St Paul's, Big Ben and Westminster.

Then suddenly we were on a flight to Australia! It was amazing how quickly things moved once agreements were in place. We were to meet with the two Australian writers, with whom we spent a week nailing down a new format and 'bible'. I felt a little uncomfortable with them, but I guessed it was because I'd been told they were to write the first two episodes of the series. Our Park partners said it was inevitable, since the Australians were putting up the lion's share of the cash, that they should have control over the series; and since government money was involved it meant using Australian talent to the full. I felt, however disbelieving, that I had to accept this, knowing no different at the time. However, I was script editor so I felt that if it was like my experience with the Canadian situation I'd still have overall control of my character and series.

Things didn't turn out that way. I asked the Oz writers to come up with an outline of a couple of pages so that we could get the detail and direction of episodes one and two, before going ahead with scripts. I waited several weeks for the outlines to arrive. To my utter consternation they were not two or even three pages, but thirty to thirty-five pages long! Virtually scripts, without the dialogue. Furthermore, episode two had only two pages which featured the star of the show, K9!

I hit the roof and demanded to know what was going on. I was told in no uncertain terms that these writers were Disney's chosen men and that they would not only be in charge of the writing, but would have editorial control over other writers, directors and even actors in the series! I was new to all this and quite frankly shell-shocked by it. Paul and I had worked on the K9 series for eleven years, moving it toward getting a production made, and now things looked as if they were crumbling before our eyes. I was unsure what to do and so returned to the UK leaving Paul to hold the fort.

When I got back I felt like pulling out of the whole deal. I was miserable and pissed off. I tried not to think about it, but then I received more and more desperate emails from Paul, begging me to return and telling me that the Aussie writers were now dictating costume, props and even design which was Paul's specialist area. When I brought this to the notice of Park Entertainment, I was told to get out to Oz and change things for myself.

I flew back to Brisbane determined to set things straight, only to find – and I had this on good authority – that the writing pair, with the power they'd been handed by Disney, were rejecting writers and directors because either they didn't like the person, or they were worried that they might be better than them! I could see how this might happen in the relatively small pool of Australian film people: they all pretty much knew each other and had worked with (or against!) each other at some time. For the show's line producers it was a shackle they could well do without.

I returned to be part of the script department, which has a different set-up to British TV productions. There is a script producer in overall charge, and as many as three script editors – and on a twenty-six-part half-hour series you really need them, especially when episodes one and two had to be rewritten totally. Perhaps the worst thing I had to bear was that these writers had got their names on the cover of each script as co-creators. This was the last straw for me and I had to have it understood that Paul Tams and I were the creators of *K9* and that it was imperative to get that clear, otherwise problems could arise regarding the chain of rights in any future deal. I had to hire a lawyer to clarify our rights over the show. Finally we got them to change their credit to 'developed for television', but it had been an unpleasant and very expensive exercise.

It also meant a return to England which turned out to be a happy coincidence. I was delighted to find that *A Matter of Loaf and Death* had been nominated as Best Animated Film at BAFTA and even more thrilled to find that I had again been nominated too. This was such a fillip to my morale, since I'd begun to wonder while in Oz if I really was a writer? Receiving this accolade did my spirits a lot of good, especially when I went back to Oz to find blow-ups of the award ceremony on the wall of the studio.

I heard that the two writers had visited the studio while I was away, but after that they didn't come near the place. That suited me fine.

I did my best to keep abreast of the rewriting going on and got to meet the rest of the production team. The design department and all the crew were fantastic people; I got on extremely well with all of them, and they, to a man/woman, were right behind the project. It was especially pleasing to dump our Australian writers' ideas on the costumes and sets into the bin and start afresh. Paul and I were very impressed by the time and energy the crew put into getting details right. Things were beginning to get on track again.

I'd hired a car and began to look around Brisbane and started to relax a bit. I'd been given a one-bedroom apartment, a mere stone's throw from the studio where the series was being shot. It had a balcony and it was magnificent to eat outside every evening as the sun was going down and watch swarms of metre-wide fruitbats flying home; sometimes they flew within five metres of my balcony, a strange and rather frightening experience at first , but you soon get used to it… honestly!

As it was coming up to Christmas, my first one in a hot climate, my PA Lou Henry very kindly asked me to share Christmas Day with her family at a beachside barbecue. Marie had flown out for a couple of weeks and we went to meet them on a beach just north of Brisbane. It was cool by Aussie standards, overcast and only about seventy-five degrees. I was surprised to learn that Lou's family had got to the beach at six A.M. to be sure to get one of the electrically powered barbies along the beach promenade, which, apparently, are provided by the council. It was a very enjoyable and enlightening day. The beach was packed and the whole area was taken up by loads of families of different nationalities and religions, each chatting and kids shouting in their own language. The noticeable thing was that there was not even a hint of anger, frustration or drunkenness. It was perfectly 'mellow'… Those who had to wait for a barbecue to free up, waited patiently; others were playing ball games with children or flying kites or splashing around in the sea. There was an air of genuine peace and happiness abroad on the beach that day. A sort of ideal do-it-yourself-United Nations; 'peace and goodwill to all men' in practice… I'll never forget it.

The designer on the series, and his wife who also worked on the show, told us of a resort that was a 'must' to stay at called Noosa. They gave us the address of the apartment they stayed in every year; fortunately it was available for New Year. Noosa is about ninety kilometres north of Brisbane and has a long sandy beach and lagoon which becomes a sort of crystal-clear sandy-bottomed river as it weaves its way around the town, so that as many houses as possible can be on its bank. Each one has its own boathouse and slip. The river/lagoon is held in by a sandbar at the end of the beach. We found it a marvellous place to relax in and used it as a base to explore the interior of the country.

The series was coming together pretty well even with the constriction put on us by Disney's men. Every script they wrote, as was the agreed opinion of all in the script department, would have to be totally rewritten. Furthermore, these fellows had awarded themselves a massive twelve episodes to write. They still didn't seem to understand that the series was called *K9* and that, like it or not, the robotic dog was the star of the show, around whom the story must be built. We, and they, soon realised that they had bitten off more than they could chew. They still had eight episodes to write and we were right up to schedule on the filming, ahead if anything. We were crying out for their episodes; but, as usual, we had the inevitable overlong outline followed by a script that practically always had to be completely rewritten. By this time we had a really sharp team in the writing department, and as we were *in extremis* I wrote an episode and collaborated on another, thus busting the myth that UK writers couldn't be used. In addition it eased the logjam, but the other two script editors in our team had to work all hours to get the scripts into shape.

Despite everything we managed it and were able to get a super last episode where the director David Napier really went to town with the CGI. There was very little else I could do; so, as the end of the shoot was coming up, Marie came out again for a real holiday. We went to Port Douglas and then flew on to Alice Springs for the obligatory visit to Uluru, calling in on a pub with a singing dog en route!

Once the show was in post-production with a really keen and committed Brisbane company, Cutting Edge, doing wonders with the special effects, I came back to England for rest and recuperation, and to reflect on what I'd learned from the experience.

I thought I knew a bit about co-productions, but what I didn't appreciate is that the whole exercise is the manipulation of money. I reflected on John Boorman's marvellous expression that film was 'turning money into light'! To sum up: the trouble began at the very moment we started our endeavour in late 2007... precisely the same time as the credit squeeze and the beginnings of the banking debacle. The arrangements made for the money to be raised as the British investment fell through. Nobody in banking wanted to put money into film and TV. This left the co-production rather one-sided with the Australians raising what was to be almost the whole budget with Disney taking a small share, but placing their agents – our recalcitrant pair of writers – at the beginning in a position of complete power over the whole series. On the other hand, by the exemplary work of the crew, actors and the writing team we came up with a series they, Paul and I can be proud of. K9 was a reborn, rebooted and redesigned character and he looked good; plus we got some real humour out of the dog. We were especially keen to get the excellent John Leeson to do the dialogue because not only was he perfect in the new situation, using him kept a link with the previous mutt and his erstwhile master – who we were not allowed to mention…

The *K9* project was, to use a cliché, a roller-coaster ride where my heart was in my mouth at times, contrasted with the deep satisfaction of seeing that the series was actually going rather well and that the dream Paul Tams and I had started in – well, in the previous century! – was actually, despite all the frustrations, working.

Since then, Paul and I have been trying to set up a second series; and the good news that series one will be showing on the Syfy network in the US in 2013 should help no end.

So, whilst I'm waiting for that, I think I might sit down and write my memoirs!

There's no rest for the wicked…

THE END

Acknowledgments

I WOULD LIKE TO thank the following people for all their advice, help and support.

They are Laurie Booth, for photographs and hours of recordings, Celia Martin, Patrick Dromgoole, the family, Martin, Avril, Holly and Amy, Kathy, Paul, Andy, Laura, Sarah Jane, Rachael and Joanna and Clare and my earlier wives, Vicki and Angela.

I would also like to thank Tom Baker (no relation!) for being a brilliant Doctor Who, Pamela Gillis, my agent throughout the *Who* years, Robert Banks Stewart, and of course, Nick Park, Dave Sproxton and Peter Lord, for just being the Aards. Also Terrance Dicks, Jim Buckingham, Victoria Byard, John Miles, Malcolm Windsor, John Fortune, Roger Crago, and – oh – the Bristol Royal Infirmary, for saving my life.

The Anchor pub in the village has played a big part in my life, so thanks to Mike Dowdeswell, Mark Sorrell, the boules teams, the people I meet at the pub (including the fantastic Tractor Boys!) and friends and neighbours in the village, especially Peter and Joy, who look after my gay cats when I go away.

There are lots of people I haven't mentioned. You know who you are and you have all been part of my eventful life and I would like to thank you for putting up with me.

I also thank Mike Sharland for being an astute agent and believing in me.